Praise for *Six Figu*

An honest, enjoyable, practical look at what it takes to make money in your business and be the parent you want to be without losing yourself.

JODIE THORNTON | PARENTING COACH

Any parent and entrepreneur will tell you they were never handed a roadmap for what unfolded after the birth of their babies. (Yes, our businesses feel like our babies too.) Kate has done a pretty stellar job in this book of highlighting the terrain, the bumps and turns, stop signs, red lights and green lights when it comes to the journey of running a business and being a parent. I highly recommend putting this on the must read-list for any parent juggling a business and kiddos.

SAM JOCKLE | FOUNDER AND CEO | PARENTTV

It's about bloody time someone wrote this book. For far too long, people with a business and kids have been suffering in silence without a map to navigate this merciless minefield. Kudos to Kate for finally putting it all out there in such an intelligent, insightful and humorous way. If you want to make significant money around kids, this book is for you.

DALE BEAUMONT | FOUNDER & CEO | BUSINESS BLUEPRINT®

This book is a delightfully honest blueprint (with touches of perfectly timed humour) to banish parent guilt and work on your terms. It's affirmation from the business-parent trenches that you don't have to work like you don't have kids or parent like you don't work. I wish I had this when I started my business while pregnant with a toddler in tow, surrounded by five piles of laundry waiting to be folded just out of vid-conferencing view.

CARRIE KWAN | CO-FOUNDER | MUMS & CO

I had to keep checking behind me while reading *Six Figures in School Hours*. Surely Kate was somewhere in the house looking over my shoulder? I felt seen. She has perfectly captured what it's like to manage the competing pressures, priorities and pleasures of being a parent and a business owner. This is a book I'll return to again and again – so practical, so readable and so wise. It's truly a gift.

ERIN HUCKLE | CHUCKLE COMMUNICATIONS

As a parent and business owner, this is the book I didn't know I needed. Filled with Kate's humour, easy-to-implement tips and stories of her own struggles, this book is real, kind and genuinely helpful. *Six Figures in School Hours* will gently sit you down, hand you a pen, notepad and a cup of coffee, then guide you towards less stress, less guilt and more success – for you, your family and your business.

LAUREN MINNS | LUMINOUS COPY

I just wish I had read the book 50 years ago. Really looking forward to seeing the published version.

DAD

SIX FIGURES IN SCHOOL HOURS

SIX FIGURE$
— IN —
SCHOOL
HURS

How to run a successful business
and still be a good parent

KATE TOON

MAJOR
STREET

I dedicate this book to my son, Orion,
who is just a wonderful human.

And to my Viking, Tony Cosentino,
who reminds me every day I can do whatever
I set my mind to, and for being my recharge mat.

MAJOR STREET

First published in 2023 by Major Street Publishing Pty Ltd
info@majorstreet.com.au | +61 421 707 983 | majorstreet.com.au

© Kate Toon 2023
The moral rights of the author have been asserted.

NATIONAL LIBRARY OF AUSTRALIA

A catalogue record for this book is available
from the National Library of Australia

Printed book ISBN: 978-1-922611-73-4
Ebook ISBN: 978-1-922611-74-1

Cover design by Tess McCabe
Author photo by Jade Warne
Internal design by Production Works

10 9 8 7 6 5 4 3 2 1

Contents

Introduction

The sun is setting in my back garden, and my desk is cluttered with the remains of a busy day: three coffee cups, half a bowl of soup and a keyboard full of biscuit crumbs.

I'm talking to Barry in my Facebook group. Barry doesn't understand some aspect of marketing and I'm trying to explain it to him, but it's not going well. So, we go back and forth in the comments. Barry is being a little bit rude, but he's a potential client, so I need to keep him happy.

I consider my next post, letting out a deep puff of coffee breath and looking through my home office window. Across the back garden, I can spy the lounge room. My four-year-old son is on the sofa in furry pyjamas watching *In the Night Garden* on TV, the garish colours of Upsy Daisy lighting up the walls and his face.

He looks a little small and a little sad.

'I'll just be five minutes,' I'd told him. But it has not been five minutes. It's been way longer.

Barry's notification pings again and my heart sinks.

I should be in that lounge room. Because it's not Barry who deserves my time right now. It's my son. And I'm slapped with the slightly vomity realisation that I'm sacrificing my family on the altar of my business.

I'm trying to be a successful businessperson and a great parent, and right now I'm doing a terrible job of both.

Barry pings again.

*

Now that memory feels like, well, a distant memory. Back then it felt impossible to find any kind of balance. I'd been brought up on the idea that 'if you work hard, you can have it all', and I was pushing myself to the absolute limits to get that 'all'.

My priority was to be a good parent – the sort who does craft with their child and bakes homemade oatmeal biscuits. My *other* priority was to be a killer businessperson who does impeccable marketing, feels confident about their cash flow and relentlessly dreams big. *(The irony that 'priority' means one thing does not escape me.)*

These two goals fit together like two ill-fitting, damp jigsaw pieces.

I was exhausted, wracked with guilt, struggling with debt and piling on the pounds. I had a constant anxious feeling in my chest and a to-do list longer than a long thing. There were never enough hours in the day, and I felt like too little butter spread over too much bread *(I'm a big Bilbo Baggins fan).*

Something had to change. And so, I changed it.

Over the next few years, I worked hard to re-evaluate my ideas about parenting, quality time and 'parent guilt'. I managed to improve my productivity and squeeze the maximum amount of juice out of my short days. I got comfortable with my money and stopped kidding myself about my cash flow. I learned smart ways to explain my business needs to my son, helped him understand and even got him involved. I focused on my own mindset, managing my ego, dropping the 'burnt chop' martyrdom and learning to prioritise my own self-care and mental health.

Of course, I made mistakes. And I faced some hideous challenges along the way. But here I am today with a business I'm proud of and a teenage son who genuinely wants to spend time with me. *(Well, sometimes.)* And I call that winning.

That's why I wanted to write this book. Because for me, having a small business while having a family was impossibly hard for a long time, and then I found a way out – and I want to show you that way out.

While it may look like I'm all about digital marketing, copywriting and getting to grips with Google, those aren't my *real* superpowers. Rather, those skills are just the basic bricks I used to build my business powerhouse.

My true skills – the real reasons I've been able to build a financially successful and fulfilling business in between pick-ups and drop-offs – have more to do with persistence, productivity, profit, persuasion and practical parenting. All the 'P's'. I love me a P list.

My success is about my values and my why – which I'll touch on later – and the ability to be flexible and learn from my mistakes. I also don't beat myself up too much – not just as a business owner but also as a parent.

And finally, it's down to the fact that, while I take my business seriously, I don't take myself too seriously. When all else fails, the tumble dryer breaks and I accidentally burp on an important Zoom call, my sense of humour will see me through.

The big question

If you're flicking through this book in a shop or reading it in the few minutes you get to yourself at the end of the day, I'm betting you've asked yourself this question:

Can I have a successful business *and still* be a good parent?

Perhaps you're already running a business and trying to balance everything, but you feel as though the business you're supposed to love is eating you and your family alive.

Maybe you have a 'real job' and hate every living minute of it. You desperately want to start your own thing, but you're worried you'll never be able to match your current salary.

Or, you could be about to start a family of your own and wondering whether having your own business could make life a bit easier.

You're not alone.

I've worked with thousands of business-owning parents, and very few of them are trying to build a global empire or make a gazillion dollars a year. *(I'm not saying it wouldn't be nice, but let's get real.)* Most of us *(yes, me included)* are simply trying to earn a decent income and have time to read our kids a bedtime story without having a meltdown in the process.

But instead, we're trying to sound professional on business calls while our kid throws a hissy fit in the supermarket. We're wrestling with gut-wrenching guilt as we plop our small humans in front of whatever device is available so we can just finish that 'one last thing'. And we're struggling to make enough money in the precious few hours a day we can work without distraction.

What makes it worse is the business world can't see us. While Australia has around 2.4 million small and medium-sized businesses[1] and no shortage of business-owning parents, there's precious little help out there for the likes of us.

And the challenges of the past few years have seen more parents working from home, bringing the struggle into sharper focus.

Do you remember the dad on the BBC newscast during COVID? (If you don't, google 'kid interrupts dad's live TV interview'.) Just a parent, working from home. Books neatly arranged on the bed, serious expression, shirt and tie. He was desperately trying to look professional on a newscast but I'm guessing he had pyjama bottoms on.

His ridiculously cute, pigtailed, yellow-jumpered daughter had different ideas. Despite the closed door and probable firm warnings not to enter the office, she wanted to talk to her dad. She strides in, pigtails wiggling, full of confidence, not a care in the world. And we see her dad frantically trying to remain composed, to keep talking – even as his wife, accompanied by a baby in a mobile play gym, bursts through the door to remove the small intruder on all fours.

It's both hilarious and horrifying. Because we've all been there. *(Sidenote: I highly recommend locking yourself in the loo to take Zoom calls. Just make sure you blur the background.)*

This eternal piece of pop culture is a shining example of how hard it can be to juggle work and family. Yes, it's funny. But it's also deadly serious. The business and parenting struggle is having a massive impact on our wellbeing.

According to the initial findings of the *National Working Families Report 2019*[2], 62% of respondents said they had difficulties managing their own physical and mental health as they juggled working and caring for their families. And around a third said it was contributing to stress and tension in their relationships with their partners and children.

But where's the help?

Yes, there are plenty of business productivity books out there, and I'm sure you've looked at a few of them in your desperate search for

So, again, while I give you my action plan in this book, there's zero expectation that you will implement every single aspect of it, or even that every single aspect will suit you. Because, just as every family is different, so is every business and every business owner.

Even if we set aside privilege, prejudice, education and wealth, the playing field clearly isn't even. Many business owners suffer from disabilities, chronic illnesses and mental health issues. Others work with neurodiversity, which can be both a blessing and a curse. It would be absurd for me to say 'Do this' *(in a rumbling Morgan Freeman voice)* and guarantee you'll have immediate success. Instead, I'd rather offer 'Try this' advice *(in a soft Cate Blanchett voice)* while patting your bottom encouragingly and making you a nice cup of tea.

I know that, as a middle-class, middle-aged white woman in Australia with only one child, I have it easier than possibly 99% of parents. *(I believe 98% of statistics are made up on the spot.)* So, I've been careful *not* to include smug advice like 'only cut your organic zucchinis on a Wednesday' and 'six ways to get more out of your hessian tote'.

How this book works

The book is broken up into five parts:

1. Mindset
2. Productivity
3. Money
4. Family
5. Communication and self-care

Each section includes chapters that outline core ideas, advice and little snippets of insight from other business-owning parents.

Here are a few things to look out for:

- **Toon Tips:** Occasionally I highlight a point to really drive it home.
- **Member quotes:** This book is peppered with comments from members of my business mentoring group the Digital Marketing Collective (DMC), as well as from guests on my *Six Figures in School Hours* podcast (available on iTunes, Spotify and all good

podcast players). I think they add a lot of interesting perspectives and flavour.

- **TL;DR (too long; didn't read):** If you're busy *(of course you are)* and had to skip or skim a few a sections, I sum up the entire chapter in one line.

- **Exercises:** I've set short 20-minute exercises to complete at the end of each chapter. They're optional, but they'll really help the information stick.

- **Benefits:** I summarise the benefits of doing the work I suggest you do in each chapter.

After you've read *Six Figures in School Hours*

My hope is that, by the end of this book, you'll be able to reach the nirvana of business parenting and eradicate parent guilt, be present for both your family and your business, and build a business that supports and enhances your life. Yes, there's hard work to do. But I know you can do it.

Get involved

If you're loving the book and want to get more involved, here are some fun ways to do so:

- **Listen to the podcast:** Search for 'Six Figures in School Hours Podcast' to hear interviews with other business parents on topics covered in the book.

- **Follow on Instagram:** Search for '@sixfiguresinschoolhours' or post your own content using the hashtag #6fish

- **Grab the accompanying workbook:** You can grab a copy of the *Six Figures In School Hours* workbook that goes with the book at sixfiguresinschoolhours.com.

- **Join the Facebook group:** Hunt for 'The Misfit Entrepreneurs' Facebook group to share your experience of reading the book.

PART I

MINDSET

STOP FEELING TORN IN TWO

WHETHER YOU'VE BEEN in business for a few years or you're just about to start, getting your brain to behave is so important.

It took me years to realise that mindset matters. I was always a deep thinker *(often too deep)*, but it's only recently that I started analysing *why* I think the way I do.

I was also a 'just get on with it' doer – minimal navel-gazing and not much planning. I just strode boldly forward without ever knowing why I was striding or whether 'boldly' was really working for me. *(Spoiler: it wasn't.)* I never addressed my preconceived beliefs about parenting, my business desires and fears, or my foolish belief that I could do it all. As a result, I ended up with my mental knickers in a giant twist, and it took me several years to untwist them. It was a painful process.

I want to save you from getting lost in your business by helping you understand your mindset from the get-go. Because unless you get your thoughts on parenting and business straight, you're going to struggle every single day.

I want to save you from feeling torn in two and like you have to choose between your business and your kids.

As sleep-deprived parents, we've had to process a huge mental load before we even sit down to work each day. We don't get to create our ideal, distraction-free morning before we head to our perfectly arranged desks. Instead, we've spent the night with a small child's foot in our armpit, dealt with a tantrum about toast, handled an argument with a grumpy teen or cleaned up a puddle of dog wee on the living-room floor.

By the time we sit down to work, we're already befuddled, our stress levels rising, a damp pressure on the back of our neck. We know we need to get as much done as possible before the baby wakes up from their nap and needs a feed, the child returns from school and demands a snack or the teen needs to book in the 'parent taxi service'.

It often feels like we're running downhill too fast, our legs almost going out from under us. It's hard enough just to stay focused, let alone have clear vision or a strategy. We stumble along blindly in the business dark. We make mistakes, and it takes us far too long to get to where we want to be.

In this part, we dig into some core mindset issues so we can get clear on our whys before we start tackling our 'to-dos'. We cover:

- the reasons behind your business
- what could potentially kill your business
- how you can define business success
- how you can define good parenting
- the best ways to eliminate parent guilt.

Ready? Let's get stuck in.

Chapter 1

Why start your own business?

'If you have a clear mind... you won't have to search for direction. Direction will come to you.'

Phil Jackson

Before we start examining parenting, productivity, money and the rest, let's take a deep breath and tackle the mindset stuff.

First, I want you to answer the big question *(I've used big font here so you can see just how big a question it is)*:

Why do you want to start your own business?

Or if you've already started your business, think back and ask yourself why you started your own business.

Write down your answer somewhere. Try to sum it up in a few lines, not in some *War and Peace*–length essay.

Okay, now I'm going to close my eyes, put my fingers on my temples and see if I can imagine your answer. *(Think of me as a mythical business mind-reader.)* Here goes. *(Begins humming.)*

Got it. I'm going to take a stab in the dark and say you wrote down one or more of these reasons:

- You want to escape the nine to five.
- Your boss is a shitgibbon and you're sick of working for them.

- You'd love to spend more time with the family.
- You're sick of paying exorbitant childcare fees.
- You want the potential to earn more than a set 'salary'.
- You want to feel more in control of your life.
- You've been sacked or made redundant and can't face getting another job.
- You hate having to put on a bra/tie every day and act like a human.
- You want to follow your passion.

Was I right? If yes, then BOOM! Mind-reader status confirmed.

But, of course, I cheated a little. Having worked with oodles of parent business owners through my mentoring programs and memberships, I know the most common reasons. *(Unless you threw a real curve ball answer in there, like you have decided to take a new direction after being mauled by an otter.)*

Here are a few examples from my members.

Lorraine Sleep from Lorraine Sleep Digital Marketing Services, mum of Jonathon (32), Jordyn (29) and Ridge (25), said:

> 'I wanted to be in the driver's seat of my life. I love a challenge, and I'm keen to make more money.'

Kate Merryweather, mum of Alice (13), Jessica (11) and Lucy (8), said:

> 'My employer was completely uninterested in accommodating me with babies, and I wanted to keep working and use my brain.'

I think all our 'why we started a business' reasons – apart from that pesky 'passion' one, which I'll deal with in Chapter 2 – can be summarised with one word: **flexibility**.

In my experience, flexibility generally falls into three categories:

1. time
2. money
3. creativity.

Time flexibility

For some, flexibility means being able to work how and when you want. We imagine that running our own business will mean we can set our own hours, run our day how we want, finish early and pick our kids up from school, and miss a day of work to go to our kid's cake baking day, award ceremony or trumpet concert.

It means we no longer have to stuff tissues up our noses and hang our heads off the end of the bed to sound extra sick when we call our bosses. *(It works. Try it.)* It means we never have to suffer the eye-rolls of our childless co-workers as we leave early for the 100th time to pick up our sick kids.

Time flexibility means you can finally balance your family and work time. Right?

Well, it's a beautiful dream.

And it was my dream. In fact, work flexibility was the main reason I decided to do my own thing. *(I also hated the living crap out of my job – the awkward kitchen conversations, the endless pressure and the regular sobbing on my daily bus commute.)*

Before I became 'with child' I was working at a digital agency in Sydney on a contract. Yes, it was only four days a week, but it meant long hours, a lot of stress and a pressure to do 'all the things'.

Then I got pregnant, somewhat miraculously. *(My son's dad and I had been told we couldn't get pregnant due to various fertility issues, and we were weighing up IVF or just being the kind of couple who travels and owns a white sofa.)* Unfortunately, my highfalutin agency job wasn't exactly baby-friendly. I'd waited a long time to get up the duff, and the last thing I wanted was to squeeze out my son, take six weeks' leave and then return to the grind of office life.

If I was going to make a human, I was going to spend time with him.

So, when I was five months pregnant, I quit my day job and started my own business. For the flexibility.

Bless me. I really had no clue.

For those of you already running your own business, you'll know that working for yourself means you get to choose whatever 80 hours you'll work each week. Your business seeps into every single crack of time available. There are never enough hours in the day. Your inbox is never empty. Your to-do list is endless.

My advice?

If *time flexibility* was your core, why? I want you to think about something that backs this why up, then perhaps write it on a Post-it Note and stick it somewhere prominent. It could be something like the following:

- 'I'm in charge of my own time.'
- 'I'll make the best use of my time.'
- 'My time is valuable.'
- 'I'm careful how I invest my time.'

Why is this important? Because the time flexibility you crave will be challenged again and again. You'll constantly be asked to compromise this why:

- You started your business so you could pick up your kid from school, but then one of your clients requests a call at 3 p.m.
- You dreamed of being fully present during your kid's bedtime routine, but you have a deadline looming and you're not quite finished.
- Your plan was to volunteer at the school canteen, but can you really afford to spend those hours helping when mortgage rates are going up?

I'm not saying you can't be flexible with how and when you work, but you can easily lose sight of that initial goal when you're in the thick of it.

So, if time flexibility is your goal, remember that.

Money flexibility

The other big desire behind starting a business is the flexibility to make more money.

No longer will you be a wage slave, snuggling up to your boss at your annual review in the hope of getting a piddly bonus or salary increase. Working for yourself means you can decide just how much – or how little – money you'll earn.

At first, your goal might be to earn half of your previous salary *(because you'll also be working fewer hours, right?)*. Then you might want to match your previous salary, if not exceed it. After that, maybe become a six- or seven-figure earner. Get a new car. A bigger house. A new pair of boobs. *(Blokes, I suggest thinking of a boob equivalent. Golf clubs?)*

Our money goals tend to grow as time goes on because enough is never enough for very long. That's just human nature: we're always striving for more. And while this is a great thing – we'd still be that little fish-like thing in a pond if we hadn't craved land and grown little legs – it can also be our undoing.

Money was not my primary goal when I started my business, but it quickly became everything, far exceeding my desire for time flexibility. I replaced my 'real job' salary fairly quickly and then just kept pushing my annual financial target higher and higher – from 5K months to 10K, from six-figure revenue a year to seven.

But oh, the compromises I made to get there.

For one, I had to totally compromise my time. It simply was not possible to make that kind of money in a few hours a day *(at least at the start)*. I also compromised my health and wellbeing, piling on weight and drinking way too much wine. It put stress on my relationship and my friendships.

And, ultimately, my desire to make money undermined my focus on my real priority: my son.

Money is less important to me these days, which is easier to say now 'cos I actually have a little bit. But even if I didn't, I think time has taught me that money is a cold reward.

Of course we want to be comfy: there is no glamour in struggling. But I wish someone had explained to me that money goals need to be connected to something tangible. With my copywriter hat on I'd say the amount is just the feature. What's the benefit?

Connecting money to a real-life 'thing' makes it more manageable. It also makes your money goals more realistic. And when you reach your goal, instead of feeling empty and dead inside *(well, I did)*, you feel a sense of satisfaction that you can now pay for the real-life thing you planned.

In short, if I had my time again, I'm not sure I'd make financial flexibility my goal. But you live and learn.

My advice?

If money flexibility is the core reason you're starting your business, write something that backs it up. Again, find a large Post-it Note and stick it somewhere prominent. Maybe something like:

- 'I have the power to earn the money I want.'
- 'Money helps me reach my life goals.'
- 'Money is a means to an end.'
- 'I want to earn money to… (insert goal here).'

Because, when you hit your first financial goal, I want you to think about how it feels:

- Does it give you a rosy glow or leave you feeling unsatisfied?
- Do you feel content, or did you immediately create a new financial goal?

I'm not saying you can't be flexible with how much you want to earn, but you need to be realistic and appreciate the compromises you'll need to make to hit your self-created goals.

Creative flexibility

Creative flexibility is another huge factor for most people starting a business. And when I say 'creative flexibility', I don't mean making memes on Canva. I mean being able to decide how to plan your day and what you'll tackle next; being able to create products and services, processes and procedures; and marketing yourself however you want.

You could call it 'autonomy' or 'self-determination'.

Being able to create your own business reality is a powerful driver, especially if you've had a shitty boss. But again, creative flexibility can be both a blessing and a curse because, while it works great when you have a clear direction, it can be absolutely debilitating when you're not sure.

And being a creative type means you'll be more easily distracted by shiny objects. Personally, I've never met a shiny object I didn't like.

Being full of ideas is wonderful, but it can leave you paralysed by choice. In those moments of self-doubt, imposter syndrome, low motivation and gloom, you'll be crying out for someone to JUST TELL YOU WHAT TO DO. *(It's why business coaches make so much money.)*

We all think we want to be the captain of our own ship, but it's often more fun being the first mate. As the captain, you'll need to build your own life raft, learn to swim and do your best not to panic when things get salty. *(Wondering how far can I push this nautical metaphor? Me too.)*

Creative flexibility needs boundaries. It also needs structure and process. Because, in truth, you haven't got rid of your old boss: you are now your own boss, and you have to manage yourself well. We'll talk more about this in Parts II and V.

My advice?

If creative flexibility is the core reason you're starting your business, write some things that back it up *(again with the Post-it Notes)*. Maybe something like:

- 'I won't sacrifice my creative freedom for…'
- 'I'm the captain of my ship.'
- 'I get to decide.'
- 'I am the boss of me.'
- 'Even though I can do what I want, I will have boundaries.'

But I also think you creative types need to be honest about who you are as a person:

- Are you driven?
- Are you great at planning your day?
- Do you find it easy to see the big picture?

While you may well be creative, you may also be all over the place from a project management point of view. So, you might need some support in this area *(not that there's anything wrong with that)*. We'll talk more about this in Chapter 10.

I'm not saying you can't enjoy the creative freedom of being your own boss, but at times you might find forcing yourself to make a plan and sticking to it a bit of a challenge.

Help! I'm motivated by all three

Right now, you might be thinking, 'Oh dear. I'm motivated by all three'. That's perfectly okay. But I'm sure that, if you dig deep, you'll realise one is more important to you than the others right now.

Mind you, it can also change over time. As I said earlier, I started with time and then moved to money. After that, it became creative, and now it's all about time again. I've come full circle.

We're evolving beasts and, while simple definitions are lovely, they often don't quite work. If you feel all three could fit you, then you'll need more Post-it Notes.

TL;DR

If flexibility is your goal, that's great. But you'll need to be flexible about it.

Benefits

Thinking about why you want to start your business will help you:

- have a clearer idea of what's important to you in your business
- be more realistic about your goals
- have something to look back on when times get tough
- set boundaries to avoid being eaten alive by your business.

Over to you

Based on your answer at the start of the chapter, here are a few exercises to really pin down why you want to start your business:

1. If **time flexibility** was your main goal, write a list of non-negotiable boundaries. Start each sentence with 'I will always make time to...'.
   Example, 'I will always make time to read my kids a bedtime story',
   or, 'I will always make time to have a proper lunch'.

2. If **money flexibility** was your main goal, write out some financial goals. I dig further into this in Part III, but for now, just think about what you'd like to earn and connect it to a life goal. Start each sentence with 'If I make [amount] in [time period] then I can...'.

   Example, 'If I make $5K in a month then I can cover all my expenses,' or, 'If I make $20K profit in year one then I can pay off all my credit card debt'.

3. If **creative flexibility** was your main goal, think about some challenges you might meet when you actually have that much freedom. I tackle this more in Part II, but for now, just think about how you like to work. Start each sentence with 'I work best when I...'.

   Example, 'I work best when I get a good night's sleep,' or, 'I work best when I make a time-based to-do list'.

If you want to dig into these exercises further, head to sixfiguresinschoolhours.com and grab the accompanying workbook.

Chapter 2

The biggest business killer

'If passion drives you, let reason hold the reins.'
Benjamin Franklin

People often say they want to start a business because they have an idea they're truly *passionate* about. When I hear this line, my eyes roll so far back into my head I can see the goblin who controls my brain.

Why? Because I believe passion is the biggest business killer. I put the blame firmly at the feet of those passion-pushers who believe it's all you need to make your business a success. I'm not sure whether it was Confucius or Barry Manilow who said, 'Choose a job you love and you'll never work a day in your life,' but whoever *did* say it is wrong.

Yes, passion is delicious, fiery and exciting, and gives you a fizz in your belly. But it's also incredibly short-lived. Just like any new relationship, you begin by wanting to rip off your new lover's knickers. After that, it's sex five times a day, chocolate-dipped strawberries and legs akimbo. And it's the same with a new business. You stay up 'til all hours working on your business plan and wasting entire days fiddling with your website and faffing about in Canva.

But passion doesn't last. One day you will wake up with zero passion for your business. But you still need to bring home the bacon *(or vegan ham)*. So, what are you going to do now?

You know what else kills passion? Being a parent.

It's hard to feel the tingle in your undercarriage for a new idea when your battery's running low. The 'cut me and I bleed coffee' state most parents exist in doesn't lend itself well to feeling enthusiastic and excited.

The most passionate thinkers, artists and business owners in the world are often childless. They have the time to indulge their ideas, wait for great ideas to bubble up and work only when inspiration hits.

You don't.

You have to do the do when you're tired, unmotivated and uninspired, and when the passion has well and truly died. Oh, how I miss the energy I had when I was child-free; how fast my brain moved from idea to idea; how much I could achieve.

But after a night *(okay, four years)* of not enough sleep, there were times where I could barely remember how to type. Every day felt like wading through mud, and my brain felt like it was on permanent mute.

If you're thinking of starting a business because you're passionate about a particular project or industry, stop for a minute and think about it:

- There's no quicker way to fall out of love with something you adore doing than to try to make money from it.
- All relationships become boring after a while – and so do businesses.
- A boring business is often a successful business.
- Predictability, persistence, consistency and hard work aren't sexy, but they're often the key to long-lasting success.

Now, I'm not saying you can't choose a business idea you're passionate about. Having enthusiasm, a deep interest in an area and a giggly, delightful feeling when you even think about your passion is a wonderful way to get started. And when times get tough, passion and a strong belief in your idea may well be the things that keep you going.

But you need to ask yourself: 'Can I love my idea for the long term?' Is it a one-night-stand business idea, or can you grow old together *(or at least into middle age)*?

In business, we all crave stability – a time when everything is running smoothly and we're not riding the rollercoaster of business every single day. But what happens when things start working? We get bored and lose interest. Stupid humans that we are, we crave excitement.

You also need to ask yourself whether passion will be enough to keep you going when your kids are sick and screaming for the iPad, or when the dog has vomited on the carpet, the car has a flat tyre and your kid tells you at 7 p.m. that they need to make a diorama of a Roman amphitheatre by tomorrow.

Here's what some of my members had to say about passion. Jennifer Crawford from Our New Home Coach, mum of two kids (16 and 12), agrees:

> 'Business is more boring than passion. It's determination, grit and commitment. Passion? Pffft.'

Felicity Bent from The Book Basket Company, mum of Oliver (27), James (27) and Annabel (24), added this:

> 'I do think you need a passion – as in, a strong belief in the importance of what you're doing – as it will help get you through the hard times. But the other parts of your why are possibly more important. Keeping them in the forefront of my mind is the main thing that keeps me motivated.
>
> 'And the passion for what you do needs to be tempered with some business smarts. Passion and ideas are great, but they aren't enough on their own.'

And finally, Rhi Sugars from The Atypical Educator, mum of Dallas (7) and Evanna (19 months), summed it up perfectly:

> 'I am incredibly passionate about what I do. But the reality is, I need more than passion to survive in business and as a disabled person existing within an ableist society. Frustration at the way things currently are, determination to change the narrative, resilience, and commitment to get past the pushback and the bad days are what keep me going. Passion was the start, but it comes up short when the reality of business life hits.'

How I choose my business ideas

These days, whenever I'm considering a new business idea, product or service, passion is rarely a part of my thought process. Instead, I base my decision on three questions (see figure 2.1):

- **Do people want it?** There's no point launching a new range of otter galoshes if there's no market for them.

- **Will it make money?** If you can't make a profitable margin on each pair of boots, you won't survive. (I talk more about this in Part III.)

- **Will I enjoy it?** This is the enthusiasm bit. I need to enjoy what I'm doing. There needs to be a sprinkle of passion. But the additional question embedded here is, 'Can I keep doing this for a long, long, long, long time?'

Figure 2.1: How I choose my business ideas

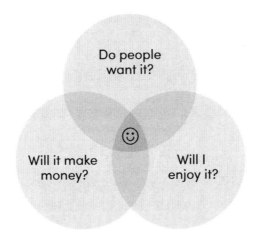

Now, I'm not here to poo on your passion bonfire. I just want to add a smidge of reason to the inferno, along with a few fistfuls of reality and common sense.

The 'Baby one more time' approach

Imagine being Britney Spears.

This somewhat controversial figure is known for her musical achievements, her tough times and her family challenges. But some will only remember her in a school uniform, shaking her pigtails around and singing 'Baby one more time'.

I'm sure that at her concerts, despite having a dozen amazing new tunes, the audience would at some point – probably around song ten – start a low rumble. A few would call out 'Sing "Baby one more time"!', and everyone around them would take up the call until they were all shouting it together.

Now, maybe Britney would know they want this song. It may already be on the set list. Or maybe not; maybe Britney would rather stick a fork in her thigh than sing that damn song one more time. But she has to, because that's what her audience wants and that's what makes her money.

And it's the same with your business.

In my opinion, the biggest factor for success in business isn't passion. It's persistence. It's:

· the ability to turn up day after day without motivation or inspiration

· the ability to treat both success and failure the same; or, as Rudyard Kipling says in my favourite poem, *If*, 'Treat those two impostors [triumph and disaster] just the same'

· the ability to keep loving your business even after the passion dies

· the willingness to appreciate reliability and regularity more than excitement.

Maybe you won't have to be Britney. Maybe you'll get to be Madonna and have a core fan base that lets you evolve and change your style, product or service. Maybe you'll get to spice up your flagging business with a few new ideas, a rebrand, a staff member or a side hustle.

But you still have to turn up, even when you don't feel like it. And that's why, when thinking about your passion, you should think of Britney.

The Stephen King approach

I saw an interview with Stephen King many years ago in which he said that, when he started as a writer, he forced himself to sit at his desk from nine to five.

It didn't matter if he was highly motivated or flat as a roadkill possum, he sat at his desk from nine to five. Some days the words flowed from his eager fingers like a tsunami of creativity. On other days, he barely managed to push out a colon *(or a semicolon)*. But he sat at his desk from nine to five nevertheless.

And he probably still does. It's probably just a much nicer desk, and he gets to sit on million-dollar cushions.

And that's what we need to do – if not from nine to five then at least from nine to three, or between drop-off and pick-up.

Passion will wane, inspiration is fleeting and motivation isn't a flowing tap. We need to find determination and the ability to put in the hours no matter how good it feels. We need to plod on, keep on swimming and generally STFU (Shut The Fuck Up) and get on with it.

TL;DR

Passion is great, but you need to consider how you'll keep the love alive.

Benefits

Thinking about your level and longevity of passion in a more rational way will help you:

- test your idea to see whether it genuinely has long-term legs
- think about your customers and marketing
- be more realistic about your financials and profitability
- separate the one-night-stand ideas from the serious-relationship ideas
- create a micro business plan to get started with.

Over to you

Now it's time to scrutinise your idea – not so much that you squash all the life out of it, but enough to see if it will really stand up if you give it a few gentle prods. Think of this as a micro business plan:

1. **Define your business idea in a few lines.** Imagine you're describing your business idea to an informed friend: what would you say? It can help to say it out loud. Record yourself and write down what you say.

   Example: 'I want to make a brand of animal gumboots to stop animals suffering from foot-related diseases, to keep out the cold and to help animal owners keep their properties clean'.

2. **Who is the target audience for your business idea?** What market gap are you filling? Try to define your audience using more than simple demographics. Use the BDF methodology to dig into true customer insights by thinking about their preconceived **beliefs**, deepest **desires** and darkest **fears**.

   Example: 'My market is Australian animal owners who may think it's foolish for their animals to wear shoes. They want to stop expensive vet and cleaning bills, and they're worried the product won't work or that people will laugh at their gumboot-wearing animals'.

3. **How much does it cost to make your products or deliver your services? How much can you sell them for?** Hopefully, you've done a little research into the costs involved in producing whatever you'll sell, or the market rates for your service. But you also need to think about the profit you want to make. (More on this in Chapter 13.) It doesn't have to be exact; you just need a rough idea.

   Example: 'Unit production cost for gumboots is around $6. Shipping TBC; marketing, advertising etc. $10; my salary TBC; taxes etc. TBC. Other pet shoes are selling for around $25 to $33'.

4. **Rate your passion for your idea now and consider how passionately you'll feel about it in three years.** You may evolve your idea over the years, and even expand and diversify. However, in my experience, it takes around three years for an idea to take off.

Chapter 3

What is a successful business?

'*Success is not final; failure is not fatal:*
it is the courage to continue that counts.'
Winston Churchill

If you're reading a book about how to have a successful business and be a good parent, then it's kind of important to understand:

- what a 'successful business' means to you
- what being a 'good parent' means to you.

Let's tackle the successful business bit first.

We must decide the success metrics for our business in the early stages and revisit these metrics often as our business grows. Why? Because we can easily become so busy looking for the next bright shiny object that we forget to acknowledge how far we've come and what we've achieved. Goalposts move; our desire is an insatiable beast; yadda yadda.

Often, our definintion of success changes over the years. Once we wanted to simply stay afloat, then we wanted to earn a bit of money – now we want something more.

I asked lots of other business-owning parents in my membership what success means to them. Most measured success financially; they answered the question 'When will you feel successful?' with answers like:

- 'When I hit $200K a year.'
- 'When the business pays all the bills and I'm able to save a little.'
- 'When I hit $120K and get five new clients.'

I loved this answer from Jo Violeta from Violeta Finance, mum of Eva (21) and Marcus (8), as it really showed the evolution of her business success metrics:

> 'Our definition of success is primarily financial; we have targets each year. But we link those financial metrics to other factors. For example, our first "success milestone" was my partner Carl being able to work in the business full time.
>
> 'The next was about me being able to join him in the business because our business income could sustain our family consistently, reliably and with a surplus.
>
> 'Then, being able to support our family with the business income without having to work such crazy long hours. Carl actually has at least one day off per week now. Most recently, we were able to purchase a commercial property.
>
> 'The next big thing will be being able to take time for a holiday. Still figuring that one out.'

My success metrics

Now, you've no doubt heard of Maslow's hierarchy of needs, as this pyramid gets rolled out by every business coach and their cat. Essentially, it identifies life stages – from basic and safety needs, through to belonging and esteem needs, and ending up at the tippity top with self-actualisation.

This pyramid can be applied to business, too.

When I started out, I lived in Maslow's 'basics' land for a long time: just food, rent and enough money to scrape by. During the first year of my business, I was pregnant and then had a small baby to look after.

We were living in a one-bedroom flat. My son's dad had just started his French tutoring business and had exactly one client.

I was in absolute survival mode. I needed to make enough money to pay my bills in as little time as possible.

It wasn't until I was about two years in that I thought about anything beyond the basics. At that stage, I moved into 'safety' mode: working out systems and processes, focusing on my customer loyalty and starting to market myself more effectively. I wanted to climb off the feast-and-famine roller-coaster and create some financial certainty. At this stage, hitting a particular financial figure – for me, six figures of revenue in a year – felt like success. *(This happened in year three of my business.)*

As I started to hit my financial goals and the money pressure wasn't an ever-beating drum in the back of my brain, I moved into caring more about customer love. I'm a people-pleaser at heart and really wanted to feel popular and adored. *(There, I admitted it; hate me.)* At that stage, having positive reviews and loyal customers felt like success to me.

But I learned quickly that customer love is a double-edged sword. The love is lovely – but you can't have the love without the haters.

Not everyone is going to like you and that's okay. Or at least you have to be okay with that.

I've had so many trolls and haters along the way. I've endured comments on everything from my appearance to my incorrect use of semicolons. A personal favourite was a particularly kind woman who emailed me to say, 'You're too ugly to send me emails.' I mean, WTAF?

And I learned that, to ensure I'm not impacted by the negative comments, I couldn't let myself get all joyful about the positive ones either.

The next stage of my business success adventure was all about self-esteem. I decided that success looked like being 'famous'. I began feeding my furry little ego until it became a bloated mammoth. I entered awards, appeared on about six million podcasts and jetted off to speak at conferences in the USA and Europe. Seeing my name in the conference brochure sure made me feel like I had made it as a 'successful business owner'.

But guess what? It didn't last. It soon felt empty.

And oh, how I missed my son.

Yes, it was fun to stay in fancy five-star hotels and feel like a superstar, but the mum guilt was horrendous and, honestly, the trips took a huge toll on me emotionally and physically. I decided I wasn't willing to travel the world and miss my son in order to feel like a success. This is a perfect example of when your business goals directly conflict with your definition of what it means to be a 'good parent' – more on this in the next chapter.

Then I began to feel like I needed a bigger purpose. Something worthy. A loftier why.

Surely, I should want to work more so I could give an even bigger chunk of my revenue to charity? *(At this stage I was already donating a portion of revenue and had a number of do-good initiatives set up but wondered whether it was enough.)* Or perhaps I ought to have a why that involved doing more for people and the planet. I needed a mission – fast.

Finding your why

What self-respecting business owner or entrepreneur type doesn't have a copy of Simon Sinek's *Start with Why* gathering dust on their bedside table? *(Psst: I don't)*.

If you're not familiar with Simon, he created the Golden Circle theory, which argues that many of today's most successful businesses think beyond the practical, rational benefits of the products and services they offer. Instead, they start by examining the how and the why behind their business.

The idea is that your business needs a bigger purpose than just selling stuff and making money, and that purpose is born out of your business values. So, Apple, for example, doesn't just 'sell computers', but rather they 'Think different'.

From Apple's perspective, people choose their products for more emotional, nebulous reasons than simply needing a new phone. Instead, Apple customers want to associate themselves with a brand that's driven by similar values and beliefs. As Simon says, 'People don't buy what you do; they buy why you do it. And what you do simply proves what you believe'.

Let's start with values

As I was still struggling to find my bigger, sexier why, I decided to start thinking about my values.

To work out what my values were, I had to ask myself some tough questions *(and you can ask them of yourself at the end of this chapter)*:

· What do you stand for?
· What do you believe in?
· What don't you like about your industry that you want to take a stand against?
· What beliefs would you stick to no matter what?

I had to do some soul-searching, finally start navel-gazing and take some long beach walks to get through this, but here's what I ended up with. I decided my brand values were HONESTY, OPENNESS, DIRECTNESS and GENEROSITY.

Now, these aren't entirely positive. I can be overly direct, even a little abrupt; my honesty is sometimes not appreciated. And my generosity sometimes bites me on the bum. I give away a lot of free content and, of course, that means it gets ripped off, repurposed and resold. And that's made me question whether being generous works as a brand value. But I just can't stop giving people things. It's who I am; it's what I stand for.

As Mr Astronaut/Amazon Jeff Bezos says, 'Your brand is what people say about you when you're not in the room'.

What would people say about you if you left the room? Would it be the same as if you were still in it? Would you enjoy what you heard, or would your sphincter clench in abject horror?

Brand values aren't the same as brand personality

If brand values are what you stand for, your brand personality is how you come across. It can be a little confusing; for example, honesty can be a value, but also you can come across as honest.

I'd say brand personality is more about who you are as a person. And, again, we must consider the good *and* the bad.

I like to think my personality traits are FRIENDLY, SMART, FUNNY and ODD.

One of my members said that I'm also 'not a dick in a space where most people are' (SEO) and I kinda like that too. Not being a dick is both a brand value and a personality trait I'm proud of.

If you run your own business then it's likely that your personality will in turn become the personality of the business, no matter how far up Maslow's hierarchy pyramid you climb.

Once I had my values and my personality sorted, I felt a little closer to finding my why. But not entirely.

The next step

Despite this deep work and introspection, I still struggled to find my sexy why. And because I didn't have one, I found myself questioning my direction, my business and my success a lot over the years.

At first I made money my success metric, but I wasn't clear on the number or what it was connected to. So, it was never enough.

Then I made popularity my success metric, but that came with trolls and haters and I still felt unloved. So, it was never enough.

After that I made peer respect and accolades my success metric, but there was always someone, somewhere doing better. So, guess what? It was also never enough.

And here's the kicker: if you can't define why you're doing what you're doing and what your metrics for success are, you'll never feel successful. You'll constantly push yourself to achieve more and more.

And guess who suffers? You and your family. This lack of a why will lead to long hours, relentless effort and burnout if you're not careful.

Finding my why

It took a while, but finally it clicked. After years of searching, looking under sofa cushions, asking others and retracing my steps, I found my why exactly where I'd left it.

Flexibility.

My why was simply to have the flexibility to work with good people, make enough money to be comfy and be able to spend time with my family. The exact reason I started my business, the place where it all began, was actually my destination.

I'll admit I was a bit wobbly with my why at first. I remember being asked on a podcast by a successful entrepreneur what my why was and, when I came back with my answer, she scoffed, 'Is that it? Don't you want to make more money? To help more people? To have more impact?'

Yes, of course I'd love to do all of that, but here's the important bit: I don't want to do all of that at the cost of my family and my mental health.

Some people may be able to do more with their time, help more, donate more, but I've realised my limitations and I've also accepted them. So yes, I'm afraid I don't have a big, lofty purpose. I don't believe I'm changing the world. I don't feel I have a huge mission. I generally just want to have a good, enjoyable day, help a few people, have some giggles with my team, finish at 3 p.m., make my son a snack and watch a bit of Netflix.

It's not that impressive, right? And I've beaten myself up about it for years, but now I'm confident that there's nothing wrong with wanting to have a business that you're proud of, enough money to get by and a great relationship with your family.

As Nick Gale from NicksDigital, dad of Ted (5) and Olive (2), said so beautifully on my podcast:

> 'We all know we need to pay off the bills, but that's a shitty reason. Really, we're doing it for them, our kids. Okay, so I haven't made much money today. But I've made enough that we can buy groceries and I can walk my kids in the bush in their gumboots at two o'clock on a Friday afternoon – that's perfect. The work will always be there, but I make it about them.'

Success is a slippery little sucker, ever-changing, ever out of grasp, and *(not to get all woo-woo about it)* mostly it's not about money or popularity or ego. Rather, it's about having a warm, contented feeling in your belly at the end of the day.

TL;DR

Your why will change and evolve over the years. Don't compare your metrics of success to anyone else's.

Benefits

By thinking about the reasons behind your business, you can get clearer on:

·   the core values that guide you as you move forward
·   understanding that your success metrics will change over the years
·   seeing when you've moved beyond the basic business needs
·   gaining freedom from having to have a huge impressive why
·   realising how unhelpful it is to compare your success to others.

Over to you

1. What do you stand for? What do you believe in? Try to think of a few points.

    Example: I believe it's important to be transparent about where my products come from and how they are made.

2. What is it you don't like about your industry that you'd like to take a stand against?

    Example: I hate it when people claim their products are sustainable when they're really not.

3. Based on the above what are your business values? Try to think of at least four.

    Example: Transparency, honesty, reliability, creativity.

4. What is your business why? Have a go; even trying to come up with something will help.

5. Identify your success metrics. Finish the sentence, 'I will feel successful when I have...'

Chapter 4

What is a good parent?

'There is no such thing as a perfect parent. So just be a real one.'

Sue Atkins

Okay, so we've taken a look at what it means to have a 'successful business'. Now let's tackle what it means to be a 'good parent'.

I'm going to take a wild poke in the dusk and say that, since you're reading this book, you fundamentally care about your kids. And you probably care more about getting a tick for being a good parent than for being a successful business owner.

But what does 'good' even mean?

There's no such thing as a good parent

Of course, words like 'good' and 'bad' aren't actually that helpful when trying to describe your parenthood as they're totally subjective.

We all have our own value systems.

My goal in this chapter isn't to give you a universal standard to measure how good a parent you are, but rather to help you think about the kind of parent you want to be.

Because I'm going to bet that you're a little harsh on yourself.

You know how most people think they have a good sense of humour and great dress sense *(even when they so patently don't)*? I've found that, when it comes to parenting, the outlook isn't so positive. When I ask other humans if they think they're a good parent, their answer is inevitably, 'Well I try to be, but...'

And oh, those buts. Those big, big buts.

It seems we all think we're failing in one way or another. We keep measuring ourselves against an idealised notion of parenthood and falling drastically short:

- A good mum does sensory play with their child and bakes muffins.
- A good dad kicks a ball around with their kid and teaches them how to build a go-kart.
- Good parents are never too busy, distracted or tired.
- Good parents are always present, calm and engaged.

But, of course, they're not. Despite what you see on their perfectly curated Instagram feeds. Despite those cute 'Guess what my wonderful child just said' quotes on Facebook. Despite the relentless sharing of their sporting or academic achievements *(guilty)*.

The perfect parent doesn't exist. Other parents are likely struggling with all the same things you are.

I'm sure most of us thought we could be perfect parents before we actually had kids. And to understand why we judge ourselves so harshly, I think we need to look at where these notions of 'good parenting' come from.

In this chapter I'd love to help you:

- understand what type of parent you are
- determine the effect your parenting style truly has on your kids' behaviour (and to what degree it's just their temperament)
- dig into the nature versus nurture idea
- take a look at a few newer ideas about parenting.

All this is food for thought when you're thinking about who you are as a parent and how you'll juggle it with who you are as a businessperson.

Now, while I love this topic, I'm not a parenting coach, so I enlisted help from Jodie Thornton (who *is* a parenting coach) to provide her perspective. You'll see her comments dotted throughout this chapter.

Okay, let's get stuck in.

The four styles of parenting

Back in the 1960s, a smart woman named Diana Baumrind, a developmental psychologist at the University of California, Berkeley, determined that there were four broad styles of parenting[3,4]. (Maccoby and Martin further refined the model in the 1980s[5].) Her study of parents was one of the first to include mothers *and* fathers, which was kind of revolutionary at the time.

She followed children from preschool age through to late adolescence and identified two core dimensions to parental behaviour: demandingness (the degree to which they controlled their children's behaviour) and responsiveness (the degree of warmth and sensitivity they showed to their children's needs).

She believed these two dimensions combined revealed four main parenting styles:

· Authoritative (Democratic)
· Authoritarian (Disciplinarian)
· Permissive (Indulgent)
· Neglectful (Uninvolved)

If you're anything like me, converting two dimensions into four parenting styles might make your brain melt a little, so I've drawn you a little diagram to explain (see figure 4.1).

Figure 4.1: The four styles of parenting

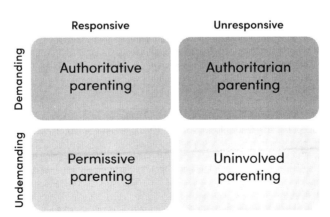

The Authoritarian Parent

Let's start with the Authoritarian Parents, who score high on the Demanding scale and low on the Responsive scale.

If you're an Authoritarian Parent, you're likely to enforce harsh rules and not prioritise your kid's feelings or emotional needs. According to Baumrind, you could be a little cold and a little tough.

Authoritarian Parents tend to do all the talking and use phrases such as 'Because I said so' and 'Just do as you're told'. Authoritarian Parents often justify their discipline and rigidity as tough love, but Baumrind believes it masks a deeper desire to be in full control of their children.

Kids with Authoritarian Parents tend to be:

· unhappy
· less independent
· more insecure and with low self-esteem
· more likely to have behavioural problems and temper tantrums
· less academically capable
· more prone to internalising their feelings
· less likely to cope socially.

It's quite a depressing list, right?

Baumrind clearly wasn't a huge fan of this mode of parenting, and I can say for sure that it's not the kind of parent I want to be. And I don't think I am, although I admit to having thrown out the odd 'Because I said so' in times of great need. I also believe tough love works sometimes, both for my son and myself. Sometimes we do need to push ourselves just a little, rather than being all fluffy and gentle.

The Permissive Parent

Permissive Parents score low on the Demanding scale and high on the Responsive scale.

If you're a Permissive Parent, then you're likely to have good chats with your kids. You probably talk openly and let them decide things for themselves rather than giving them strict directions.

Permissive Parents rarely set rules or enforce them. Instead, they go to great lengths to keep their children happy – often at their own expense. *(I look down sheepishly as I realise my people-pleasing ways also extend to my own child!)*

Permissive Parents offer less guidance and often want their kids to see them as friends rather than parents. They'll also do anything to avoid conflict and tend to give in to their kids at the slightest sign of distress or meeping (this may be a Toonism – it means 'whinging and moaning').

Kids with Permissive Parents are likely to:

· have poor self-control
· be unable to follow rules
· struggle to form relationships
· be a little egocentric.

While I would never have thought of myself as a Permissive Parent, I can see a flicker of myself here. I find it uncomfortable when I have to set firm rules for my son and sometimes avoid it so he will love me.

The Authoritative Parent

Authoritative Parents score high on the Demanding scale and high on the Responsive scale. They're nurturing and supportive and, while they do set rules and expectations, they balance them out with flexibility and understanding.

If you're an Authoritative Parent, you're likely to be a good listener, more open and honest and take into consideration your kids' feelings and thoughts. You're also probably good at letting your kids understand consequences – 'If you don't eat your dinner now, you'll be hungry later'; 'If you don't do your homework, you'll fail your exam' – and you'll use these consequences to help your kids learn and reflect.

According to Baumrind, kids with Authoritative Parents are more likely to:

· be happy and content
· be independent
· achieve higher academic performance[6]
· have competent social skills
· develop good self-esteem[7]
· have better mental health[8].

As you've probably guessed, this is the 'good' list. It's the kind of parent Baumrind wanted to be and the kind of parent I want to be.

That being said, I still feel I have a thin streak of Permissive Parent running through me.

The Uninvolved Parent

Uninvolved Parents score low on the Demanding scale and low on the Responsive scale. They tend to let their kids fend for themselves, providing little (if any) nurturing, support or guidance. Uninvolved Parents rarely implement rules and have limited engagement with their kids. They're often distracted or busy with other things. They can also be indifferent, cold and uncaring, although not always intentionally.

Unsurprisingly, Baumrind found that kids with Uninvolved Parents are likely to:

- be more impulsive
- struggle to self-regulate their emotions
- encounter behaviour and addiction problems
- have mental health issues.

Again, I kind of inner cringe at this parenting style. While I don't think I'm cold or uncaring, I do look at my phone a lot. But I guess that's just being human.

Boundaries and communication

It's not hard to see which parenting style Baumrind felt was the best. She believed warm and responsive Authoritative Parents who set limits, provide structure and listen were more likely to raise kids with strong social, emotional and cognitive skills.

And even though this whole notion was developed a while back, psychologists and psychiatrists still believe Authoritative Parenting is the most effective style, and setting boundaries is still an important part of a parent's role.

Jodie Thornton, Parenting Coach, has this to say:

'Marshall Rosenberg uses the phrase "protective use of force" when it comes to boundaries. Obviously, this "force" might be verbal rather than physical.

'So, say for example your child is using disrespectful language with you. If you can stay calm, help them to unpack what is going on, figure out what they are trying to communicate and how could they get that across without using the disrespectful language, then there's no need for protection.

'However, if the words are pushing all of your buttons, you and your child do need some protection in that instance because, if they push enough of your buttons, you are going to do something. If you don't lash out, you might withdraw and become more emotionally numb, even if it's just for that moment. So, there is some protection required there. So, when you're deciding if a boundary is necessary, a useful question can be, "Is there a need for protection in this moment?"'

You may be thinking it's going to be extremely tough to set boundaries. Young kids won't understand. Teenagers don't listen.

But perhaps we underestimate how much children can communicate and forget that a small child's ability to understand may be far greater than their ability to verbalise. I believe you can set boundaries and talk to your children about what you expect of them, even at a young age. Jodie agrees:

'I'd say with a two-year-old you absolutely can talk with them about their behaviour. Just manage your expectations about how they will respond.'

Just like many other parts of parenting, having boundaries with children is a skill we can learn. It helps if we allow ourselves to be imperfect during the process and accept that it's not something we'll master overnight.

I found it interesting to consider where I could plop myself on Baumrind's grid.

And I'm guessing most of us consider ourselves a combination of the various styles. Erin Huckle from Chuckle Communications, mum of Finley (9), Walter (6) and Lachlan (4), told me:

'While I'd love to say I'm an authoritative parent, I've definitely been authoritarian, permissive and even neglectful at times.

But I don't think this makes me a bad parent. It just makes me a human one who's doing her best to juggle the demands of three energetic kids. It's easy to read parenting descriptions on paper and see how they make sense, but it's harder to apply them in the constant, noisy day-to-day of parenting.'

Take note of what gave you pause in the list of parenting styles and save it for the tasks at the end of the chapter.

Is it all about our parenting?

All of this kind of sounds like how our kids turn out is entirely down to how we parent. That's a lot of pressure, right?

But, obviously, other factors come into play, such as:

- cultural differences
- ethnic differences
- the child's temperament or nature.

In short, many child psychologists believe that parenting style isn't the only determining factor in a child's development. In fact, many believe your child's temperament can influence your parenting behaviour. It's a chicken-and-egg thing.

You could say that, if a parent is warm and listens, they will have children with fewer behaviour problems, or that warm, responsive parenting results in well-behaved kids. But, equally, you could argue that well-behaved kids *allow* their parents to be warmer and more responsive.

You see the problem?

While it's important to make decisions about how you want to parent, you also need to adapt to the child you have. And I think that's clearly the case with multi-child families.

My brother and I were brought up in the same family, and I'm sure my parents felt they were parenting us the same way. But there was so much more at play:

- My parents were five years older when they had me, and so they were more mature and more confident.

- Their financial situation had also hugely improved, and so they were less stressed.
- My brother was quite unwell as a child, whereas I was a chubby ball of health.
- We moved when I was about seven, which disrupted my brother (who was 13 at the time) a lot more than it did me.

And there are probably thousands of other tiny factors I'm not aware of.

My brother and I are similar in many ways but starkly different in others. So, is that nature (we popped out of the womb like this) or nurture (the differences in the ways we were parented)? Or is it a bit of both?

It's hard for the average parent to work it all out and come up with an exact answer. But I hope this has helped you reflect and stop blaming yourself for everything you do.

Psst! I saw a Facebook post the other day that said, 'My kid just got a face tattoo. Go ahead, bottle-feed your baby. It doesn't matter'. Which I think sums it all up nicely. All this effort trying to make the 'perfect' human, and they will likely go ahead and do things you don't approve of anyway.

Style versus practice

While you may identify with a particular parenting style, the way you implement this style (your way of 'doing' parenting) might be hugely different from other parents. This means even parents with similar parenting styles may choose different approaches.

For example, if you're an Authoritative Parent and pride yourself on your honesty, you might find you're a bit *too* honest for most parents.

I remember explaining where babies come from to my son when he was five – not in graphic terms, but also without pulling any punches. The school told us that other parents were slightly horrified when he started regaling their kids with the details.

If you're a Permissive Parent, your level of 'no rules' living may not fit with parents who have some basic rules. Are you the type of parent who lets their kid run around a cafe having a wild old time, or is that reserved for your own home?

So again, while these broad-sweep parenting types may help you find your parenting 'tribe', you may discover you have less in common with the other members than you expected.

Nature versus nurture

We've all heard the nature versus nurture debate. Do our mini humans turn into who they are because of how we raise them, or are they pre-coded from birth?

A recent study by the Queensland Brain Institute and the Vrije Universiteit Amsterdam collected and analysed almost every twin study ever done in the past 50 years[9]. Their study found that, on average, a person's behaviour, traits and character are influenced almost equally by genetics (nature) and environment (nurture). Dr Beben Benyamin from the Queensland Brain Institute said:

> 'When visiting the nature versus nurture debate, there is overwhelming evidence that both genetic and environmental factors can influence traits and diseases. What is comforting is that, on average, about 50% of individual differences are genetic and 50% are environmental.'

So, we're only 50% responsible for how our kids turn out. Phew!

New parenting styles

Over recent years a few new types of parenting have popped up, so let's run through those quickly while we're here.

Attachment parenting

In 1993, William Sears wrote *The Attachment Parenting Book,* which is about parenting practices based on the attachment theory developed by psychiatrist John Bowlby.

Attachment parenting is all about meeting the emotional needs of your kids and being super responsive. It involves a lot of physical contact and emotional connection. These types of parents create a warm, safe, positive environment that encourages their kids to develop trust and closeness, giving them enough time to feel comfortable with the larger world.

Again, I like to think this is me. I'm a hugger and a talker. I talk about emotions a lot – so much so that my now-13-year-old son begs me to stop:

'No more feelings talk, Mum.'

'Yes, I know you love me.'

Hugs have also been rationed to one a day. He's a teenager.

And now my poor dog bears the brunt of my attachment parenting.

Tiger parenting

Tiger parenting refers to a stricter parenting style with harsh rules and regulations. These parents tend to create rigid environments where kids have little freedom and few choices. They may even resort to shaming and insults to force their kids to comply with the rules. (It's a bit like Baumrind's authoritarian parenting style.)

It all sounds a bit full-on, but we should probably take a minute to reflect why they become tiger parents in the first place. Most tiger parenting is coming from a place of good: wanting their child to succeed, wanting the best for their future, and feeling that the only way to get that is to push them every day.

I know a fair few humans who were tiger-parented into choices that didn't feel like their own and then, much to the distress of their mums and dads, rebelled in their early 20s – that medical degree thrown aside to become a graphic designer. I guess it's important for these types of parents to let go a little and realise that their child will one day be an adult.

Helicopter parenting

Helicopter parenting refers to an over-protective parenting style with constant involvement. These parents 'hover' over their children and control every aspect of their lives. Helicopter parents tend to step in whenever a problem comes up, controlling activities and potentially not letting kids have the chance to learn things on their own.

This parenting style is thought to interfere with a child's development, leaving them with poor coping skills, less independence and a fear of failure.

Erm, guilty. I live in morbid fear of my son climbing any kind of tree. I've told him he's going to live at home until he's 47 and never can learn to drive a car.

I'll admit I still get super anxious when he's out for more than five minutes with his friends. For me, it's a battle between letting him enjoy life and keeping him safe.

Here's what Anastasia Geneave from Chalk and Cheese Occasions, mum of Samuel (3) and Emily (1), said:

'I try not to be a helicopter parent. However, I find it creeping in now and then. When it shows up, it's usually because I'm feeling anxious, either about the kids or something else. It makes me hover, lowers my risk appetite and stops me from letting the kids take as many risks. I have to stop and remember all the research I've read about bringing up resilient and confident kids by letting them go a lot more than we're comfortable with as adults.'

And here's what Lauren Minns from Luminous Copy, mum of Bella (9) and step-mum of Jaxen (10) and Olliver (9), has to say:

'As a helicopter parent, I think it can also be about protecting our kids from emotional "danger" as well as physical danger; for example, protecting them from social problems, failures and other mentally/emotionally tough learning opportunities.'

Free-range parenting

Free-range parenting is the total opposite of helicopter parenting. Free-range parents offer less control and supervision and give their kids more freedom. Free-range kiddos are allowed to explore their environment, make choices and learn from the consequences of those choices.

Again, there are pros and cons to this. Many see this style as a great way to emphasise self-direction and respect for a child's needs, but others believe the lack of boundaries and rules places this style firmly in Baumrind's Uninvolved Parenting category.

My own parenting style

While researching this chapter and chatting with Jodie, I obviously reflected on my own parenting style. And to be honest, I found it hard to fit myself in any given box.

You might feel this way too.

I can be helicopter in the morning and free-range in the afternoon. I've been known to be uninvolved when I'm distracted, but I also feel I'm warm and responsive.

I think your own parents will be an influence too. You'll either want to be just like them or the total opposite.

I grew up as a child of the seventies. We were the generation of broken arms from falling out of trees. I once disappeared for the day to swim in an abandoned quarry without my mum having a clue.

We played doctors and nurses in our friends' lounge rooms while our parents drank Blue Nun in the kitchen. We were the latchkey kids.

But on the flip side, I was also loved and listened to. I was given rules and boundaries. I was allowed to do my own thing but also given help and advice.

Were my parents perfect? Far from it.

Have they influenced my parenting style? Absolutely.

A little bit of 'Do that' and a bit of 'Don't do that' – which is probably true for most of us.

Sam Jockel, Founder and CEO of ParentTV, mum of Eden (15), Maisie (13) and Ellis (9), agrees:

'A lot of how we show up and who we are with our kids is just what was programmed in us from when we were kids. Sometimes that can go either way.

'If you had one really extreme experience as a kid, you may actually flip to the other side because of the trauma of even being close to that kind of behaviour. But for other people, they can have that kind of experience and still show up with that, because that's actually just how you were coded.'

What if your parenting style differs from your partner's?

It's highly unlikely that your parenting style will gel completely with your partner's, even if you 'agreed' on certain values and ideas before you had kids. You don't have the same tastes in music or even Netflix shows, so how can you expect to be on the same page with your children?

Jodie explains it:

> 'Ninety-nine out of 100 disagreements about parenting styles come from the baggage we're each trying to protect our children from. What resonates with you may not resonate with your partner because they have different baggage. So, while you can want the same things for your child, the path you both need to take to get there will probably be extremely different.

> 'Having different parenting styles is fine. Who of any of us had parents that said the same thing to us?'

This is true for me. Mum was one way, Dad was another. I learned to be a little diplomat.

And I know there's an abiding idea that both parents should be united and that, if both parents give their child the same message, everything will be okay. But will it?

Jodie thinks not:

> 'Soon enough, our children will be looking at the million different ways of living in this world. They need the skills to be able to see what someone else is doing and decide whether that's what they want for their life. And so, instead of worrying about giving them the same message so they don't question it, we want to look for, "Why is my child not taking on what I'm saying?"'

Understanding lack of control

Once we understand our children will be exposed to different parenting styles and strategies and influenced by the world around them, we need to start accepting the limits of our control.

Which is both a good thing and a scary thing.

As soon as our child goes to day care or school, they're exposed to new ways of thinking, new influences and new ideas.

Jodie adds:

'I saw a quote on Facebook that said, "If your first child is best friends with my third child, I am sorry," because the third child is exposed to so much.

'If it's your first child, you think you've controlled the environment and you're not exposing them to these things. But that's not reality. I'm not saying we shouldn't try and control anything, but let's not overestimate how much control we have.'

So, if we don't have absolute control, all we can do is help our child process things, feel confident and make decisions about their behaviour.

Can we really define 'good' parenting?

I know we all love a personality quiz and many of us love a label. We all want someone to give us a hug and tell us we're doing a good job, or a crystal ball to see how it all turns out.

But I think it's hard to definitively say what makes a good parent.

Rather, I think it's important to work out what being a good parent means to you. How do your values translate into parenting? What is your list of requirements for yourself?

And because you might not know where to start, I asked some of my members what they think makes a good parent. Here are their suggestions. Do you agree with them?

- You tell your child you love them and show them your love every day.
- You listen to your child. (Put your phone down and give them your full attention.)
- You keep your word when you make a promise. (This is a huge one for me.)
- You're aware that actions speak louder than words. (Don't tell your kids off for yelling and then yell yourself.)
- You manage your child's expectations. (You admire the differences in their personality, behaviour and preferences rather than endlessly wishing they were a mini you.)

- Your child feels they can come to you with problems. (They're not scared of how you'll react.)

- You encourage your kids to pursue their interests and talents. (Don't live out your prima-ballerina or pro-soccer-player dreams through them.)

- You teach your child to fail and to trust themselves. (Don't try shielding them from all the bad things.)

- You create boundaries to keep your child safe. (Set limits around bedtime, respectful language and behaviour.)

- You work hard to manage your emotions and stay calm. (But you forgive yourself when you can't.)

- You acknowledge your mistakes. (While you may not always be perfect, you can apologise for your behaviour.)

You think you're failing

'You think you're failing' could have been on that list, but it was a big one that came up a lot, so I thought it deserved its own little section.

The general feeling among the parents I spoke to was that if you're worried you're not a great parent, then you're probably doing something right. It's the parents who are supremely confident (and a tad smug) who are often the worst.

It's that whole Dunning-Kruger effect thing. The Dunning-Kruger effect suggests that the more we know, the more we realise what we don't know; it often refers to those who don't have expertise or overestimate their ability.

I think Hannah Potter from THINKercise, mum of three (9, 7 and 4), provides a great perspective:

'It's so tricky to articulate what makes a good parent. I think you can look at it from different perspectives. What a child considers a good parent in the moment could be quite different to what an adult thinks is good parenting.

'Thinking about it now, a good parent is someone who brings their child up with the skills for living. But that said, there's no guarantee because every child is an individual. Arrgh!

'I know I'm doing the best I can in the situation I'm in. Sometimes, on reflection, it could have been better but, in the moment,
what happened happened. Second-guessing and regretting isn't
helpful for me.'

Knowing you're doing the best you can, and aiming to be in the moment
and not living in a state of permanent regret, might be all we can hope
for. It's not idealistic but it feels realistic.

Comparison isn't helpful

Becoming clear on what makes you feel like a good parent will help you
stop comparing yourself to other parents.

Whenever I'm doubting my parenting, I find it helps to be mindful
and honest about my strengths rather than just focusing on my flaws.
Sure, I can't volunteer for the school canteen *(and even if I could, my
son would die of embarrassment)*, but I'm really into doing craft projects
with him. I'm not sporty and won't kick a ball around, but I'm willing to
spend hours playing Minecraft.

I know my strengths and my flaws as a parent. I genuinely feel that,
like Hannah, most of the time I'm doing my absolute best.

Understanding your parenting values

Now we have a deeper understanding of different parenting styles, the
impact of nature and nurture and some suggestions for what others
value as parents, I'm hoping you feel about ready to make your own
list of 'good parenting' ideas. And once you have your list, you need to
think hard about how your business could support (or will challenge)
those ideas.

For example, is listening to your kids important? Well then, you
need to put down your phone and make space for that.

Do you want to set strict TV and gaming limits with your kids?
Then you need to finish working when you said you would.

There's simply no point in setting out ideals of parenting that you'll
never be able to meet. You need to get real with yourself now. By all
means, create your list and have some non-negotiables. But don't set
yourself up to fail.

Giving your child life skills

At the end of all of this, what we probably want to give our kids is what we may not have had ourselves: the ability to explore who they are, be themselves and be confident in their choices. Even as a near 50-year-old woman, I'm still unpacking what my thoughts actually are and what was expected of me as a child.

Jodie sums it up beautifully:

'We'll need to wrestle with the idea that our children will inherently be something we didn't see coming. And so it then becomes this interesting exercise in not having certainty. I think it's useful to hope that they are physically healthy and mentally well, and have the skills to cope with life.'

TL;DR

There's no such thing as a perfect parent. Instead, you need to work out your approach to parenting and be comfortable with it.

Benefits

Thinking about your definition of a good parent will help you:

- attain a deeper understanding of your parenting style
- get clear ideas about how you want to parent
- create a more realistic list of parental attributes that don't set you up to fail
- realise there's no such thing as a perfect parent
- stop comparing yourself to others.

Over to you

I hope you now realise there's no such thing as a universally good parent. Rather, it's about deciding when you feel good about your parenting. To help you really get clear on this, here are a few exercises:

1. Make a list of parental attributes that are important to you.
   (Feel free to use some of my suggestions in this chapter as a guide.)
2. Make some notes about how your business will challenge these attributes.
3. Discuss them with your partner (if you have one).
4. Discuss them with your kids (if they're old enough to understand).

Chapter 5

How to banish parent guilt

*'There is no way to be a perfect parent and
a million ways to be a good one.'*

paraphrased from Jill Churchill (who originally
wrote 'mother' instead of 'parent')

Remember me sitting in my backyard office laboriously tapping out an answer to a marketing question in my Facebook group from some dude called Barry?

I felt like a terrible mother.

My inner narrative went something like this:

I shouldn't be trying to build a business. I should be spending time with my son. He's going to grow up hating me. I am a horrible person. What's wrong with me?

Every day I suffered chronically painful attacks of parenting guilt. *(I know this is more often known as 'mum' guilt, but for the purpose of this chapter we're going to call it 'parent guilt' because I know it's a dad thing too.)*

And back then then I had no idea how to deal with it. As time went on, I suffered a million parent-guilt paper cuts. I've not turned up at school sports days due to meetings, forgotten birthday cupcakes while on a business trip and missed out on hearing a story because my brain was abuzz with spreadsheets and deadlines.

Does that sound familiar?

These days, I'm older, wrinklier and somewhat wiser. I've 'toughened up' a bit and learned some tactics and mindset shifts that allow me to deal with these icky guilty feelings. In this chapter, I want to share them with you.

Childhood is a new concept

Okay, here's one for the history and sociology buffs: you may not realise it, but the notion of 'childhood' is a social construct. Which means it's a made-up thing.

Back in 1960, French historian Philippe Ariès argued that the concept of childhood was a very modern invention. He declared that in medieval Europe the idea of children as entities to be loved and cherished just didn't exist. There was no special treatment for them in terms of preparing them for adulthood: no emotional investment (affection, time, attention) and no separate activities given to children.

He argued that, up until the 1680s, kids were actually considered mini adults. They were dressed like small adults, and from the age of seven they were deemed capable of helping their parents around the house or farm or leaving the house altogether to earn an income.

I don't believe that humans back in the old days didn't love their children just as much as we do now. But I do believe the idea of being a 'good' parent wasn't such a huge thing. In most working-class and middle-class families, kids were born (often a lot of them), but not all of them survived to adulthood. Those who did were looked after and then sent out to work as early as possible to support the family.

Even in the 19th century, parenting tactics were harsh by modern standards. Charles Dickens – he of *Great Expectations* fame – was sent to work in a boot-blacking factory at age 12, which can't have been much fun.

The 1880s edition of *Cassell's Household Guide* generally encouraged a deep terror of spoiling your kids and cautioned that, with children, 'Overindulgence is the stumbling block of life'[10]. This resulted in hugely hypocritical behaviour. For example, while parents could often stuff down 13-course dinners, they would happily serve their children bread and porridge at every meal. Fancy foods, such as sweets and fruit, were seen as the route to creating a spoiled brat. And there was deemed nothing worse than being spoiled.

We all know that 'be seen but not heard' is a bit of a Victorian catchphrase, but it was quite common – especially for upper-class parents – right up until the 1960s. It was deemed perfectly acceptable to barely see their children, possibly speaking to them just once a day at teatime. Physical affection was discouraged beyond a shake of the hand and a pat on the head. Nannies for wealthier families were the norm, and working-class children in the UK were often put out to work as young as eight until the *Chimney Sweepers Act* was passed in 1834 outlawing kids working before the age of ten. *(My grandad started working in a coal mine when he was 14. Poor lump.)*

And while I'm not arguing for a return to stuffing six-year-olds up chimneys, I think it's interesting to consider how much pressure modern society puts on us to be 'good parents'. In the UK, where I grew up, we've gone from sending kids down the coal mine at 14, to an hour of reluctant parenting after teatime, to 'Go play outside until dinner', to hands-on helicopter parenting – all in less than a century.

The history lesson may not help with the guilt, but it certainly provides some perspective.

Here's what Jodie Thornton, Parenting Coach, told me:

'The act of parenting was not a verb until recently, and I think it's fascinating to think about how little thought was going into parenting previously and now how much almost obsessive thought is going in. But I think that's how we change. This generation of parents is overthinking, overanalysing and overworking – but we have to get through this stage to something that feels more natural and easy.'

Why do we feel parent guilt?

Parent guilt often comes from expectations about how you *should* be parenting your child and meeting their needs. It's often exacerbated by comparing yourself to your own and other parents – both real and fictional – or measuring yourself against a self-created list of impossible proof points.

Now, of course, there needs to be some 'guilt', or a least a modicum of 'care factor'. On a primal level, it helps us stay focused on our children rather than letting them be chewed on by the mammoth outside our cave.

Caring about your kids, worrying about them, is normal and natural. But, left unchecked, it can become a monster that makes your life miserable.

Some might argue that parent guilt is all in the mind, but of course it can feel very real. Those thoughts turn into feelings, those feelings into actions – and all of a sudden we're splashing $200 on a LEGO set just to assuage our feelings of being a poo parent.

And when you're trying to build a business, the guilt can become so totally overwhelming and debilitating that it impacts your productivity and profit. Parent guilt can also lead to mental health issues such as depression and anxiety. *(It did for me.)* And, if it's ignored, it can result in complete burnout and total neglect of your own wellness. (More on this in Chapter 20.)

What makes you feel parent guilt?

I asked my members to identify the last time they felt parent guilt, especially around their business. Here are some of their answers (*I've kept these quotes anonymous because I know some parents feel ick about this stuff*):

> 'I promised to watch a show with my son but got caught up in what I was doing and missed it completely. What's worse is he didn't come and tell me because he didn't want to disturb me.'

> 'I turned my phone onto silent during a Zoom call and missed calls from my daughter's day care saying she was unwell. I made it there in less than an hour, but I felt dreadful.'

> 'School holidays are the worst for me. Even though my kids are older, I always feel the pressure to be doing something big and adventurous but just don't have the time.'

The truth is we're constantly faced with parent-guilt-inducing decisions, and everyone has an opinion.

Take Carla Ellerby from Composed Communication, mum of Maxwell (10) and Ivy (8):

> 'I had a grim moment last year when I asked my seven-year-old if she'd miss me when I went to Melbourne for a client conference.

> '"No. I never see you anyway. You're gone when I wake up and you work every night."

> 'At that point, I knew I'd taken on too much and my whole reason for starting my own business – to see more of the kids – had flopped. Sure, I was finally earning the same as I was in corporate land. But at what cost? The guilt was horrendous.'

How do we tackle parent guilt?

I think it's important to recognise that most parents feel guilty at one time or another and that, as I said earlier, it's perfectly 'normal'. I'd be a little worried if you *didn't* feel guilty. I'm not sure it ever goes away completely, but there are ways to mitigate and minimise the feelings.

Tip 1: Find your triggers

Try to identify the triggers for your parent guilt and avoid them. I often found the school gate a real problem. I hated listening to the other mums semi-torture me with tales of all the awesome things they'd done with their kids while I'd spent the evening up to my armpits in a spreadsheet.

So, rather than put myself through that every day, I waited away from the gate until the last minute and then dashed over to grab my child and run, or I wore headphones or pretended to be on a call. 'Don't make eye contact' was my mantra.

Was I being antisocial? Yes. Was I improving my mental health? Also, yes.

Here's my permission to stop talking to those annoying parents. Stop following the Instagram accounts of perfect parents who make you gag. Leave the judgy-wudgy parenting Facebook groups. You're already criticising yourself enough. Don't encourage others to join in.

Learn to recognise when you're using parent guilt to reassess your priorities and when you're just using it to beat yourself up.

Tip 2: Practise self-care

Learn to forgive your flaws. Recognise that parent guilt is just a thought that's become a feeling. It doesn't need to lead to any kind of action.

Recognise when you're spiralling into negative self-talk. Take a minute to meditate. Or lock yourself in your bedroom for a minute and scream into your pillow.

Tip 3: Talk to others

I remember when my son was very small, about eight months old, I was sitting in a cafe, trying to enjoy a coffee after a sleepless night, my son wailing in my arms.

A man came over to my table and leaned down. I thought he was going to chastise me for my inability to calm my son down. Instead, he said in a low, friendly voice, 'Don't worry, the first year's just shit'.

The relief flooded over me like warm bathwater.

Yes, it was a bit shit. And I needed someone to say that.

Surrounded by mums who breastfed with ease and seemed to enjoy their children so much more than me, I felt like a failure whenever I had negative feelings about parenting or when I did anything other than be with him.

Not being able to communicate or share how you feel with others is part of the problem. Yes, other parents might be sharing their perfect families on Instagram, but you and I both know it's just their highlights reel.

Try to find someone – either a friend or a professional – who you can share your real feelings and thoughts with. Parenting does suck at times and it's okay to admit that.

Tip 4: Ask for help

As well as telling people how you feel, remember to ask for help. No-one is a mind reader – and that includes your partner, friends and family.

What do you *really* need? An hour to enjoy a warm bath? A night in a hotel, away from everything? Someone to go shopping and cook dinner?

While practical help won't always relieve the emotional stress, it can certainly give you time to process it. And if you don't ask, you don't get. Remember that even the smallest things can often make a big difference.

And here's a big fat dose of reassurance: there's no shame in asking for help. We all sometimes feel a bit embarrassed to put our hand up and say, 'I'm not coping'. But if we all did it a little more, we'd be much better off.

Tip 5: Reject the notion of 'quality time'

Redefining quality time helped me a lot.

Before I became a parent, I thought quality time would be baking homemade muffins with my child while simultaneously doing a wooden jigsaw and listening to Bach; or taking an outing to the zoo, eating fairy floss while carrying balloons and feeding the monkeys.

But let's face it: cooking with kids is a nightmare. 'JUST LET ME DO IT.' And the zoo is exhausting, fairy floss is sticky, balloons always pop, and both you and the child end up having a tantrum. Trying to create a 'perfect day' is often a recipe for disaster.

These forced 'fun' events are often a struggle.

Instead, I now view *all* time as quality, including:

- shopping at the supermarket – quality
- driving to pick up your dog from the vet – quality
- mowing the lawn – quality
- cleaning the loo – quality

I find kids just want to be with you. They don't hugely care what they're doing.

Remember this mantra: it's about presence, not presents.

Kids don't need to be lavished with adventures and cool things. They just want attention, security and time to play with you.

Here's a tip from Sally Westra from Flow-On Plumbing & Gas Fitting, mum of Hazel (6) and Sage (3):

'One way I avoid the guilt is to spend 10 to 15 minutes of quality time doing whatever my kids choose before getting into a big task. My eldest will always choose crafts, my youngest pretend play.

'Once they are settled into play and I've joined in for a short period, I explain that I have to do some work now and will join them again just before lunch.

'I can't say it works every time, or that I don't get any sighs or whines when I depart, but for the most part it works well and they have had their cups filled with mummy time, even if it is in short bursts.'

Tip 6: Create time blobs

In Part II, we'll look at how we invest our time, and how getting really organised allows us to commit to clear periods spent working and periods spent parenting.

'Zoning' your day into work time and parent time is far easier than trying to be all things to all people all the time. And I find kids are more accepting if you're clear about when you'll stop working and spend time with them. As long as you stick to it.

Tip 7: Accept the good and bad days

Sometimes you'll eat cereal for dinner and the washing won't get done. On other days you'll take them to the park, cook some nutritious muffins and have every item of clothing washed and ironed. *(Okay, I'm pushing it now.)*

You may not win every day, but there's always tomorrow.

Parenting isn't a competition. There are *(sadly)* no prizes at the end of it all. I like to aim for a 70% success rate when it comes to parenting – it makes life easier.

Tip 8: Make a list

Okay, so perhaps you didn't play that one game with your child when they asked.

But what about all the things you *did* do? The early morning cuddle. The nice breakfast. Getting them dressed. Brushing their teeth. Going to the park. Having lunch together.

Or, for older kids, the endless lifts and meeting the endless demands for food.

It's easy to focus on the one minor 'wrong' of the day rather than thinking about all the 'rights'.

Tip 9: Remember who you are

It's also easy to lose your sense of self when you have kids and forget you're anything beyond a 'parent', but never forget that you're allowed to do things other than stare at your child 24/7.

You're allowed to have hobbies and interests. You're allowed to socialise with other adults *(and not just those with kids)*. You're allowed to have your own business and be excited about it.

You did not lose your right to be happy and fulfilled when you made a child. You owe your child safety, love and LEGO, but you don't owe them your very soul.

Tip 10: Be proud

Remember that, by creating your own business, you're teaching your kids an amazing life lesson. You're showing them what it means to be brave, persistent, confident, hardworking, inventive and so much more. So, rather than trying to hide your business, tell them what you're doing and how your efforts contribute to the family.

We'll talk a lot more about this in Parts IV and V.

Tanya Abdul Jalil from Hayzel Media, mum of three kids (11, 9 and 7), said this:

> 'I tell myself that if I had a nine-to-five job, I'd be out of the house from eight 'til six anyway. So, they're getting more of me than they would if I worked somewhere else. It's also about being a good role model, showing my kids that they can do hard things, that they can be whatever they want to be and that sacrifices pay off with rewards later on.'

Tip 11: Learn to accept

I doubt parent guilt ever goes away completely. Even if we did hug our children continuously all day and give them constant attention, we'd still find something to beat ourselves up about.

Accepting that parent guilt is normal and shows that you care is an important step in handling it each day. Just learn to ride the roller-coaster of emotions and let parent guilt pass over you rather than consume you.

Belinda Owen from Belinda Owen Website Design, mum of Isaac (9), said this:

> 'I don't think parent guilt is altogether a bad thing. The fact we feel it means we care about our work and our family. But I think it consciously takes us away from our work to spend time with the kids, which is a good thing. It's the reason most parents choose to work from home or run their own business.'

Tip 12: Tell it how it is

When I spoke with Jodie Thornton, she suggested being 100% honest with your child:

> 'You might say, "I love you, and I play Barbies or Transformers with you because you love it. I hate it, but I do it because I love you and you love to do that with me". We want to be honest.'

I'm not sure I'm quite ready to be *that* honest – even now, and my son is nearly 14. But it might work for you.

TL;DR

Cut yourself some slack. If your kids are clean, fed, loved and relatively happy, that's enough.

Benefits

Thinking about parent guilt and how to minimise it is vital as it's going to help you:

- stop wasting your time feeling guilty and spend more time getting the things done that you were worried about in the first place
- find the headspace to focus on your business when you're working and enjoy parenting when it's parenting time
- get yourself off the emotional roller-coaster and live a calmer life.

Over to you

1. Make a list of three times you felt parent guilt in the last few months.
2. Review each one and assess whether you genuinely feel it was worth feeling guilty about.
3. Identify triggers for your parent guilt and do your best to eliminate them. It's fine to unfollow people on social media (or just mute them if you don't want them to know).
4. Make a list of all the things you do for your kids each day.

Remember, if you'd like to work through these exercises in detail you can head to sixfiguresinschoolhours.com and grab the accompanying workbook.

PART II

PRODUCTIVITY

SQUEEZING THE MOST
OUT OF YOUR DAY

I'M YET TO MEET a business owner who feels they have an excess of time. And it's rare to find a parent who doesn't feel utterly frazzled every single day.

And yes, like you, I was horrified when I had my son and realised just how little 'me' time I now had. Horrified!

But if there's one thing I've always been good at, it's time management. My brain has a knack for being able to assess a task, estimate the time it will take to fix and then stick to that time allowance.

I also have the seemingly rare ability to sit at my desk even when I'm tired, have no motivation or inspiration, and just get the hell on with it. And that, my friends, is a superpower.

Because here's the truth: I know you wish you had more hours in the day. But you don't, and you need to get over that.

You need to realise that the key to being a successful business owner and parent isn't finding a secret hack or a get-rich-quick scheme. It's not about following some fancy-pants entrepreneur success strategy. It's about making more of that finite resource called time.

You need to understand that it's less about the myth of 'balance' and more about the truth of focus.

I believe you can achieve the dream: the ability to be either off or on. The freedom to be present for either your business *or* your kids.

No more desperately trying to catch up on emails while also making your kids an afternoon snack. No more tapping out typo-filled emails to clients at the supermarket checkout. No more forcing yourself to get up at 4 a.m. just to get in a solid hour of work before the kids wake up. And no more missing half of what your kid is saying because your mind is wrapped up in some work dilemma.

You see, it's not one big thing that helps you become a better business owner and parent but lots of little shifts. The discipline to start on the important tasks rather than leaving them until the last minute. Writing a to-do list and then actually doing it. Setting workable boundaries and sticking to them.

Now, I'm not promising to turn you into a robotic machine of extreme productivity, powering through tasks like a hamster on crack. You'll still have good days and bad days. But, using a combination of realism, basic project management, smart productivity tips and firm boundary-setting, you can get to the point where you can tell your kids, 'I'll be done in an hour,' and actually keep your promise.

In this section we're going to tackle:

- genuinely assessing the time you have
- creating workable schedules
- finding planning methods that work
- implementing small productivity wins
- asking for help.

Okay, let the productivity adventure begin.

Chapter 6

Getting real about your time

'Don't get sidetracked stomping on ants
when you have elephants to feed.'

Peter Turla

Lack of time is the single biggest issue most business-owning parents talk to me about:

'There aren't enough hours in the day.'

'My to-do list never ends.'

'I'd love to spend more time with the kids but I can't squeeze it in.'

'I'm just bloody exhausted all the time.'

And yet so often these same parents have few time management strategies in place.

I'm guessing it's because they never have the time to sit down and think of them. I mean, when was the last time you had the luxury of an empty hour with no distractions? Either that or they're horrendous procrastifaffers – possibly a Toonism, it's a dangerous combination of procrastination and faffing, which means being a busy fool to avoid doing the important things in your business. Or they have learned the dark art of doing 30 minutes of work in eight hours and eight hours of work in 30 minutes.

In this chapter, I want to encourage you to think about your days and weeks, and how to manage your time intentionally and intelligently for both your business and your family.

Why is understanding time important?

Most of us are fully aware that we face time limitations as parents. I mean, duh!? But rather than take a calm rational approach to this reality, we frantically try to jam as much as possible into the pathetic amount of time we have.

We fall into a pattern of dramatically overestimating what we can achieve and failing miserably to get everything done. This leaves us constantly feeling like we're underperforming, when the truth is we were *never* going to tick off all those things on our to-do list anyway.

As I write this, my list for today looks something like this:

· walk elderly dog
· make school lunch
· drive my son to school (raining) so back at my desk at 9-ish
· pick up son at 2.40 p.m.
· take son to the gym, then shopping, post office
· make dinner
· family time
· one hour of me time before I'm drooling on my pillow.

That 9 a.m. to 2.40 p.m. slot equates to 5.5 hours of available working time. But today I had 3.5 hours of online meetings (Mastermind × 2, 1 × podcast, 1 × team), leaving me with just 2 hours to do actual work – really 1.5 if I allow myself time to wee and grab a bite to eat.

1.5 hours isn't very much, so I gave myself a reality check and decided to only:

· send one big important email
· balance my Xero accounting software *(Xero is a financial management software tool – more on this in Extra Bits at the end of the book)*
· clear my inbox *(I'm one of those disgusting 'inbox zero' people)*
· do a Facebook live.

That's it.

By taking a realistic approach, I'm able to feel like I've had a productive day within the bounds of what time I had available to me.

Is it moving my business forward in huge sweaty leaps and bounds? No. Is it the best I can do? Yes.

Your time reality

I'm going to assume that you're working within the parameters of school (or day care) pick-up and drop-off *(hence the book title)*. I want you to take a minute now to map out the time you have in any given week.

My weekly time map would look something like table 6.1.

Table 6.1: My weekly time map

	Available between	**Hours available**
Mon	8.30 a.m. – 3 p.m.	6.5
Tue	8.30 a.m. – 3 p.m.	6.5
Wed	8.30 a.m. – 3 p.m.	6.5
Thu	8.30 a.m. – 3 p.m.	6.5
Fri	8.30 a.m. – 3 p.m.	6.5
Total		**32.5 hours**

I'm being relatively realistic here. I'm acknowledging the following:

· I'd love to be the sort of person who gets up at 5 a.m. and does a few hours of work before my son gets up, but that ain't ever going to happen. I LOVE MY SLEEP.

· My brain turns to soup at around 3 p.m. each day so I'm never going to be a burn-the-midnight-oil type.

· I loathe and resent working weekends and want to keep them for family time or for myself.

But it's still not a true picture. It assumes I start work as soon as my son leaves. Also, it assumes I don't eat and never go to the toilet. (I do, in fact, have a bladder of STEEL, which I shall donate to medical science upon my demise.)

So, let's try that weekly time map again (see table 6.2).

Table 6.2: My slightly more honest weekly time map

	Available between	Hours available
Mon	9 a.m. – 12 p.m.; 12.30 p.m. – 3 p.m.	5.5
Tue	9 a.m. – 12 p.m.; 12.30 p.m. – 3 p.m.	5.5
Wed	9 a.m. – 12 p.m.; 12.30 p.m. – 3 p.m.	5.5
Thu	9 a.m. – 12 p.m.; 12.30 p.m. – 3 p.m.; 6 p.m. – 7 p.m.	6.5
Fri	10 a.m. – 12 p.m.	2
Total		**25 hours**

Now I've been a little more honest – and can have wees *(winning)*.

You'll notice Friday is a little lighter: this is because I acknowledge that on Fridays I often book in essential life admin things, like taking the dog to the vet and getting my nostril hair waxed.

I've added in the one late night a week as I regularly have coaching calls with my European clients (ooh la la!). By being a bit more honest, I've unfortunately already shaved a fat 7.5 hours off my available working time. Bugger!

But the problem is, it's still a big fat lie. Because it doesn't account for billable time.

What is billable time?

In my advertising agency days, we were forced to keep comprehensive time sheets tracking every millisecond of the day. Why? Because that's how the agency knew how much to bill each client to pay for all the free booze and beanbags.

There was a general acceptance that not all time would be billable. But only a teeny bit.

We were allowed a few hours for admin, for faffing about and for heating up tuna pasta in the office kitchen microwave – but we were never allowed to go over 20% non-billable.

For those who are poor at maths, that meant we had to be 80% billable.

In truth, most of my time sheets were a glorious work of fiction, and I apologise to all the clients who were billed for the time I spent flirting with the design team and endlessly googling romantic mini breaks. But the practice of tracking billable versus non-billable hours was deeply ingrained in me. When I work, sometimes I'm making money and other times I'm most definitely not.

From discussions with hundreds of my community members, I'd say that most business owners are not hitting the lofty heights of 80% billable; it's way more likely to be around 60%.

Most small business owners will lose at least 40% of their available weekly time to:

· faffing about
· disappearing down social media wormholes
· working on new business
· overtalking on client and customer calls
· cleaning their desk – and shaking biscuit crumbs out of their keyboard
· mindlessly watching Reels and TikToks
· gazing into space while having an existential crisis.

Now, while some of these tasks (new business and social media) might generate money in the long term, often there's no clear or immediate return on investment (ROI). And mostly the rest is just procrastifaffing.

Belinda Owen from Belinda Owen Website Design, mum of Isaac (9), said this:

'Now my son's at school I find it easier to track hours and set schedules. I work the five hours he's at school and that time is billable, with a few non-billable hours attending workshops, group calls or commenting on social media posts building my reputation. I work a few more non-billable hours in the evening doing admin, social media, blog writing or planning the next six months.

'Realistically, I probably work 15 billable hours a week based on income. But I'm working to increase productivity and my billable hours to 20, which will move me closer to my financial goals.'

TOON TIP You can use a tool such as Toggl Track to track your time and work out the percentage that is billable versus non billable.

If we add the 60% billable factor into my weekly time chart, then my working hours look more like table 6.3.

Table 6.3: My weekly billable hours

	Available between	Hours available	60% billable
Mon	9 a.m. – 12 p.m.; 12.30 p.m. – 3 p.m.	5.5	3.3
Tue	9 a.m. – 12 p.m.; 12.30 p.m. – 3 p.m.	5.5	3.3
Wed	9 a.m. – 12 p.m.; 12.30 p.m. – 3 p.m.	5.5	3.3
Thu	9 a.m. – 12 p.m.; 12.30 p.m. – 3 p.m.; 6 p.m. – 7 p.m.	6.5	3.9
Fri	10 a.m. – 12 p.m.	2	1.2
Total		**25 hours**	**15**

Oh, the sweet horror of realising I actually only have 15 hours to make all the money I want to make. But it's a truth I need to face if I'm going to be realistic about what I can achieve.

The time mindset shift

So, if I took my time at face value, I would think that I had 32.5 hours a week to work and, if I don't question this, I'm going to think I can achieve a lot more than I actually can. That mentality will set me up for failure.

It will also make others – like my partner – think I have more time than I actually do and wonder why they don't come home to a clean house, a home-cooked meal and a much happier human.

Without this time reality check, I will forever feel like I'm not doing enough, making me question my ability as a business owner. And because I'm regularly not finishing the unrealistic tasks I set myself for the day, I will:

· resent leaving what I'm doing to pick up my child because I have tasks to finish
· try to squeeze in work when my son is around, making him feel neglected and making me feel frustrated
· force myself to wake up at stupid o'clock or work late into the night – when I'm neither switched on nor productive
· feel mentally and physically exhausted by everything I have on my plate.

Hourly rates help

Working out how many hours you have can also help you calculate your hourly rate. Whatever type of business you have, whether it's an ecommerce store or some kind of service, hourly rates matter.

> **TOON TIP** I am not recommending that you necessarily charge by the hour – product or project rates are far more effective, allowing you to build in contingency, amends, material costs etc. But, to work out these rates, it's good to know how many hours you spend doing the do.

However you choose to charge, knowing your base hourly rate helps you:

· set budgets and cash flow expectation
· understand your high-margin and low-margin tasks and projects
· compare your rate with those of suppliers that may offer opportunities to outsource.

We talk more about setting budgets in Chapter 12 and outsourcing in Chapter 10.

Let's calculate your hourly rate

Imagine I want to earn around $10K a month *(we talk more about how much you need and want to earn each month in Chapter 12)*, which would bring in revenue of $120K per year – a comfy six figures. The calculation would look something like this:

1. **Calculate billable hours:** total weekly hours × 60% = billable hours per week

2. **Calculate working hours in a month:** billable hours per week × 52 (working weeks in year) ÷ 12 months = monthly billable hours

3. **Calculate hourly rate:** financial goal ÷ monthly billable hours = hourly rate

For me, this looks like this:

1. 25 weekly hours × 60% = 15 billable hours per week

2. 15 billable hours per week × 52 weeks ÷ 12 months = 65 monthly billable hours

3. $10k ÷ 65 billable hours per month = $154 per hour

So, based on my 25-hours-a-week realistic goal, I'd have to charge around $154 per hour to hit my budget.

But wait, you're a parent

Oh, hang on a minute, I didn't allow for holidays, did I? Goddammit. We could change my possible working time to 48 weeks in a year, giving me a nice four weeks off.

But, of course, we're parents, so we need to consider school holidays of around 12 weeks a year (possibly more if your kid/s attend private school). Of course, you might be able to work a little but not at full pelt.

And even then, we need to remember teacher training days and public holidays. Depending on what childcare options you have in school hols, you're going to have to factor that in too. (More on handling school holidays in Chapter 7.)

Oh, and kids tend to get sick sometimes too, don't they? *(And by 'sometimes' I mean all the damn time.)* And possibly you might too. All those nasty little germs they pick up at day care and school seem to hit us poor adults twice as hard.

So, let's assume I only have 44 working weeks (giving me eight weeks off) and recalculate:

1. 25 weekly hours × 60% = 15 billable hours per week
2. 15 billable hours per week × 44 weeks ÷ 12 months = 55 monthly hours
3. $10k ÷ 55 billable hours per month = $182 per hour

Based on this, I'd need to hit $182-ish per hour to hit my revenue target.

Now, of course, this hourly rate is entirely doable – depending on your product or service – but it's vital that you're aware of this rate when you're working out all your financial metrics.

Also, accepting that you really do only have so many hours in a week to work kind of forces you to accept the concept of sacred time.

What is sacred time?

Sacred working time is something I strongly believe in. It's the idea that, when you're working, you are working. Simple, right? But it's so hard to stick to. I find most working parents are hugely distracted by household chores, especially if they work at home. (We talk more about workspaces in Chapter 15.)

The average work-at-home parent's day looks something like this:

1. Head to luxurious office space (kitchen table)
2. Open inbox
3. Remember you didn't put the washing on
4. Put washing on
5. Have a wee
6. Make a cup of tea
7. Check emails again
8. Consider starting project
9. Washing finishes – decide to pop in tumble dryer
10. Have a wee

11. Check fridge for inspiring food
12. Make a cup of tea
13. Write up shopping list
14. Return to desk
15. Check emails again

Oh, the constant, endless, unproductive loop! So, let me be firm here *(this might be the most important thing you read in this book, so grab a highlighter).*

As a working parent, it's vital that you learn how to be either 'on' or 'off'.

You're either parenting or you're businessing.

You can't be 'on' for both all the time.

Boom! Mic drop. The downfall of most business-owning parents is that they try to blend parenting and business into one homogenous blob. But I want you to think of business and parenting like oil and water (for the most part).

They don't mix.

This is especially true when your kids are small, when you can't leave them alone for one minute without them trying to flush themselves down the loo or eat the dog's kibble.

It gets easier as they enter tweendom – the awkward time between being a little kid and being a teenager – and teendom, as they're able to wipe their own bums and make themselves snacks *(even if they do destroy the kitchen in the process).*

So, let me repeat: when you're working, you're working. That time is sacred. No popping out after that Zoom call to just quickly vacuum the entire house. No nipping to the shops after school drop-off for some random vegetable purchase. Instead, you must focus on your business 100% and leave those household jobs until you're in parent mode.

But, equally, when you're parenting, you're parenting. That time is sacred. No taking business calls in the supermarket checkout queue. No writing social media posts when you're supposed to be playing Minecraft. Instead, you must focus on your family 100% and leave the work stuff for the 'official' working hours.

Creating division and treating both your work time and parenting time as sacred has been key for me.

Time as an investment

Another great way to reframe your attitude to time is to think less about 'spending' it and more about 'investing' it.

Spending feels frivolous, like you're splashing your time about with no thought for the consequences.

Investing feels more solid, like you're laying down the foundations for the future.

For a long time, I had a Post-it Note on my screen that said:

'Is this the best use of my time?'

I can't tell you the number of times this caught my eye before I fell into a pit of social media time wasting and it pulled me back from the brink.

My partner has little Post-it Notes in strategic places in his house *(my favourite is the one on the back of the loo door!)* saying:

'What's important now?'

It helps him refocus and think about priorities in his day.

Thinking of your time as an investment helps you stop and think before starting an activity. Ask yourself, 'Is what I'm about to do intentional or mindless?' Are you choosing to watch 73 reels about pimple popping for customer research, or are you using it as a tactic to avoid starting that important task? Do you really need to load the dishwasher at this exact moment, or could it wait until after school pick-up?

Or – continuing that nautical theme – are you bobbing about aimlessly like an empty crisp packet in the ocean, or are you an eager dolphin, swimming porpoisefully (!) towards your goal?

It's fine to have downtime – in fact, it's essential – but be sure you're choosing the time to relax and not using it to faff away your day.

TOON TIP I think it's really important for kids to see you doing household jobs so they can appreciate all that you do. There's no pack of dutiful cleaning fairies coming in while they are at school to pick Coco Pops off the kitchen counters. You are doing it.

The world will wait

The second biggest struggle for business parents is an extreme lack of patience: we want it all now *(or, ideally, last Tuesday)*.

We're fed a barrage of 'hustle culture' messages. We see 'successful' male business types lying on Porsches counting their wads of cash, or kaftan-wearing females in clean, white kitchens sharing their million-dollar strategies.

The reality rarely compares with the cold, hard truth: building success takes time.

Now, that may feel depressing as you watch others climb the success ladder faster than you and achieve the things you wish you were achieving. But do you want the good news?

You have time.

Oodles of it. Gallons. Bags full.

Of course, you could be eaten by an overeager toad tomorrow but, barring that, you have plenty of time to get things done. You just need to be patient.

I used to long for a week when there were no dramas. No sick child. No cupcakes to make for cake sale day. No random tradie turning up at my door. A beautiful, clear week of 32 hours (or so I believed) when I could just work, work, work.

'Imagine what I could do with 32 hours!' I said to my partner.

But, of course, that clear week never came. There was always something. And there always will be.

But here's the rub: I *did* have those 32 hours; they just weren't consecutive. They were often spread out over two or three weeks rather than one, but they were still there.

Still usable. Still productive. If I was patient.

Right now, maybe you can't work 10-hour days. Right now, maybe you struggle to get more than 20 minutes of work done without interruption. But it won't always be that way. Soon enough, your children will be grown and gone. Too soon. And you'll genuinely miss someone shouting 'Mum!' or 'Dad!' or leaving sticky fingerprints on your laptop.

I remember, when my son was small, feeling exhausted by the sheer volume of LEGO everywhere in our house. It seemed like there was a half-built kit permanently on our kitchen table *(which was also my desk)*. But I caught myself, and fast-forwarded to a point when the LEGO would be gone and tried to appreciate the moment.

Now the LEGO is gone, replaced by grunts and YouTube. And I do miss it. I miss it so very much.

So rather than wishing your now away, rather than feeling resentful, try to *be* present, enjoy the moment and appreciate that the world will wait. You're not in competition with the competition. There will always be space for you when you're ready.

Don't compare

There's absolutely no point continuously comparing yourself to a 40-hour-a-week human (or 38 hours, as is the general legal limit in Australia). It's just plain daft to compare yourself to people who have no kids, or can afford a daily nanny, or have oodles of family help.

Of course they have more time. And there isn't a damn thing you can do about it.

I mean, we're often told we should never compare ourselves to anyone about anything, but apparently time isn't one of these things. If I hear one more person say, 'You have the same number of hours in a day as Beyoncé', it will break my soul. (This is incredibly witty because Beyoncé has a popular song called 'Break my soul'.) Clearly Beyoncé is loaded, has an army of helpers and is a multi-talented, gorgeous goddess. I am none of these things. And I suspect you aren't either.

So, let's not play the comparison game. It's not the length of your time but rather how you use it that matters.

TL;DR

Without a proper understanding of how much time you have and how you invest it, you'll never feel truly in control of your working day, and this will lead to stress in your family time and free time.

Benefits

Thinking about your time as a valuable resource and something that you need to invest wisely will help you:

- work out the true amount of time you have to work in a week; this might make you more realistic about what you can achieve
- define an hourly rate that more clearly represents what you need to charge to reach your goals
- reduce the pressure on yourself each day to achieve so much
- create a clear division between time invested in working and time invested in you and your family.

Over to you

Now that you understand the importance of an hourly rate, here are some exercises to help you think about your time:

1. **Conduct a time inventory:** For a week or so, keep a journal or use a free tool like Toggl Track to track how you invest your time. Ensure you track everything you do in a given day: work, social media, faffing, wees, lunch breaks. I fully expect you to be vaguely horrified by the results.
2. **Map out your working hours time grid**, including billable time.
3. **Ask yourself some tough questions** (without being too hard on yourself):
    a. At what times of the day were you most productive?
    b. At what times did you feel the least productive?
    c. What were the biggest time sucks?
    d. What did you do quickly and effectively?
    e. When could you use your time more intelligently?

Chapter 7

The sweet joy of schedules and routines

'The key is not to prioritize what's on your schedule, but to schedule your priorities.'

Stephen Covey

If the idea of a schedule gives you the heebie-jeebies, I totally get you. I used to think schedules were restrictive, suffocating and downright hideous.

'I'm a free spirit,' I shrieked. 'You can't tie me down.'

I want to be running naked through a field eating crisps, not tied to my desk and ticking off tasks in an Excel spreadsheet. But then I became a parent, and I got slapped in the face by the moist fish of reality.

Now, I realise the only way I'm going to get back to my naked crisp-eating days is to have a schedule and specifically block out time for running through fields.

Here's the shocking truth: routine is freedom.

Stick with me. In this chapter I want to make you FALL IN LOVE with routines and schedules.

Who are you?

Before we get stuck into creating routines, I want to ask you this: who are you?

Now, I don't mean this in some kind of existential way but more in a 'Who are you workwise?' way. When and how do you thrive? Are you an early bird, a night owl or a late-afternoon cockatoo?

The world feels built for early birds, and often night owls are deemed lazy or unproductive. But really, we're helpless to fight how we function. We all have an internal clock that controls our sleep and wake cycles; mostly it's influenced by light (day and night). We're mostly preconditioned to wake with the sun and sleep when it sets. But those night owls who can stay awake all night are important too: they are the ones who stopped the wolves creeping into our caves during the night and chewing on our toes.

My partner is a night owl and, as an early bird myself, it causes some issues. Even though I love my sleep, I'm perky and annoying at 6 a.m. He's perky and annoying at 10 p.m.

But for a night owl to become a morning person takes a lot of effort, including:

- shifting sleep cycles a little bit at a time and sticking to them
- getting lots of ambient light throughout the day
- eating at set times.

I rarely see early birds desiring to be night owls. So, generally, I think it's best to accept who you are and work with it rather than against it.

Obviously, if you're more of a morning person, you'll shift your most brain-draining tasks into the early part of the day and save the mindless stuff for later. If you come alive at night then you'll have to do the opposite.

As I mentioned in the previous chapter, my brain turns to soup at precisely 3 p.m. each day, conditioned from years of school pick-ups. It's almost impossible for me to do anything constructive at this time, so I try to get most of my work done in the morning.

How my routine works

I've been creating routines ever since my son was born. It started out trying to plan nap times and squeeze in little blobs of work when I could, and it's evolved from there.

Now, the majority of my day is scheduled. Without this established routine, it's super easy for me to lose track of what I'm doing and to fall into the procrastifaffing zone.

Here's how I create my routines.

1. The me, myself and I approach

As a business owner, we wear many hats and occasionally a beret. And again, rather than fight this, I like to embrace it. So, I'll wear my Project Manager hat about one day a week.

On that day – usually Friday – I review my priorities, plan out my week, update my tasks in Asana *(my favourite project management app; more on this later)* and tidy up my 'to do list' in Slack *(another productivity fave)*.

Then, when I start work on Monday, delirious and disorientated from the weekend, I don't have to stop and think, 'What should I be doing today?' Last Week Me already decided. And Tomorrow Me is going to be unhappy if I don't crack on.

I also find writing a to-do list at the end of each day helps me get started with purpose the next morning, but more on to-do lists later on.

2. Calendars and colour blocking

I use Google Calendar to plan my week, blocking out time in 30-minute and one-hour chunks.

I have a colour-coding system to keep things super clear:

- red for anything related to the SEO portion of my business
- blue for the copywriting business
- teal for my Digital Marketing Collective Membership
- grey for admin
- purple for marketing
- right now, a lovely peacocky blue colour for anything related to this book.

I use a nice, sunny yellow for personal things. I make sure there's plenty of white space for food, wees *(have you noticed I'm obsessed with wees?)* and just to take a breather.

When I started out, I scheduled all my work things first and squeezed in real life around them. Now, I do the opposite. My real life goes in first, in sunny yellow, and then I factor work around that.

It's a little like the Profit First idea (which we talk about in Chapter 12), whereby you pay yourself your profit first, before bills and staff and tax. My idea is Pleasure First – that we should schedule joy first and prioritise family time over work commitments as much as possible.

My one big indulgence is a massage once a week at my house *(I know, right – sooo Elizabeth Taylor)*. This feels hugely extravagant, but I'm not a huge spender and investing in a bit of self-Toon love feels like a fair return for my hard work.

This planning also helps me recognise when I'm removing family time from my diary or overscheduling work things to get out of difficult or uncomfortable family situations.

Carving out time for your family can be tough and it's so easy to let things slide. You start the day determined to make a wholesome family dinner and end up standing at the fridge door eating fistfuls of cheese out of the bag.

I aim to fit in just one solid parenting activity each day beyond keeping my child alive. So, when he was younger, it might have been doing some art together or going to the park. Now he's older, it's going to the gym together. Of course, some days I'm able to do more, but setting that realistic expectation helps me cope.

Apparently, family dinner is a great one to aim for because of the conversations you might have, although these days my best conversations with my teen often happen when we're in the car. So it's your call.

3. Daily goals

As you'll learn in the next chapter, I'm not huge on formal goal setting and planning. But, of course, I have a vision for my business and things I want to achieve. My project management skills mean I'm fairly good at breaking down lofty, far-off goals into doable, bite-sized chunks.

I start with project phases, trying to break the task down into, say, three or four chunks; these might include:

· planning
· creating
· designing
· coding.

Then I translate these phases into months, then divide them into weeks and then daily goals.

These smaller day-to-day goals help me not to get overwhelmed by the big picture. I choose to eat the elephant one bite at a time, sometimes even just one lick at a time.

I aim to set just one real goal a day.

I come to my desk, read through my to-do list created by 'yesterday me' and highlight the *one* task I'd love to get done that day. Some days, I give myself a break and make it something easy. Other days, I bite the proverbial bullet and choose a big, spiky thing that's been keeping me up at night. I often achieve way more than the one thing, but keeping it to just one helps me stay focused.

It's a bit like when I trained for the marathon *(okay, half-marathon)*: if I set out to run 10 kilometres, I would never have laced up my trainers, but if I committed to just run for 10 minutes, it gave me the ability to start. And once I started I kept going.

4. Light and shade

When I'm planning my day, I take note of my working style; so, as an early bird, I often front-load the 'harder' things into the start of the day. But I also think about energy levels *throughout* the day.

My job involves a lot of performance-style tasks: podcast interviews, coaching calls, Q&As, Facebook Lives and group coaching Zoom masterclasses. These are high-energy, brain-pumping and draining, so I try not to have too many in a given day.

I also split my day into 'deep work' and 'light work'. Light work tasks include:

· social media (I find it easy)
· reconciling Xero (or Rounded accounting software)

- team meetings
- inbox fiddling
- fixing typos on my websites (there are so many)
- making graphics in Canva.

Deep work tasks include:

- writing email intros
- recording podcasts
- planning course content
- creating presentations.

I know that I won't get much deep work done on Tuesdays, Wednesdays and Thursdays as they are speckled with calls and Zooms, so generally I do deep work on Mondays and Fridays.

5. Quiet days

As I said, I tend to leave Mondays and Fridays as empty as possible, with no high-energy tasks – and absolutely no calls. Then I go hell-for-leather on Tuesdays, Wednesdays and Thursdays.

I love being able to ease myself into Mondays one toe at a time, rather than having to plunge into the icy horror of my working week in one terrifying splash.

On Fridays I say to myself, 'I can work if I want to, but I don't have to work'.

And, of course, generally I do, but I also allow time for personal admin and the occasional day off. The self-created illusion of Friday freedom makes the week feel shorter and more doable.

6. Late nights

I made the decision several years ago that I would only do one late night a week *(and by late I mean finishing at around 7.30 p.m.)*. Generally, these late nights accommodate coaching calls with my European customers.

I could do more – and if I did, I could probably entice more Eurobeasts *(the term I use for the members of my communities who are based in Europe)* to my clan – but I'd rather have fewer customers and more time for myself and my family. I'm just not prepared to sacrifice dinner and Netflix with my family, and if that means I can't be a millionaire, so be it.

7. The multi-tasking lie

I firmly believe the idea that anyone can multi-task is a big fat lie. While it may seem like we're being super productive when we're second-screening with 87 tabs open, listening to a podcast while walking on a treadmill under our standing desk, we're likely not doing a great job of anything.

I like to handle projects one at a time, working through each task as thoroughly as possible until I can do no more. I've found that finishing one thing before I start another is the secret to my success. So many business owners have fingers in so many pies that they are left, well, fingerless. My recommendation: put all your fingers and possibly a toe into ONE pie. Enjoy it. Finish it. Then, bring on the next pie.

8. A time for calls

I'm not a hugely chatty person, but sometimes you do have to talk to your clients. I know, it's awful, isn't it?

But rather than take and make phone or Zoom calls throughout the day, I set aside designated time – usually across lunch between 12 and 1 p.m.

If my phone rings outside of that time blob, I let it go to voicemail, then listen back in my 'chatty slot' and return the call. I also keep calls as short as possible, often scheduling them at 15 minutes to the hour so that I can start the call by explaining that I only have a set amount of time because I have another call scheduled on the hour.

> **TOON TIP** The majority of humans are grateful for short, to-the-point calls, but if you have someone who wants to talk longer (and they're paying for it, or you see the value) you can always start with a 15-minute chat and the offer to schedule a longer one.

> **TOON TIP** I keep a spare t-shirt, hairbrush, mirror and dry shampoo near my workspace. This tip has come from far too

many incidents of coffee spilled on my boob right before a Zoom call and greasy fringes only noticed after a call is done. Save yourself the last-minute scramble and be prepared.

TOON TIP This one is slightly ridiculous and probably not what you'd expect from a serious business mentor, but I find if I schedule a call when I need a wee that it helps me get it over with faster. *(I'm sure my editor will ask me to remove this from the book, so if you're reading this, he must not have noticed it.)*

9. Space for curve balls

Of course, if you schedule yourself up the wazoo, when something unexpected pops up you'll be entirely out of whack.

Planning back-to-back calls? What happens when one overruns?

Allowing two hours for a two-hour job? What happens when your computer crashes?

Giving yourself two days to turn around that project? What happens when the dog decides to partially eat a sock and you have to take him to the vet? *(True story.)*

We can't foresee every disaster, but we know they will happen, so scheduling time to NOT WORK is important.

This might look like:

· allowing an hour for lunch when really you're happy with 15 minutes

· planning only a four-day week even if you have five days available

· giving yourself an hour of unscheduled time before school drop-off

· making sure you leave an hour of unscheduled time after school pick-up.

TOON TIP Even with these tactics in place – with the white space, the one goal, the working to your productivity strengths – accept that you'll still have bad days when everything goes to hell.

10. How you handle failure

How you handle perceived failure is also a key part of your business success and your personal happiness. Acceptance is everything, as is being kind to yourself.

If you measure your success purely through your ability to complete your to-do list and being uber productive, then you're in for some unhappy times. It's important to forgive yourself for your bad days and not spiral into a pit of despair. It's also important to carry on and turn up the next day, regardless of how bad the previous day was.

Belinda Tainsh Morgan from Morgan and Me Interiors, mum of Lola (6) and Charlie (4), said:

> 'My entire working life has been to a schedule. In fact, if I don't plan my week, I forget things that I am supposed to deliver and I am unproductive.

> 'It ensures I finish everything I have set out to do and pushes me to be more effective and complete tasks faster. And yep, totally agree that planning downtime is super important. I got the balance wrong for a while there. I ended up being behind in everything because I forgot to give myself downtime.

> 'These days I'm scheduling exercise, meditation, work, time to look at emails, time for ad hoc stuff, time to be present with the kids and downtime.

> 'I now only feel at ease when the schedule is set. It's my equilibrium. In fact, when I feel a bit discombobulated, the first thing I do is turn to the schedule.

> 'And schedule as many chances as possible to frolic naked.'

Rhi Sugars from The Atypical Educator, mum of Dallas (7) and Evanna (19 months), told me:

> 'Routines are everything in our house. We have two kiddos with disabilities, so that is nonstop in itself. Hubby has a demanding job and I hardly see him during the working week. Add being a newbie into the business world and everything quickly collapsed into a chaotic heap.

> 'A schedule has been essential for creating a balanced household, both in a practical sense and from a mental health perspective.'

The power of routine

I'm sure you've all heard about how Steve Jobs wore a similar outfit every day to save himself the wasted time and brain goo of fashion decisions. *(I expect he also had a wretched dress sense, but that's by the by.)* You probably know that a lot of successful humans are fans of routines. Why?

Because routines eradicate choice. And choice can be an emotional, exhausting and confusing thing.

With routine, your brain goes into autopilot: knowing intuitively what to do next with no deep thought or pent-up emotion. And let's be honest, we all know that how you *start* your day can influence the rest of it. Establishing a morning routine or ritual might get you off to a good start and make you feel positive for the day ahead.

Dale Beaumont from Business Blueprint, dad of two boys (15 and 12), says:

> 'What gets scheduled gets done so, really, scheduling stuff in your diary is really important. Start the day well and then you're off to a good start, but remember that the day starts the night before. So, at 10 p.m. I'm in bed and at 10.30 p.m. I pull the sheets up, go to sleep. Simple.'

Routines can be daily, weekly or monthly. *(Any more than that and I find it all becomes a little too abstract.)*

My daily routine

If you've read my previous book, *Confessions of a Misfit Entrepreneur,* you'll know that I jokingly said my morning routine involved:

1. waking up at 4 a.m. feeling totally refreshed
2. meditating and doing an hour of yoga
3. making myself a wholesome green smoothie while listening to whale music
4. jogging on the beach and swimming in the golden morning sun.

Of course, it was all a lie. Back then *(when my son was around eight)* my routine was more like this:

1. Wake up at 7 a.m., often feeling more tired than when I went to bed.
2. Lurch to the bathroom with a rigid totter, my legs having seized up during the night through extreme lack of exercise.
3. Have a quick shower and brush my teeth. On a good day I might even brush my hair.
4. Stumble out into the world to either make breakfast for my small human, prepare backpack and lunch box and do the school run, or walk my dog to the coffee shop for a jumbo three-shot coffee with half a sugar.

Because, in those early days of parenting, it was often all just an exhausting blur. *But I still had a routine*, which honestly helped me remember to pack a lunch box and put on a bra *(most days)*.

These days, now my son is older, I am able to:

1. wake up early *(around 6 a.m.)*
2. take a proper shower *(and even wash my legs)*
3. plan my food and exercise *(I'm a MyFitnessPal freak)*
4. walk the dog and get a coffee
5. come back and prepare my son's lunch *(although often that's my son's dad's job)*
6. have a proper breakfast with oats!
7. head to my desk at about 8.30 a.m. and start work – or head to the gym and start work at 9.30 a.m.

(Oh my god, I realise that I've become that person I hated/longed to be back when I wrote my previous book.)

It all sounds dreamy, right?

(Psst: My son also has a list of jobs to do in the morning. which saves me so much time – more on that in Chapter 16.)

Yes, it feels a bit groundhog day. Yes, sometimes I long to sod it all off and run away to Acapulco with a lover called Roberto. But I've also learned to accept that routine is not boredom; routine is comfort: it's stress-free and it makes me happy.

Helpful daily family routines

Having family routines for the mornings and evenings can be thigh-shudderingly awesome. I personally like to write them up and stick them on the fridge: a nice daily list of who does what and when do they do it.

Routines help everyone know what's expected of them, and help you keep track and get out the door on time. They could include:

- packing the kids' lunch boxes the night before
- setting up the breakfast table the night before
- trying to make everyone sit down to eat breakfast together
- tasking one of your kids to clear away the breakfast dishes
- having a countdown to leaving the house.

Okay, as I'm writing this, I'm thinking that many of you will be laughing and thinking, *That's IMPOSSIBLE!* And I get it; it is when your kids are small. It's like, *just feed them, clean them and let's go,* right? But it does get easier, I promise.

Now, of course, mostly my family totally ignores my beautiful fridge schedule and I seem to spend my life asking my son, 'Have you emptied the dishwasher?', but it helps me feel I have a modicum of control.

Helpful weekly family routines

You might find that daily routines are a little unrealistic for your family, so consider creating a weekly routine instead. It could include:

- one sit-down meal together a day (breakfast or dinner)
- one grocery shopping trip together – possibly with something fun afterwards
- one movie or game night a week
- paying all the family bills one day of the week (or month)
- one 'I'm not cooking' night a week, where everyone eats snacks or you order a takeaway
- set meals on each night: Taco Tuesday or Pheasant Thursday.

Chat it through with your family and ask them about their favourite things to do. My son is a huge fan of routine and knowing exactly what's going to happen. Perhaps your kids are too?

Helpful daily business routines

My morning work routine is pretty straightforward; it goes something like this:

1. Log on and review my to-do list (while listening to loud pop on Spotify).
2. Pick one core task for the day.
3. Assign a time allowance to each task.
4. Spend one hour on a tough task.
5. Check my finances and balance my Xero.
6. Open my inbox and deal with easy emails quickly.
7. Take longer, more complex tasks and drop into Asana.
8. Talk to and brief my team.
9. Head to Facebook to tend to my groups.
10. At the moment I'm also trying to make a daily TikTok, which is fairly hideous but hopefully will pay off.

I never, ever schedule calls before 10 a.m. so I can ensure I've allowed myself time to complete my routine and feel stable and ready for the day before I have to be 'human'.

Helpful weekly business routines

If daily work routines aren't your jam – or are just plain impossible at the moment – consider a weekly or monthly routine. This could include things such as:

- planning out your week on Friday so you're all set for Monday
- having one day a week when you do all your client calls
- setting up subscriptions for as many items as possible
- having one day a month when you review all your outgoings and expenses
- allowing yourself one hour a week to read articles and blog content and stay up to date on industry trends
- having a set time and day when you go to the post office
- allocating social media tasks to one day a month and using scheduling software to send them out (I use Agorapulse).

A note on school holidays

I think it's fair to say that school holidays are just a poo fight however much of a planner you are. If you're blessed with family and friends who can help, take advantage of that. I wasn't and it sucked.

I tried school holiday camps, tennis camps and surf camps, but my son wasn't keen on them and in the end I just gave up.

I set myself a few simple guides to make the holidays bearable:

1. I would not have ridiculous expectations about productivity
   (I assumed I'd have, max, a few hours a day).
2. I would try to do one 'fun' thing with my son a day – generally something that got us out of the house.
3. I would generally do the fun thing in the morning and wear my son out *(and, unfortunately myself)* and then not feel so guilty about working in the afternoon.

Now my son is a teen, it's much easier, as he wants to sleep a lot and flop – but I still drag him out at least once, even if it's just to go to the supermarket. Which, of course, he loves.

Beautiful boundaries

Now that you have a schedule, it's much easier to see when you're working and when you're not. Remember, the goal is to be on or off.

And this is when the real work begins, because now you have to stick to it.

If back in Chapter 4 you decided that, as a 'good' parent, you wanted to prioritise being present and listening to your kids, then you need to ensure that you're not taking calls during bedtime stories.

Often, I'll hear business owners complaining that customers don't respect their boundaries:

'I took a call at 7 p.m. from my client!'

'I was answering emails from one customer all weekend.'

But the truth is, often the person who is really disrespecting your boundaries is you. By setting firm rules like 'no calls after 6 p.m.' and then taking calls after 6 p.m., you're training your customers and clients to think that's okay. You're letting their urgency become your urgency, when it really shouldn't be.

Clients are mostly really well behaved. They're not pushing your boundaries because they're horrible people. They're pushing them because they don't even know they're there.

And I know you're being nice and ignoring your boundaries out of fear. Just like me answering Barry in the Facebook group when I should have been hanging with my son. I wanted to keep Barry happy; I wanted him to become a customer. So, I bent over backwards and twisted my boundaries all out of shape to try and lure him in.

And, of course, he never even became a customer.

People-pleasing and parenting do not go well together, especially when the last people you choose to please are yourself and your family.

So, start setting those boundaries: physically write them out, then pop them in your email footer or on your website.

For example:

'I'm available from 9 a.m. to 3 p.m. on Tuesdays, Wednesdays and Thursdays.'

Or, as my email footer used to read:

'I don't work Mondays. Lucky me.'

Sure, some customers will say you're unprofessional, not available enough, not keen enough. But the truth is, while you ARE professional, you're not going to be available enough for everyone, or keen enough for that eager client, and it's better that they know now.

I've found that when I'm clear with my boundaries and admit I'm a parent with responsibilities, most people 100% understand. The reality is that a lot of my customers are parents too and, quite frankly, it's a relief to admit that we can't do it all or work 27 hours a day.

TL;DR

Schedules, routines and boundaries may seem unrealistic and hard work at the start but, with persistence, they become second nature. And rather than feeling restrictive, they allow you to create space for what's important to you, your business and your family.

Benefits

Thinking about scheduling and routines will help you:

- break down tasks into small chunks over a more reasonable time frame
- appreciate when you work best and schedule time accordingly
- stop the distraction of endless business calls
- focus on one task at a time rather than zipping through multiple tasks poorly
- push back on clients and customers who have unrealistic expectations of your availability.

Over to you

1. **Take a look at my list of scheduling tips.** Which, if any, do you think you could apply to your business? Make a list and aim to lock in one new idea a week.
2. **Write up a realistic morning or weekly routine for your family** (and talk it through with them).
3. **Write up a realistic morning or weekly routine for your business** (and talk it through with your team, if you have one).
4. **Write a list of your boundaries/working hours and add them to your email footer, website and also YOUR BRAIN.**

Chapter 8

Easy-peasy planning

'An hour of planning can save you 10 hours of doing.'
Dale Carnegie

When I stand on my business turret surveying my business empire/cul-de-sac, it looks like a well thought out plan has really come together. I have three clean lines of business, marketing funnels backed up by a comprehensive social media plan, regular and predictable income, and successful launches.

'Ah,' I sigh as I pat my rotund entrepreneur belly, 'look how well my plan turned out!'

But that's another big fat hairy lie. I never had a plan in the first place.

Sadly, I suffer from a severe case of AGA (Abject Goal Aversion). Give me a goal and I'll do everything in my power to avoid achieving it. The number of times my brain has subconsciously mistyped goal as gaol is rather telling, I think. Goals make me feel trapped and restricted.

I once set myself a target to get 5000 followers on Instagram in a year. A year later I think I had 236 new followers – but in that time I built an SEO course and launched a membership.

While I love a time-blocked schedule, and I love a routine, I hate a plan. I simply don't like being told what to do, even if it's by myself. Which makes planning and goal setting hard.

A good example of this is that I have an app on my phone that tells me when to drink water. Every time the alert pops up I angrily dismiss it: 'Don't tell ME what to do, you damn app'. I finish the day dehydrated and exhausted. And, of course, it was me who set up the reminders in the first place.

Planning and parenting don't mix well

Generally, planning takes time, space and a clear head. These are three attributes that parents rarely possess.

And for the neurodivergent readers, I know that planning can often be a struggle. Being able to see that big helicopter view and break down a monster task into chewable chunks *(without being distracted a zillion times along the way)* ain't easy. My partner has ADHD and planning is his Achillies heel: he struggles to get things done unless he's fascinated by them, or until they become so urgent they're keeping him up at night.

Let's hear from two neurodivergent parents in my membership.

Rhi Sugars from The Atypical Educator, mum of Dallas (7) and Evanna (19 months), said:

'Planning is challenging for me, one of my biggest challenges really, because perfectionism is one of the most common characteristics seen in autistic people.

'I've had to start really small, like social media content, and get used to publishing not-quite-perfect content. Understanding that others feel this way too helps me feel that not being perfect won't kill me.'

Nick Gale from NicksDigital, dad of Ted (5) and Olive (2), added:

'Progress over perfection is hard but sometimes necessary. There's no way I can remember every tip and trick with all software and, being out of the game for a few years, there were some definite hurdles. Also, suddenly being made redundant forced my hand.

'I try and tick as many boxes as I can, but I'm a diagnostician at the core of what I do. There's not always a perfect route to repair (that'd be nice), but anything I create is going to last and that makes the customer happy.'

Now, I am able to plan but I just don't enjoy it that much, and in my time as a business owner I've found that even the best, most thoughtful plan won't completely mitigate risk and guarantee success. In my opinion, it's a great idea to have a plan, as long as you don't get too attached to it.

So, instead, I think we need to come up with a new way of thinking about planning.

Goal setting

I'm sure you've heard of SMART goals. 'SMART' stands for **specific**, **measurable**, **achievable**, **relevant** and **time-bound**.

It's all about defining these parameters to make sure your objectives are attainable within a certain timeframe. If a business owner comes to me and says they want to increase sales by $2K a month, I'd take that goal and drill into it a little using the SMART ideas:

- **Specific:**
  - Which product do you want to increase sales of?
  - Why that product?
  - What evidence do you have that you *can* increase sales of that product?
- **Measurable:**
  - How much are you selling now?
  - What percentage increase are you aiming for?
- **Achievable:**
  - Have you previously achieved this percentage increase on other products?
  - What actions will you take to increase sales?
  - Do you have the time to make these changes?
  - Do you have the money and resources to make these changes?
  - How will putting effort into this product impact other business activities?
- **Relevant:**
  - Is this the right time to be pushing this particular product?
  - Which audience segment is the right one to market to?

- Where/who are your ideal customers?
- Are they new or existing customers? (Where are they on their customer journey?)
· **Time-bound:**
    - What timeline are you giving yourself?
    - Is this realistic given other life constraints?
    - Have you achieved results in this timeframe before?

For me it's all about getting real about your goals because, let's be honest, most of us pull goals out of our bottoms. We become super attached to them and then fail miserably at achieving them.

But even with all these rational questions, we're missing the most important piece: **why do you want to complete this goal?**

I firmly believe that most of us can achieve pretty much anything we set out to if we have enough time, energy, persistence, confidence, a whole bag of other qualities, opportunities and luck. But just because we *could* doesn't mean we *should*.

A fish planning tale

Forgive me if you've heard this one before. The Mexican Fisherman story is often wheeled out by smooth, white-toothed business-coach types, but there's a reason for that: it's a great little fishy tale and a great way of planning in a fishy way.

It goes something like this:

An American investment b/wanker is mooching around a small coastal Mexican village when he sees a small boat with just one fisherman docking. Inside the boat is a small pile of freshly caught fish.

The American (let's call him Clive) asks the fisherman (we'll call him Bob, which isn't particularly Mexican, but I'm not a fan of cultural stereotypes) how long it took to catch the fish.

'Only a few hours,' Bob replies.

Clive asks why Bob didn't stay out longer and catch more fish. Bob replies that he has enough to support his family.

And Clive asks, 'But what do you do with the rest of your time?'

Bob, the fisherman, replies, 'I sleep late, fish a little, play with my children, take siestas with my wife, practice guitar, read books, work in my garden; I have a full and busy life'.

Clive scoffs (in an American accent), 'You should spend more time fishing and, with the extra money, buy a bigger boat. With the proceeds from the bigger boat, you could buy several boats. After a little while you'd have a fleet of fishing boats.

'Also instead of selling your fish to the cannery, why don't you open your own factory? You would control the product, processing and distribution. You could leave this village and move to the USA. Set up your HQ in New York.'

Bob asks, 'But how long will this all take?'

'Around 15 years,' Clive replies.

'And what then?' asks Bob.

'That's the best part. When the time is right, you could sell your company stock to the public, and you'd make millions!' Clive chortled. 'Then you would retire. Move to a small coastal fishing village where you sleep late, fish a little, play with your children, take siestas with your wife, practice guitar, read books and work in your garden.'

Bob then ties a fishing net around Clive and pushes him into the murky depths of the ocean. *(This isn't part of the regular story but I think it works, so I'm adding it in.)*

You get the idea.

This little story really helps us examine why we want to do what we do. Yes, more money is nice, but what will you do with that money?

Here are some questions to ask yourself:

- Are you willing to make the compromises needed to achieve your goal?
- How do your business goals fit with your family goals?
- If your goals are in conflict with your family life, which is going to win?

For me, the Mexican fisherman story teaches me the following.

1. Small is beautiful

I'm often asked why I don't expand and push to earn multiple seven figures or even eight. Why don't I build a bigger team? Why don't I get an office in the city and fill it with bean bags and a microwave for tuna pasta?

And the answer: I don't want to.

I work for around five hours a day. I walk my dog. I go to the gym. I make nice dinners and watch Netflix with my son. I lead a full and happy life.

2. Enjoy the now

Of course, planning is all about the future, and often people say to me, 'I'll be content when…'

But the truth is that you'll never be content unless you discover the source of your discontent. *(How very Buddhist.)* You'll achieve your goal, finish your plan and immediately start a new one. Well, that's what I used to do, anyhow.

Do you want to enjoy your family and business now, or work yourself into a stress ball of frazzle so you can start enjoying your life in 20 years' time?

It is a choice. You get to choose it.

3. Enough is enough

Many of us have a nagging feeling that we could do better, make more and 'level up'. *(This is a slightly up-its-own-bum phrase business coaches use to talk about scaling your business either financially or with humans, or just shifting your mindset.)* But we also know on a logical and warm-tummy level that the secret to having it all is often recognising that we already do – or, rather, that we should strive to be content with what we have.

Yes, you need to earn enough to get by and be comfy (more on that in Part III), but how much do you really need beyond that to lead a happy and full life?

It's clichéd but true: you really can't put a price on happiness.

4. One size doesn't fit all

Many business coaches will offer you advice that, on the surface, seems logical and smart:

· Create a business plan.
· Scale.
· Earn more money.
· Hire staff.

But if it doesn't fit with your why, your reason for doing all of this, then it's not going to help.

It's great to seek advice, gather information and research, but don't do all of this at the expense of trusting your own inner voice. You know yourself best, and spending $10K on a pricey business coach just to disagree with them is a monster waste of cash.

An alternative to business planning

Now, I'm not saying my business is entirely 'seat-of-my-pants' style. But I do take a slightly different approach.

I've never written a formal business, marketing or product plan, but I do have long-term goals. For example, I might decide that I want long-term security for myself and my son. To achieve this, I want to hit a certain income that allows me to pay off my mortgage, invest and build some generational wealth. I'll then investigate the best ways to do this.

And then I'll start doing the do.

Starting when you're not ready

If we all waited until we were 100% ready to do things, we'd never do anything at all.

It makes practical sense to do oodles of marketing and competitor research, but for busy parents this is often a time suck we can't afford. The single best way to find out if your audience wants something is to create it and try to sell it.

Now, obviously, my experience only extends to digital products and services rather than physical products (*other than this book!*). But even with ecommerce, it can be a good idea to trial some tester products before commissioning a whole truck full of goods.

You can ask people if they want a thing, and of course most will say yes. But, when it comes to handing over their credit card, suddenly they're nowhere to be found.

When I built my search engine optimisation course, there weren't really any other prominent SEO courses in the market. My peers told me SEO was unteachable. My customers told me it would be too hard to learn.

But I ignored the research, created a website sales page and sold 20 places to existing clients *(I was still a copywriter back then)*. Then I built the course based on a loose plan from a few SEO workshops I'd run in the past.

Was it perfect? No. But did the price reflect that these first customers were coming on the adventure with me? Yes.

I started before I was ready and launched a course based on intuition and trusting myself.

Since then, it's made me nearly $3 million.

Iterative development

Carrying on with the course example: as I mentioned, I only started with a loose plan. I'd run some eight-hour in-person workshops and I felt that format lent itself well to an eight-module course. So I went with that.

Over the years since, I've tweaked, improved, reduced and expanded the course – not based on a plan I created five years ago but based entirely on customer feedback and my own feels. The course has been updated five or six times, and the sales page has been fiddled with probably more than 20.

Now the formula works well and, yes, possibly I could have foreseen all this, planned it all out and reached my success faster – but for me, with the limited time I have, iterative development works better.

'Progress, not perfection' is a mantra I live by.

Getting your ducks in a row

One of my favourite sayings is, 'If you wait for all of your ducks to be in a row, one of them will likely be dead or, at the very least, extremely unwell'.

If there's one thing I firmly believe in, it's not waiting for the ducks. Get one duck ready, with another duck waiting quietly in the background, and go forth.

If you're super attached to planning and perfection, you're not alone.

Cindy Creighton from Eco Confetti, mum of Emily (6), shared with me:

> 'Initially, I ticked every single box. Everything was perfectly ready when I went live… except my customers were not who I thought they would be and what I had put out wasn't perfect for them.

> 'So, I had to let go of my "perfect" business to accommodate my actual customers, and when I did, my sales immediately increased by 400%.

> 'It made me realise there is no point in waiting for everything to be perfect, because until it's in the market I don't really know what might need to be tweaked.'

Kara Lambert, mum of Imogen (17) and Brennan (15), said:

> 'I started out teaching social media, then I saw the psychology behind it and added that. Then I realised business owners didn't need social media training, so I started coaching.

> 'My business changed. Trends change. Clients change. We need to learn, apply, observe, grow. It would be boring if they didn't.

> 'Sure, it might feel like wearing that stretched-out and threadbare t-shirt – familiar and comfortable – but sometimes comfortable isn't what we need.'

Micro-plans

German field marshal Helmuth von Moltke the Elder believed in developing a series of options for battle rather than a single plan: 'No plan of operations extends with certainty beyond the first encounter with the enemy's main strength.'

Today, 'no plan survives contact with the enemy' is the popular abbreviation.

If we replace 'enemy' with 'customers', I'm with Moltke. Most comprehensive, detailed business plans are pretty much useless after a few months in business, mostly because customers are unpredictable. Markets are unpredictable.

And guess what? You're unpredictable.

So, breaking down your monster plan into smaller chunks is vital, as is being flexible enough to change the plan when you come to an issue. Don't cling to your plan like Kate Winslet on that bit of wood in *Titanic* (Leonardo would have fitted), and don't hold onto mistakes just because you spent a long time making them.

Micro-challenges

While I find big long-term plans a turn-off, I do love a micro-challenge. They help motivate me throughout the day.

Here are a few examples of micro-challenges I've completed for my business:

- seeing how many emails I can answer in 25 minutes
- timing myself on how fast I can write 1000 words
- achieving ten days of posting stories on Instagram without worrying about metrics *(I'd like to achieve 30 days but a month is a long time)*
- committing to posting on LinkedIn three times a week.

I also set micro-challenges in my family life by:

- committing to making three fancy meals a week *(I cheat and use a meal delivery service)*
- planning one big family outing a month
- promising my son, when he was little, that we'd go to the park every second day
- committing to taking my son to the gym every day *(which means getting up at 5.30 a.m. – but for him I'll do that).*

The key to micro-challenges is to make them tiny, fun and achievable – and to reward yourself lavishly if you achieve them. I generally do this with crisps or gym leggings.

Where does coaching come in?

It would be hypocritical of me, as a business mentor with coaching offerings, to say that coaching doesn't work when it comes to planning and setting business goals.

I believe that if you find a coach who fits your value systems and isn't peddling some one-size-fits-all success path, they can help you get where you want to go faster. Coaches can be great cheerleaders for you and your business, giving you the confidence to push forward when you're feeling nervous, helping you stress test your ideas and giving you insight into possible risks.

But I will say that I don't think coaches are essential.

TOON TIP I would NEVER advocate putting you or your family in financial strife to afford some Mastermind retreat or coaching program that promises the world, because they rarely deliver.

I have personally never had an ongoing business coach, but I have had a few insightful conversations, especially with Robert Gerrish (formerly of Flying Solo), who told me the story of Bob the Mexican fisherman.

I've found that small peer groups work really well to help me move forward, so I've created a lot of these along the way, one of which evolved into my membership: The Clever Copywriting School.

But most importantly, I believe in trusting myself – my brain, my gut and all my other bits and bobs.

Courses and learning

Again, it would be stupid of me to pooh-pooh courses, books, podcasts and general learning as a way to move forward with your business and decide what your goals should be. It's literally how I make my money.

But I often think course addicts use these purchases as a bandaid for self-doubt: 'If I just do this next course then I can finally...'

Often, business owners get trapped in an endless cycle of personal development and education to avoid actually doing the do. Learning by doing is, of course, riskier, but it's infinitely more rewarding and powerful.

Rewards and recognition

Whether or not you set goals and plan, it's vital that you track your progress and achievements.

I started doing this by having a client work in progress (WIP) spreadsheet where I tracked the number of copywriting enquiries I received, my success rate at winning jobs, the amount I earned for each job and the level of customer satisfaction. Those metrics were super helpful for me to reflect on how far I'd come each year.

Now, as a business mentor and educator, I track my progress in various ways by:

- having a little timeline of achievements on my website: katetoon.com/who-is-kate-toon/
- setting budgets and tracking revenue and profit
- keeping a folder of 'nice things' on my desktop *(testimonials and the like)*
- having a drawer full of cards and gifts from students and members
- entering – and winning – awards.

The awards piece is interesting because, yes, winning feeds the ego rather nicely, but the true positive is in compiling the information for the award: it forces you to think about how far you've come and what you've achieved.

As I mentioned above, it's important to establish a reward for your success in advance to motivate you. *(While I'd like to believe the glow of achievement is enough, it often isn't.)* It could be a cup of tea and a biscuit when you finish a small job, or a night in a posh hotel when you complete a bigger task.

Gratitude for what you've achieved is also so important. I think Jim Rohn sums it up nicely: 'Learn to be thankful for what you already have, while you pursue all that you want.'

TL;DR

Don't spend so long planning and trying to avoid any disaster that you actually fail to start anything, and if you do set a goal or make a plan, don't get too attached to it.

Benefits

Thinking about how you set goals and how to free yourself from the traditional idea of needing the perfect business plan can you help you:

· get started faster with small steps and eat that elephant
· stop feeling overwhelmed by the big picture
· remove the need to have all the answers and instead realise you can learn as you go
· learn to trust yourself more
· stop spending big bucks on glossy business coaches who promise to have the perfect plan.

Over to you

How do you feel about planning and setting goals in your business? Here are some exercises to help you get more from this chapter:

1. Write down one goal for your business; for example, 'I'd like to increase the number of leads I receive to my business by 50%'.
2. Review it against the SMART criteria at the start of this chapter: specific, measurable, achievable, relevant and time-bound.
3. Write down three small steps that could help you get started on your goal TODAY.
4. Think about a micro-challenge you could create for your business.

Chapter 9

Simple productivity wins

'Don't confuse activity with productivity.
Many people are simply busy being busy.'

Robin Sharma

Now that we've thought about our time, mapped out our schedule, reassessed our need for a perfect plan and thought up some micro goals, how about we actually get some stuff done?

I'd say my productivity has been a *superpower* for me in my business. I don't have a huge amount of time to work, but when I do, I go hard! And yes, I do think that working hard is important.

You can 'work smart', reduce your hours and achieve more in less time, but a huge part of having a successful business is accepting that it's going to be hard work at times. If you began this journey with the expectation that you could achieve great success in just a few hours a day, you'll be sorely disappointed. Don't get me wrong, I think you can get there in time, but at the start you have to roll up your sleeves and put in that hard yakka, as Australians say.

But if there's one thing I've done well in my business, it's achieving a lot in the limited time I have.

As I mentioned back in Chapter 1, my first priority was TIME. I had a brand-new baby and I wanted to be with him as much as possible – while also earning enough to support my family.

Now, 13 years on, time is once again everything to me. I want a business that supports my life, not one that consumes it. And I'm guessing you want that too. My son may be older and no longer need his nappy changed, but having a teen is a whole different kettle of fish that needs to be carefully watched so it doesn't boil over.

That's why in this chapter I'm going to share some of my top business and family productivity tactics to help you really squeeze more juice out of your day.

> **TOON TIP** I should point out that, while I pride myself in being productive, I do not use it as a measure of success, and I don't aim for 100% productivity every day. Remember my quiet Mondays and Fridays from the previous chapter? I allow myself to have periods of unproductivity and I think you should too.

Business productivity wins

Here are a few methods I use in my daily business life to be more productive.

1. Don't start your day with emails

Most people begin their day by opening their inbox, and, generally, this either:

- throws them into a state of panic as an 'urgent thing' has popped up
- makes them feel overwhelmed and then demotivated
- prompts them to focus on minor, unimportant tasks rather than the important, chunky things that will move their business forward.

Why does this happen?

As soon as you open your inbox, you become *reactive* rather than *proactive*. Perhaps you had planned to start the day tackling that difficult task you've been putting off, but now Steve has sent you an email about something or other, and it's just a quick thing, so you'll do that first and then get onto the big thing.

Oh, but look: an email from Pam. And one from Barbara. And…

Before you know it, it's 2.55 p.m., you've achieved nothing of substance and you're late for the school pick-up.

So, instead, I recommend taking the first hour of your day, whenever it starts, and actually doing that hard thing you've been putting off, or investing an hour in your big goal project. That way you'll feel you're making progress rather than putting out fires.

> **TOON TIP** Of course, sometimes we have to drop everything for an emergency, but make sure it really is an emergency and not just an excuse to avoid doing the tough thing.

2. Don't use your inbox as a to-do list

When we do finally open our inbox, most of us start at the most recent email and work back. The inbox becomes a really crappy to-do list, not decided by you but by whoever has taken the time to email you since the day before.

Others often leave emails in their inbox until they're resolved, which leads to huge overwhelm whenever they look at the thousands of emails that haven't been dealt with. Or, they invent elaborate mail rules and filing structures – which means they can never find anything.

I aim for 'inbox zero': having absolutely nothing in my inbox at all. Because an email inbox is NOT the best way to organise your business life. It is not a to-do list.

So, how can YOU achieve inbox zero?

- **Delete:** review your emails and delete any non-essential ones immediately.
- **Unsubscribe:** if you find yourself deleting similar unwanted emails each day, make sure you unsubscribe while you're at it.
- **Separate:** Have a separate email address for marketing stuff (newsletters and the like) and non-essential emails. But also, consider not signing up for them in the first place.

- **Play ping pong:** Answer any easy emails as quickly as possible, batting them back into the other person's side of the net fast. They're no longer your problem but their problem.
- **Write three-line responses:** Keep responses as short (and polite) as possible: friendly hello, answer, friendly goodbye. If it takes more than a paragraph, then consider making a call rather than writing an epic email.
- **Turn emails into tasks:** Anything that can't be ping-ponged back or answered with a brief three-line response I turn into an Asana task. *(Asana is a project management tool – more details on my fave productivity tools in the Extra Bits section at the end of the book.)* Why? Because then it goes into my pool of existing Asana tasks, and I can see if it really is as important as everything else I planned to do today.

Your inbox will never be empty *(well, let's hope not, because if it is then you have a big problem)*, and using your email as a to-do list leads to a squeaky-wheel mentality, where the most annoying people in your life get the most attention, rather than the quiet, patient ones.

3. Use the Pomodoro Technique

The Pomodoro Technique is a time management method developed by Francesco Cirillo in the late 1980s. It encourages you to work *with* the time you have rather than against it.

Essentially, you break your day into 25-minute chunks, separated by five-minute breaks. To break it down further, you:

1. think of a task you'd like to do
2. set a timer for 25 mins (I like to use the online Tomato Timer – just search 'Pomodoro timer')
3. work on the task with no distractions
4. take a five-minute break when the timer rings
5. repeat up to four times
6. then take a longer break: 30 minutes to an hour
7. repeat from step 1.

Now, honestly, I can't manage to do more than four Pomodoro sessions in a single day.

While I love this way of working for high productivity, it's also a little draining, and days and days of working like this would lead to burnout. But if you're clear on the tasks at hand, it can be useful to use this for at least part of your day or for a few days a week. For me, as an early bird, it's the morning, and only on Tuesdays, Wednesdays and Thursdays. For my partner who's a night owl, it's the evening on the days he doesn't have his kids.

I also don't allow myself more than four Pomodoro sessions in a row on the *same* task. Let's say, for example, I'm writing a blog post: I'll allow myself a maximum of four Pomodoro blobs on it in a given day and then, even if it's not finished, I'll move onto something else and revisit that task on another day. Otherwise, I find I get stale, I'm banging my head against a brick wall and forcing it – especially with creative tasks.

Limiting the sessions to four helps me stay fresh and perky, rather than exhausted and jaded.

> **TOON TIP** If you finish the task before the Pomodoro timer goes off, then use the spare time to review the work you've just done and make small improvements. Don't move onto the next task.

4. Lick that frog

Frog munching is a metaphor for doing the hardest task first when you are freshest. But rather than eat the whole frog, I prefer to just give it a damn good lick.

Mark Twain apparently said, 'Eat a live frog first thing in the morning, and nothing worse will happen to you for the rest of the day'.

While I'm sure amphibians are an excellent source of protein, I'm not sure they appreciate the nibbles, so licking is a slightly less intimidating version of the 'eat the frog' phrase and the book of the same title.[11]

So, I recommend you start each day by doing *part* of the most hideous, dreaded, important task first. Call that late-paying client. Finalise that tax return. Edit that part of the book *(as I am doing right now at the time of writing)*.

Get it out of the way and you'll feel all warm and fuzzy inside. Licking the frog over a series of days, rather than trying to complete it in one big bite, makes it less scary and infinitely more doable.

5. Make money first

I try to make sure the first proper job I start each day is a money earner – something I'm being paid for. So, rather than working on my own marketing, faffing about on Facebook or reconciling my accounts, I focus on doing something that has direct, clear return on investment (ROI).

For me, this might mean resolving member payment issues, working on course creation or making a new template. As a copywriter, I was actually writing copy rather than doing all the work 'around the job'.

As I've mentioned, early morning is also when I'm most creative and cognisant, so it's when I usually do most of my writing. Later in the day, when I'm foggy, I do more mindless tasks, like sorting out my post, reconciling Xero and posting on socials: tasks that don't require me to be quite as creative or cognisant.

6. Start time-based to-do lists

Following on from the Pomodoro Technique, I love to use time-based to-do lists and map them in time blocks on my schedule from Chapter 7. *(I know this sounds complex but it really isn't.)*

Here's how it works:

1. I look at my to-do list *(which I wrote the day before)*.
2. I reorder and prioritise it.
3. I assign each task a time blob, usually a max of 25 minutes.
4. I add these times in brackets to my to-do list.
5. I then add them to my calendar so I can see how they fit around meetings.

Adding time to the to-do list makes it genuinely realistic and stops me setting myself up for failure. If I end up with 12 30-minute tasks but it's only a four-hour day, then I know from the get-go I'm not going to finish everything. Better to accept this at the start of the day *(and reorganise)* rather than beat myself up about my lack of progress at the end.

Parkinson's law, which says that tasks expand to fit the time you give them, is reality for me. I find if I give myself half an hour to complete a task, it takes pretty much exactly that. Try it yourself and see.

7. Stick to paper-based to-do lists

As you can see, I've thought a lot about to-do lists. For me they're simply the number-one tool for productivity.

I've tried online to-do tools and apps, but I'm still a pen-and-paper gal (see figure 9.1). I just love crossing things out. *(And yes, of course I add daft things to my list like 'have a wee' and 'empty bin' for some quick wins.)*

Figure 9.1: An example to-do list

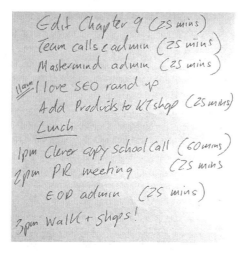

8. Create digital to-do lists

These days I also use the online tool Asana as a place to dump all my tasks. I use Asana for recurring tasks that I have to do every week or month on a certain day. I also use it for sparkly objects *(exciting new ideas that often derail you from completing things you've already committed to)*.

Whenever I have a sparkly idea, I don't add it to my to-do list for today, I add it to Asana. This way I know it's recorded and will happen, just not today. Then, once a week I go through these sparkly ideas, see if they are still sparkly and then integrate them into my to-do list. Allowing a little space between the idea bubbling up and doing it tests whether it really is something I want to do and will work, or just some daft, harebrained, random thought.

Every day, when I'm compiling my to-do list, I'll check Asana to see if:

· there are any recurring tasks that must be done today
· there are any sparkly objects I can realistically finish or at least start *(lick).*

9. Use three-things to-do lists

When I'm really under the pump, I only allow myself to add three things to my to-do list. This allows me to clarify my priorities by asking, 'If I can only do three things today, what can I do?'

When I'm in blind-panic mode – which thankfully is rare these days – I'll only commit to doing one thing on my to-do list. The relief of knowing I just have to do that one thing really helps me get started *(and obviously I usually end up doing more than that).*

> **TOON TIP** I only allow myself ten minutes to write my to do list. Yes, I'll often rewrite my to-do list several times a day, which might seem like procrastifaffing but it genuinely helps me stay clear and focused.

10. Remove distraction

We've talked about only answering the phone at key times during the day as it's hugely distracting, but here are some other tips to remove distraction:

· **Remove ALL notifications from your phone:** Nope, you don't need them – not one of them. Not the one telling you to drink water *(which, as you know, drives me mad),* nor the one asking you to close your exercise ring *(it's an Apple thing, Android people).* You don't need to know your cousin Alan has just posted a picture of his fish on Facebook, and you know there's no urgency to see your fave entrepreneur sharing a photo of herself blowing confetti at her fancy-pants retreat. Turn your notifications off. Now.

- **Turn your phone to flight mode:** This will really stop the endless pings and dings.
- **Set time limits for social media:** On my iPhone this is in Settings > Screen time. I must admit I often press ignore when they pop up, but it does help me check myself and reduce my wasted time.
- **Install restriction apps:** I like the Freedom app, which stops me accessing time-suck websites *(which I can nominate)* for a certain period.

You could take it further of course and remove all distractions:

- **Water distraction:** set up a drip to keep your fluids up.
- **Wee distraction:** wear a nappy.
- **Food distraction:** eat from a horse feed bag.

But hey, start slowly and see how you go.

Of course, the biggest distraction is going to be the kiddos knocking on your door bothering you for a snack, but we'll talk more about how to manage that in Part V.

11. Create templates

One of the biggest time sucks when working is deciding what to say, or how to say it. I find that many of my business humans absolutely agonise over what to say in emails, particularly ones that have a vague whiff of conflict, such as refund requests, clients wanting amendments or chasing money. They write, rewrite, share them in Facebook groups for a second opinion, sleep on them and generally waste time worrying about scenarios that mostly will never happen.

You'll be sending these kinds of emails again and again. So I recommend, every time you have a difficult email to write, sure, agonise over the phrasing the first time, phone a friend, share it in a Facebook group, but then create a template and save it somewhere for future use.

The same goes for documents. Work out what the essential documents are to run your business, write them up, get them proofread, then reuse and recycle them as much as possible. You can even make them look fancy in Canva.

TOON TIP I've made a lot of good money from creating email templates and process documents. These were simply items I created to make my life easier and faster; they came fairly easily to me but are lifesavers for others. So, perhaps if you're struggling to make a template yourself, do a quick google – it likely already exists on the interweb. You'll find all my email and other templates in The Clever Copywriting School shop.

12. Find great tools

I've included some super useful productivity tools in the Extra Bits section right at the end of the book. So, check that out, and also drop into The Misfit Entrepreneur Facebook Group, where I'm often found sharing my latest fave tool or Chrome toolbar extension.

Family productivity wins

Here are a few tactics I use in my daily family life to save time on the boring things and have more time for the enjoyable things. *(Psst: I also asked my members to come up with some ideas, so some of their thoughts are here too.)*

1. Meal planning

One of the most annoying things about having a family is that they have to eat – every single day. And the mental load of thinking about it is exhausting: what to cook, what ingredients you have, what needs to go on the shopping list and, of course, actually shopping for it and cooking it.

I like to plan meals out for the week on a Sunday. Breakfast is pretty straightforward; I have no shame in making my family eat the same thing every day. This goes for lunch boxes too.

Evening meals are planned out and very much on a rotation:

- **Monday:** Pasta of some sort
- **Tuesday:** Tacos
- **Wednesday:** Egg-based thing of some sort

Et cetera.

Freyja Tasci from Apiwraps Beeswax Wraps, mum of Elle (13) and Ziggy (10), told me:

'We have regular meal schedules: Friday night, pizza night – homemade. Saturday night, entertaining – usually the same standard meal because I can make it without thinking and it's food-issue friendly. Sunday, Turkish breakfast for further social time. The more you let go of novelty and change, the more chill things are. I think the routines allow me to concentrate on how we're changing and growing up as a family because there's something against which to measure it.'

We also tend to have one takeaway meal a week – budget allowing – and one 'fend for yourself' night *(now my son is old enough to do this)*. When he was younger, this was more of a basic dinner – something like beans on toast, or toasties, or dippy egg.

Or, as Shannon Lancaster from Cobalt and Co Marketing Agency, mum of Felix (3) and Lucy (2), says:

'There is nothing wrong with pasta and Vegemite for dinner. You can eat fruit cake for breakfast, lunch AND dinner when you're super low on time.'

TOON TIP Remember, kids like routine and knowing what's around the corner, especially with food. Not every night needs to be a cordon bleu experience.

If you're able to share cooking duties with a partner, make it clear to them that they have to follow the plan you came up with at the start of the week. Or, if they want to cook something different, they have to plan it and shop for it too. I absolutely hate it when my son's dad offers to cook, then immediately asks me what to cook. Thinking about what to make is the hardest part.

Finally, there's absolutely nothing wrong with porridge for dinner if you are massively struggling. Better to do something simply than force yourself to make a fabulous meal and have a meltdown.

2. Meal prepping

Several of my members mentioned meal prepping as a big part of their survival plan, often baking things in batches on a Sunday. However, I find that, if I make a big batch of something on a Sunday, by Monday I don't want to eat it. Sunday Me is a completely different person to Monday Me.

But I will often make double the amount of food – giant lasagnes – and then freeze them in individual portions for lunches later in the month. *(Today Me is so grateful for Yesterday Me who does that.)*

Another option is to grab a cheap slow cooker, shove all the ingredients in it in the morning and come home to a warm, gooey, hearty meal.

TOON TIP Pack school lunches the night before. It makes school mornings so much less stressful. I don't manage this every day but even a few days a week helps.

3. Subscription services and shopping online

I have as many services as possible on subscription.

When the budget allows, we use a meal delivery service – just two days a week for variation. I have loo rolls, cleaning products, razor blades and dog food on subscription. It often works out a lot cheaper and massively reduces my mental load.

I also find shopping online saves me a lot of time, either delivered or click and collect. I can't do this for food items as I'm just not organised or smart enough and end up accidentally ordering 18 cucumbers, but it's great for regular cleaning and household supplies once a month.

4. Direct debits

All our bills are on direct debit and paid monthly, which makes monthly budgeting much easier (more on this in Chapter 12). We even pay ahead for regular services; for example, I get our house pest-treated twice a year because of my morbid fear of spiders. We spoke to the company and they allow us to pay for this a little bit every month so there are no big hairy financial surprises.

5. Standard operating procedures

You know how in cafes you often see little posters outlining how to shut down the kitchen at the end of the day? This is something you can implement in your home – breaking down tasks into smaller tasks so it's easier to follow both for yourself *(on brain-fog days)* and for kids and partners. *(We'll talk more about this in Chapter 17.)* These are called standard operating procedures in the business world, and they can work great at home too.

Freyja Tasci added:

'Standard operating procedures are everything. We have them on the inside of the cupboards. For cleaning so there are no quibbles about the job being done half-heartedly. For lunchboxes. For after-school routines.'

6. Helpful apps

You can use the same apps you use for business for family life too.

My partner Tony Cosentino from The WordPress Guy, dad of Josh (33), Kat (30), Fynn (13) and Sam (10), recommends the Streaks app:

'I use the Streaks app to make daily, weekly and monthly household chore reminders so I don't forget to do the basics regularly, as I get tunnel vision when working and forget when I last did a chore. For example: watering plants every two days; washing towels, bathmat, etc. weekly; mopping floors; washing sheets; etc.'

Sarah Prime from BANG ON Co, mum of Adaline (5), uses Asana for her family:

'I have a "Personal" project set up in Asana with things I need to do but not necessarily straight away. I find if it's written down, there's less brain power being used to remember it. If I have a slow day or I am heading out, I can run my eye over the list and see if there's anything I can get done at the same time.'

7. Bring in the robots

If you can afford to sell a kidney, you could splash out on a robot vacuum or lawnmower.

Kara Lambert, mum of Imogen (17) and Brennan (15), told me:

'A mopping Robovac saves time on housekeeping. I can set it going when I'm not home – that's if my husband hasn't decided he wanted to set it going first. It helps having a gadget-loving partner.'

I can't justify a robot vacuum cleaner, but I do have a greedy dog that helps keep the kitchen floor free of all food waste.

8. 'Come to you' services

You might be surprised by how many services are willing to come to you. My dog clipper comes to my house, as does my hairdresser. This saves me a huge amount of time, and I can get the entire family's hair done in my kitchen while also doing other things. *(I am tempted to ask the dog clipper to do the family hair as well, but I fear this is taking my love of productivity too far.)*

9. Reduce your expectations

'Reduce your expectations' doesn't sound like a productivity tip, but it's actually the most important one.

I'm a total clean freak, just like my mum, and used to aim to keep my home like a new-build show home 99% of the time. I have no idea why. It's not like we have visitors every day. Of course, it's important for my peace of mind to have a nice, comfortable space to live in, but it can also actually look 'lived in'.

My throw cushions don't need to be perfectly arranged. The rug tassels don't need to be combed straight at 5 a.m. each morning. Letting go of my home perfection was a huge part of being more productive and being more present for my family. It also helps my family feel a lot less stressed if they don't have to maniacally wipe surfaces and tesselate the Tupperware to military standards.

10. Divide and conquer

A key part of being more productive is also to do a hell of a lot less and realise you don't need to do this all yourself. So many parents huff and puff out the 'oh I'll just do it' mantra when in fact, if they were a little less fastidious and a bit more patient, they could let it go and pass it on to a family member.

We'll cover this more in the next chapter and in Chapter 16.

TL;DR

Productivity is something you need to work at. At first, implementing these strategies will feel like more work, but pretty soon they will become habits that you barely notice. While productivity isn't a success metric, it does allow you to feel better about your day.

Benefits

Thinking about productivity and making active steps towards improving it will help you:

- reduce mental load and stress around not getting everything done
- help you feel calmer around your business and family life
- genuinely free up time and generate hours you can choose to invest in your business or your family
- help you to feel in control of your life, your business and yourself.

Over to you

Now it's time for you to think about how these productivity wins could work for you:

1. Review the business productivity ideas listed in this chapter and pick three you think you can implement in your business.
2. Review the family productivity ideas listed in this chapter and pick three you think you can implement in your family.
3. Is there a productivity hack I missed? Share it in my Facebook group The Misfit Entrepreneurs.

Chapter 10

It takes a village

'In order to grow, you must be able to let go.'
Richard Branson

In recent years, the term 'solopreneur' has flopped into the common vernacular, basically meaning an entrepreneurial type who does it all themselves. 'Sole trader' is another term and 'martyr' is another. We business-owning parents do like to try and do EVERYTHING ourselves.

However, I am of the firm belief that you cannot run a business on your own. And thinking you can do it all yourself is the fastest track to burnout at the least, but at the worst, total failure.

We used to say it takes a village to raise a child. I believe it also takes a village to run a business. But the sad truth is that many of us often feel villageless.

Now, this might sound hypocritical since I'm a purveyor of DIY courses, templates and memberships that are designed to give people the know-how and skills to tackle everything from copywriting and SEO to finances and project management completely solo. But there's a big difference between knowing how to do the thing and actually doing the thing. Learning the what, the why and the how is vital, but doing the do? Not so much.

For example, I teach SEO. In fact, I've taught nearly 15,000 people how to grapple the Google beast via my courses and resources. But not everyone who takes one of my courses decides to manage their own SEO; rather, when they understand how it works, they have a choice: they can DIY or they can outsource.

The difference is that now they can outsource with confidence. They're no longer worried that they're going to be bamboozled by jargon and gobbledegook. And they're no longer fretting they'll be ripped off.

Knowledge is power. The knowledge that you don't have to do all the work yourself is more powerful.

In this chapter, I want to talk about outsourcing, how to overcome mindset barriers around 'hiring staff', and how to bring people into your business and your family to help – without stress and anxiety.

I know that for many of you the idea of 'staff' has you thinking about the kitchen in Downton Abbey: a plethora of humans sitting around a table waiting for a bell to ring. And while you may be able to overcome some of the icks around hiring people to help run your business, hiring people at home feels somehow weirder and harder. Well, it did for me. But I got over it and you can too.

Let's address the fears and mindset blocks for both.

1. I'm not the sort of person who has staff

I come from working-class stock. The idea of having people working for me feels extremely 'other'. It's something 'rich' people do.

One of the first family hires I made was a cleaner, and this felt very odd. I mean, I'm not so fancy that I can't clean my own loo, right?

But I realise it wasn't about feeling better than someone else; it was about getting help where I needed it. There's just something about working and parenting all week, and then having to do the cleaning on top of it, that's utterly exhausting.

And yes, it's a privilege and a luxury – I acknowledge that. But, personally, I'd rather sacrifice a lot of other things in order to pay for my cleaner. That's how important she is to me; that's how much I look forward to her coming. And I have learned not to feel odd about her seeing my messy house, or about her working for me. It's an exchange that works. And in actual fact, my cleaner has a cleaner for her own house.

Here's what Anastasia Geneave from Chalk and Cheese Occasions, mum of Samuel (3) and Emily (1), had to say about cleaners:

'When I was earning more, we outsourced the house cleaning. It was amazing, just knowing that every fortnight things would get more than just the quick wipe down than I had time for gave us such peace of mind.'

And Sarah Walkerden from The Rural Copywriter, mum of Oliver (10) and Sophie (7), said:

'We've outsourced cleaning for the past 12 months. Just two hours a fortnight has made such a difference. It saves hubby and me stress, keeps the house far more spotless than we could manage and forces us to stay more organised with keeping things tidy. We're finding the more efficiently our home life runs, the better and clearer we feel mentally, giving us more energy and mental capacity to pour into our businesses.'

I found that hiring a cleaner was hugely hard for my son's dad to accept. He felt it was a waste of money and something we could do ourselves (and by we, obviously he meant me).

The problem being, he just didn't care about cleaning the way I did. He honestly doesn't even notice the muck – or so he says. I had to sit him down and explain how important it was to me to have a clean home and how much I was struggling mentally to get it done. We started small – just an hour a fortnight. He saw the difference and eventually appreciated it, but yes, it was a struggle.

2. How do I spend money if I'm not making money?

Whatever stage you're at in your business, the idea of handing over ANY of your hard-earned cash to someone else seems daunting, but especially if you're not reaching your income goals.

Belinda Owen from Belinda Owen Website Design, mum of Isaac (9), said this:

> 'My biggest fear is being able to afford it. As a sole trader, income can be up and down, and I have fears that in the downturns I will be committed to more than I can afford.'

Here are a few points to think about.

They cost less than you

Hopefully, if you completed the exercise in Chapter 6, you're clearer on the time you have to work and the hourly rate you want to charge. Generally, you want to be hiring someone who costs less than you so you can clearly justify it. So, if a cleaner is charging $40 an hour and you're charging $100, then you're winning – you're freeing up an hour of your time and making $60 for every hour they work *(as long as you're also working)*.

They're more skilled than you

My first business hire was an accountant. Now, at the time, their rate was actually more than my hourly rate, but it was justifiable because they had a skill set I didn't have. So, in one hour they could do well what I would do badly in three. And I was purchasing the peace of mind that my accounts would be perfect, which would have saved me potentially thousands if I'd messed something up myself.

One of the biggest lessons I learned in business is that just because I can doesn't mean I should. I am not a genius at anything *(big shock)*; instead I'm an all-rounder who's okay at a lot of things. I can code. I can design. I can do my own bookkeeping. But I have to ask myself two important questions:

1. Is it the best use of my time?
2. Am I the best person for the job?

As an in-demand specialist SEO copywriter, I could demand quite a high rate, so it literally made no sense to waste my time fiddling around in Xero when I could be working for clients and making four times as much as my bookkeeper charged.

You can start small

No-one is asking you to go out and hire a team of people tomorrow. I started with my accountant, and then a virtual assistant at just two hours a week; it wasn't a huge commitment, and it grew from there.

You can dial up and down

If you're working with subcontractors, it's perfectly fine to dial up and down the amount of work they do. So, if you're having a few rough months, sure, you can ask them to do fewer hours; or you can ramp up when things are going well. Just explain this from the get-go, then you can commit to exactly what works for you – and them.

3. It's faster if I do it

Yes, it is faster if you do it. And it will be for a while. But outsourcing isn't just about efficiency, it's about mental load and scaling.

The 'it's faster if I do it' mentality will keep you small, stressed and up to your ears in work. Because there are quite literally only so many hours in a day. No matter how efficient you become, you will eventually run out of time, and the only way to make more time is to use other people.

Here are some points to ponder.

Three-month investment

I think that hiring any human for anything should be considered a three-month investment. By this, I mean that for those first three months they may actually cost you money rather than make you money.

Now, this is hard.

I recently employed an online business manager and spent three months carefully and patiently training her, accepting that for this period she wasn't going to be efficient, speedy or profitable. Then, after three months, she left for a job with a salary I couldn't match, and all the investment was for nothing.

So, yes, you may get burned occasionally, but don't let that put you off.

Obviously, the more experienced the person you hire is, the shorter this investment period will be. I asked my members recently, 'Would you rather have 20 hours a week of a $40 person or 10 hours a week of an $80 person?'

The answer was resoundingly the $80 person.

So, while cheap may feel like it's the best way to save money, remember that it doesn't always work out that way. Time has a cost too.

Don't hire a clone

If you are stuck on the 'do it myself' idea, consider the job description of the person you're hiring – is it a bit too similar to your own job description?

You shouldn't be hiring a clone of yourself.

If your core skill is, say, WordPress web development, you might not want to hire another developer; rather, you might hire an accountant, a graphic designer or a copywriter – people with skill sets that mean it would genuinely not be faster for you to do it yourself.

Or, you can hire a new you, but ensure they're a mini you: for example, a more junior WordPress developer who can handle updates and maintenance but would struggle with more complex work.

Belinda Owen from Belinda Owen Website Design, mum of Isaac (9), said this:

> 'I have two people who I outsource to now and it took six years to get the confidence to do it. But it's great as they have skills I don't have, and that makes my life so much easier. One is paid monthly on set hours so I can budget for it and the other is my developer who I pay as needed, so it works well.'

If you hire clone of yourself, you may find that setting boundaries between what they do and what you do is challenging.

4. I don't like relying on other people

Ugh I just hate having to trust other people to do things, don't you?

If this is how you feel, it can be a toughie both at home and at work. Let's break it down.

At home

Hiring people to work in your own home is terrifying, especially when it comes to your children. But even for cleaners there's a fear of them going through your knicker drawer, or just seeing what a slovenly beast you are.

Here are some tips that helped me:

- **Get a personal recommendation:** Find someone who a friend is already using and trusts.
- **Get police checks and references:** For all our babysitters, we've done police checks and several references, and I've taken the time to call each referee.
- **Be around:** As I work at home, often cleaners are working while I'm there, and babysitters are just a room away, and that helps me keep an eye on things and not have a complete panic attack. Of course, there are also cameras hidden in bears' bottoms and so on that you can use to keep an eye on things if you're not home, but I've never invested in these.
- **Get over yourself:** If you're anxious about people thinking you're not coping or the cleaner thinking your house is a mess, stop it. It's quite literally what the cleaner expects – and I'm sure they've seen much worse.

Yes, it's super challenging and we've been lucky. I would say that, if hiring someone at home gives you more anxiety, then it's absolutely not worth it. Instead, try to hire someone in your business so you have more free time to do home things.

In business

Hiring people in your business is hard. It requires a lot of trust, and of course there's always the worry that they won't do what you need and may damage your business reputation. So, here are few tips to mitigate that:

- **Keep them back of house:** Your helpers don't need to be public-facing – you can still be the face and voice of your business – and check all their work before the client sees it.

- **Invest in training:** Make sure you set aside time to train your staff members to do things as you want them done. I do this by:
  - creating Loom videos of me doing the tasks and storing them in Asana *(Loom is a video recording tool with freemium pricing – more on this in Extra Bits at the back of the book)*
  - creating standard operating procedures – essentially lists of how to do a task – and processes.
- **Keep an eye on them:** I have access to my team's email addresses so I can see the emails they are sending and receiving without needing to be CCed. After a few months, I no longer feel I need to check on them – but in the early days I do, and I'm upfront about that.
- **Keep things secure:** Don't give them access to everything immediately. Set up separate logins that can be removed quickly, and use software like LastPass *(a password storage tool – more on this in Extra Bits)* so that team members can access things without knowing your passwords.

5. What if it all goes wrong?

In business, as in life, nothing is going to be perfect. You will hire people and have them let you down horribly. Others will pretend they can do stuff and be woeful at it.

You'll have to kiss a lot of frogs *(no licking now)* and get your gentle heart broken, but don't give up! It's taken me a long time to find a team of humans who are solid, reliable, talented, honest and just wonderful to work with.

And, yes, there have been times when I've never wanted to use an external person again. But, quite simply, I could not have built the business I have without the help of others – not just practical implementation help but the support, encouragement and confidence. It's extremely lonely running a business, and having people to talk to is part of why I've been able to be brave and achieve more.

On the home front, yes, we've gone through a number of cleaners; some have just moved on, others incessantly broke stuff, but they were all good people who really helped our family.

We've had a few babysitters over the years who I now count as friends and who added wonderful dimensions to my son's life. *(Jennifer, Nikita, Jessica and Nanny Hamill, I'm looking at you.)* I've used more gardeners than you could shake a stick at – or a hoe.

Some people you outsource to for a lifetime, some for a season, some for a reason, and even those that don't work out often teach you something.

Overseas or local?

There's lots of debate online about whether you should hire business help from overseas or from your own country.

One advantage of hiring overseas is that it can be much cheaper *(depending on where you are)*. The cost of living in Australia (where I am) makes rates higher than in other countries. However, the disadvantages include:

·   **Language barriers:** Even if your supplier is fluent in your language, often nuance and humour don't match, which can make daily communication feel strained. I had a VA who relentlessly called me 'marm', even after I asked her not to. It made me feel odd and elderly. It didn't work out.

·   **Working hours:** Often overseas humans aren't available when you are, and these time differences can make communication and speedy responses difficult.

·   **Reputation:** Hiring randoms from freelancer sites can be risky because, if they mess up, they can often just delete their profile and start again. They have no reputation to protect. A lot of platforms try to overcome this with reviews and ratings, so be sure to choose carefully.

I have both Australian and overseas humans working for me now. I am proud to help them support their families wherever they are.

Hiring or subcontracting

We could dedicate a whole chapter to hiring versus subcontracting, but I'll keep it short and sweet.

If you're starting out with outsourcing in your business, then I highly recommend starting with subcontractors – it's much less of a commitment. Yes, you'll pay a slightly higher rate, but you won't have to worry about insurance, pensions, KPIs and the rest. *(In Australia we also have to think about WorkCover, which ain't cheap.)*

Once you're able to offer a more solid commitment, you can move to some kind of retainer agreement where the subcontractor works a set number of hours per month for a slightly lower rate. *(I have a retainer agreement template in The Clever Copywriting School shop if you need one, as well as a subcontractor agreement template.)*

After that, when you're really sure you have the cash flow and the ongoing work, you can consider hiring someone. It's a lot more faff to get started but definitely feels more committed and is often more affordable.

> **TOON TIP** Be super careful about how you employ people and talk to an accountant. Often, although you may think it's fine to have someone as a subcontractor, your tax office may consider them an employee. It's a fine line and not one you want to overstep.

Outsourcing in the community

Of course, hiring people is not the only solution: you can take the 'back scratch' approach as well *(as in, you scratch my back and I'll rub yours)*. Here are a few ways I've been able to get 'free' help for my family and my business.

Kid-swap mornings

Often, when you meet other parents with kids, the nice thing to do is meet for coffee while your kids play in the playground and you try to keep a conversation going with constant interruption. But I often arranged play dates for my kids that didn't involve me.

So, one morning a week, my mum friend would drop her kiddos off at my house for two to three hours, and then I returned the favour for her on another day. There was no pressure to hang around and have a coffee; instead, we were free to work, or go and lie on our bed to nap and groan.

Overcooking and shopping

Another thing that worked well for me was overcooking: if I was making any food or baking, I would make double the amount and drop some off at my friend's house, and she would do the same for me. I took a neighbourly approach to shopping with friends too, often picking up their bits for them and vice versa. It seems insignificant, but not having to pop to the shops to get a random egg or onion often saved me from having a mental breakdown that day.

Contras

In the early days of business I often did contras for services in my business: exchanging a few hours of copywriting for, say, a photo shoot or some graphic design.

My key advice here is to be very clear on what you're offering and treat it like a real job with a proposal and a budget or invoice (even if the invoice is for $0). And agree on expectations clearly at the start. Because often, one person feels like they've done more than the other, and that leads to resentment and friendship breakdown.

But when it works, it's great.

My team now

Although I started out with just a virtual assistant for two hours a week and an accountant, my team has grown substantially. And it evolves all the time as my business evolves.

Figure 10.1 (overleaf) shows my current team structure.

In terms of hours, see table 10.1 (overleaf) for the set-up. Some are on retainer, some charge by the project, and now I have only one proper employee.

As you can see, my son is part of the team. More on that in Chapter 17.

Figure 10.1: My current team structure

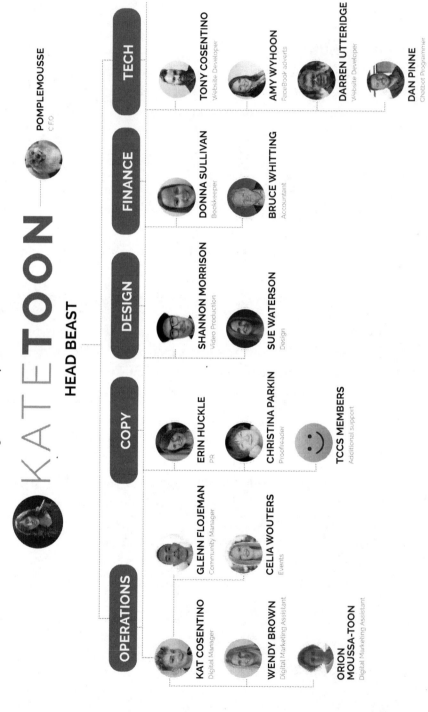

KATE**TOON**

HEAD BEAST

POMPLEMOUSSE
CFO

OPERATIONS

KAT COSENTINO
Digital Manager

WENDY BROWN
Digital Marketing Assistant

ORION MOUSSA-TOON
Digital Marketing Assistant

GLENN FLOJEMAN
Community Manager

CELIA WOUTERS
Events

COPY

ERIN HUCKLE
PR

CHRISTINA PARKIN
Proofreader

TCCS MEMBERS
Additional support

DESIGN

SHANNON MORRISON
Video Production

SUE WATERSON
Design

FINANCE

DONNA SULLIVAN
Bookkeeper

BRUCE WHITTING
Accountant

TECH

TONY COSENTINO
Website Developer

AMY WYHOON
Facebook adverts

DARREN UTTERIDGE
Website Developer

DAN PINNE
Chatbot Programmer

Table 10.1: My team hours

Person	Role	Hours
Kat	Digital Manager	Employee: 80 hours a month
My son		Employee: 20 hours a month
Sue	Designer	Contractor: 40 hours a month
Leanne	Secret squirrel special projects	Contractor: 40 hours a month
Tony	Developer	Contractor: 10 hours a month
Darren	Developer	Contractor: 40 hours a month
Erin	PR	Contractor: 10 hours a month
Donna	Bookkeeper	Contractor: 40 hours a month
Christina	Proofreader	Contractor: 10 hours a month
Wendy	Marketing Assistant	Contractor: 10 hours a month
Celia	Events	Ad hoc project fees
Dan	Chatbots	Ad hoc project fees
Amy	Facebook ads	Ad hoc project fees
Shannon	Videos	Ad hoc project fees
Bruce	Accountant	Ad hoc project fees

Don't outsource too much

At one point, I went a little outsource-crazy in my personal life. It was in the period when I pretty much burned out and made myself ill, and I think my over-outsourcing actually made the burnout worse.

I had a cleaner and gardener, which was great, but I also had a dog walker and a babysitter. And I began to increase the babysitter's hours.

It didn't take me long to realise I was outsourcing all the wrong things, the things that gave me joy. Yes, it gave me more time to focus on my business, but perhaps too much. I'd lost the balance of working to live, and instead was removing all the living and just working.

Walking my dog in the morning to get a coffee at the beach is one of my fave parts of the day. It gives me joy, settles my mind and is vital exercise.

Doing dinnertime, bath time and reading a bedtime story with my son when he was small, although stressful at times, was so important to me as a mum. And the parent guilt and longing I felt when I missed these things was just not worth what I got in return. I've since redressed this balance.

Be careful not to outsource the joy in your life as I did.

The benefits of outsourcing

Obviously, hiring other humans can come with stresses, but when it works the relief is just beautiful!

Kate Redman from RBI Australia, mum of Maggie (5), told me:

'My husband and I both work in our business. We outsource cleaning and lawn mowing once a fortnight. I find it's worth the money as it takes some of the pressure off with the boring housework – and it's one less thing to argue about.'

On the home front

My son's dad and I no longer constantly squabble about cleaning. We even went further and hired a garden person to do the lawns once in a while. Our son was babysat by some amazing humans who brought so much joy into his life.

My home is cleaner and easier to come back to after a long day of work. My mental load is much, much lighter and the knot in my stomach has gone.

On the business front

As I've mentioned, my business would not have grown as big as it has without other people, and I would not have grown as much as a person.

My endless chats with my calm, wise Secret Squirrel Special Projects Leanne have genuinely reframed the way I think about my business. The ideas and input from the rest of the team just improve things exponentially. Now, turning up to work with these people each day is a large part of what motivates me to keep going.

Keeneena Fanning from Kablooie, mum of Elisha (14), Josiah (12) and Elya (10), said:

'Because I started out cutting and making all my products myself, outsourcing when I got too busy to cope was really scary because it felt like I was losing control of the process. As a maker, I wondered if it made me less authentic if everything wasn't made by my own two hands.

'I had to decide whether I wanted to stay within my own capacity and keep making everything (very labour intensive) or expand to where the business started to really contribute to our household finances by outsourcing some of the sewing work to other makers working for me.

'In the end, the business was about generating an income, not my own internal creativity, so I made the switch. I loved that I did because I found way more scope for creativity in shaping the way the business grew and designing new ranges and fabrics.

'I also then outsourced admin work, both on-site and virtual. Outsourcing has its challenges but I don't regret it.'

TL;DR

Outsourcing can require you to take a leap of faith, trust yourself, trust others and also be ready to accept that it may go wrong, but it's the only way to grow beyond the restrictive hours you have. Also, it's a great way to share the mental load of your business.

Benefits

Thinking about hiring people both at home and in your business will help you:

- scale up your business and potentially make more money and/or spend more time with your family
- reduce stress and worry by sharing the physical and mental load
- focus on more high-value tasks
- bring new skills and ideas into your business.

Over to you

Now it's time for you to consider how you could make outsourcing work for you. Here are some exercises to help:

1. Think about your biggest barrier to hiring someone and try to challenge it using the points from this chapter.
2. Create a list of repeatable tasks in your business.
3. Create a list of tasks you think could be done at less than your hourly rate.
4. Think of three tasks you do that could be outsourced. Make a Loom video and/or standard operation procedure for each.
5. Consider signing up to Slack and Asana or similar to help you to manage people.

Remember, if you'd like to work through these exercises in detail you can head to sixfiguresinschoolhours.com and grab the accompanying workbook.

PART III

MONEY

GET REAL WITH YOUR NUMBERS

AH, MONEY. It's a funny one, eh? We want more of it, but at the same time we're encouraged to appreciate what we have and not be greedy.

We all know it costs somewhere in the region of $83 billion to raise a child to adulthood. We all feel the pressure to give them everything and, without a regular wage from 'the man', simply providing the essentials can feel daunting.

As a small business owner, the pressure to buy 'all the things' and invest in personal development is huge. There's always another tempting course to buy, or the lure of more beautiful stationery.

I'll admit I was a money muppet for many years: joyfully clueless about what I was earning and how that translated into real life. I was spending like a footballer's wife for the first two weeks of the month and living the last two eating only beans on toast.

And it got me massively in the poo. Credit card debt, tax debt and a crippling sense of financial stupidity – I had it all. Even when I started to earn decent money, I never seemed to actually have any more to spend beyond the basics.

And so, I decided to fix that.

Here's the thing: we have to learn to talk about money and get comfortable with our money if we want to hit our financial goals.

Yes, I know talking about money brings up all the 'feelings'. It's often triggering, upsetting and confusing. Whether we admit it or not, we often have weird hang-ups about money. We're heavily influenced by our own parents' attitudes to money, by society, and by our partners and friends. Even those who *do* talk about what they're earning often don't share what really goes into earning it.

For many parents, an important part of their business why is the ability to earn more money to give their kids a better life. And yet, surprisingly, few spend time examining their hang-ups and working to improve their financial literacy.

In this part, I want to examine how you feel about money, and force you to wade through your discomfort and get real about your numbers.

We'll also discuss profit and examine feast and famine, and I'll even give you some passive income ideas.

Again, the path to six figures – whether that's revenue, take-home pay or pure, juicy profit – is rarely about stumbling upon some lavish financial pot at the end of your business rainbow. It's about a million micro-changes to mindset and habits. It's about doing the work.

In this part I cover:

· how I changed my money mindset
· the cold hard truth about your numbers
· understanding profit
· implementing small business financial wins.

Okay, show me the money, honey.

Chapter 11

My money mindset

'The more of it one has, the more one wants.'
Benjamin Franklin

If I asked you right now how much you earn in your business each year, what feeling would bubble up in your chest as you thought about your answer?

- Does the very idea of money make you anxious?
- Do you think of the figure and then feel you need to justify it?
- Are you slightly ashamed of what you earn?
- Are you afraid it's too little or too much?
- Do you dread tall poppy syndrome *(the tendency to disparage anyone who achieves wealth or success)*?

We all have the 'big feels' when it comes to money. And unless we acknowledge and understand them, it can be hard to move forward and see money for what it really is. For me, it's a tool that helps me live the life I want to, but it's not the only weapon in my lifestyle armoury.

I asked my members how they'd feel answering the 'How much do you earn?' question. Here are a few of their responses. Do any of them resonate with you?

Jessica Staines from Koori Curriculum, mum of Shirley Pearl (1), said:

'It depends who's asking me. If you asked me in certain spaces amongst business peers and colleagues, there is no shame but a sense of pride and accomplishment

'However, as an Aboriginal business, if someone from another community asked me directly about my income and business profit, I definitely wouldn't tell them. There is a bit of a thing about being too successful as a Black business. To struggle is almost seen as a sign of legitimacy (something that I hope will one day change).

Keneena Fanning from Kablooie, mum of Elisha (14), Josiah (12) and Elya (10), added:

'I think I seem to have a hierarchical way of looking at myself, always trying to work out where I fit within the group I'm talking to. I have some work to do to just be happy with myself and my business publicly, as privately I really am, and I'm right where I want to be in terms of income.'

And finally, Erin Lightfoot from Erin Lightfoot Studio, mum of Ren (4) and Ira (1), had this to say:

'I have anxieties around financials not being impressive enough for the number of years I've been in business. And there's a fear that this could be because of personal lacking that will forever hold me back. Perhaps its money mindset, perhaps lack of social networking ability, perhaps too much time locked in the basement making art. So, yes, financial questions poke at the soft tender underbelly, and when a friend recently asked directly what I earn I spent the next day feeling anxious that I hadn't contextualised it (justified).'

Parents and money

Our thoughts and feelings about money and the work needed to earn it are often formed in our childhood. So, they're obviously heavily influenced by our parents' attitudes.

I can only speak about my own experience, so I will. Briefly.

My parents are working class. Their fathers worked in coalmines or factories. Their mothers were housewives.

My dad was the first in his family to go to university. *(I was the second.)* He was a bit of a pioneer and also a hard worker. His parents couldn't afford to fund his studies, so he worked canning beans and at other drudgy jobs. The link between hard work and money was drilled into him at an early age, and he then drilled it into me.

My mum met my dad when she was young and took the family route, rather than studying to be a teacher as she'd planned. She stayed at home with my brother and me until I was about seven, then went out to work. Even at that early age I was aware of what a juggle it was to work all day and then come home and have to do family things. And, of course, now I'm experiencing that for myself.

Both of my parents were open about money and the cost of things. We were by no means rich, which was brought into sharp focus when we moved from the north of England to the south. I realised then that, despite my dad having a well-paid job, our family wasn't quite as affluent as some of my friends' families. They had swimming pools while we had a paddling pool; they holidayed on the ski slopes of France while we stayed in B&Bs in Wales – you get the idea.

We were savers, not spenders

Our family was definitely comfy. We had a nice house and all the mod cons you would expect: decidedly middle class with two cars, regular outings and a pile of gifts under the tree at Christmas.

But my parents weren't credit card creatures. Spending was considered, risks weren't taken and there was always an air of caution. And frugality. 'Neither a borrower nor a lender be' was an adage I heard a lot as a child.

My parents involved us in the family budgeting. I remember them keeping a large bottle of loose change that we'd empty each year and count out, using the funds to give us extra spending money for treats. *(On a side note, this led me to develop a serious phobia of coins. It's a thing – cuprolaminophobia. Touching coins makes me feel physically sick, so the fact that we're moving to an electronic economy is a great thing for me.)*

My dad eventually left his job and started his own company, and my mum joined him in the business a few years later. My brother and I were actively involved, packing envelopes and visiting the offices. It felt awesome to be working as a family *(more on this in Chapter 17).* It went well for several years, and then the recession arrived and the company folded.

My family took a huge financial hit. Just after I went to university, my parents packed up our life and moved back to the north of England to consolidate funds. It was a tough time. There were some difficult conversations and a lot of stress and upset. Since then, my parents have recovered and now lead a comfortable, if not luxurious, life.

Did my dad's business demise put me off starting my own business? Clearly not. But boy did it make me cautious.

It feels odd and slightly vulnerable to give a potted history of my family's financials. *(Also slightly uncomfortable for my mum and dad, who proofread this book. So, thank you for letting me discuss this so openly.)* But I feel it's necessary to frame how I think and feel about money.

The lessons I learned from my parents (good and bad) include:

- money only comes from hard work
- all credit is bad
- it's better to delay and save than spend now and pay back
- don't spend beyond your means
- don't take risks.

Clearly, my parents had a huge influence on my financial attitudes. And it seems they do for most of us.

Here's what Kara Lambert, mum of Imogen (17) and Brennan (15), learned from her mum:

'My mum was a credit controller. She budgeted and saved. She taught me that some credit is good and to live within your means. She talked about investing in high-yield, short-term investments. I feel very fortunate.'

Shannon Lancaster from Cobalt and Co Marketing Agency, mum of Felix (3) and Lucy (2), had an upbringing that led her to be a free spender *(like me)*:

'My parents had a scarcity attitude towards money and in response I've always been a little too free with my spending. It's taken me years to stop and think before making a purchase as the dopamine hit I get from spending tends to override all logic!'

And Jennifer Gale from Pink Hat Digital, and mum of Nick (36), told me this:

'My mum and dad, as immigrants, worked so hard. My dad worked seven days a week for all of my known memory and my mum always worked even when we were tiny, which was a social no-no in our small village.

'We were very, very poor and that struggle out of poverty taught me so much. I've always worked. It's a great ethic, but it's taken years to understand that I don't need to and that you can enjoy money too. From them I learned you can work your way out of trouble and what you do does not define who you are.'

I'd love for you to take a minute and think about how your parents have influenced your money attitude, both for better and worse.

My early money experiences

Now, I promised this book wouldn't be a giant 'me' festival, but I need to share a little of my background for context. I want you to see where I've come from – the mistakes I've made and also a few of my wins – in the hope they will both deter and inspire you.

So, stick with me.

As a child, I was given a decent chunk of pocket money each week. But I was a girl with high expectations *(those rah-rah skirts and pixie boots weren't going to buy themselves)*, so I was always looking for ways to earn more.

My parents encouraged me to do jobs around the house to earn extra cash – everything from ironing my dad's shirts and polishing shoes to mowing the lawn. I found it delightful that I could put in the effort and see the money come rolling in.

From an early age I had the entrepreneurial spirit. At first I was a maker, creating anything I could to sell to my family, then to friends and at markets:

- I painted little faces on rocks and sold them to neighbours at age eight.
- I created a rather cool range of modelling-clay tortoise keyrings when I was nine.
- I launched a lovely line of lavender-scented bags and padded hangers at around age ten.
- I even launched a membership for my friends at around age 11, with badges and a weekly publication. It only lasted two weeks. (Memberships are hard, people.)

My brother got a paper round and subcontracted it to me when I was about 12. I helped him by lugging a heavy bag packed with papers around my estate in the dead of night for a piddling amount *(get out your tiny violins)*. But it allowed me to save, and I was happy.

After that it was a series of weekend jobs at a bakery, cleaning the school, and folding underpants at British high-street store Topman to fund my love of records and tasselly indie skirts.

And finally, off to university. While my richer friends went jetting off overseas in the term holidays, I worked in bars, clubs and the university offices, maxing out my student loan and in a perpetual state of poverty. I remember distinctly going to a corner shop in Leeds to purchase one egg and half an onion with my meagre funds. Who even sells half an onion? *(From these ingredients – and some cheese stolen from a flatmate – I made 'eggy mess', which is a household favourite to this day.)*

Now when I say poverty here, it was kind of self-inflicted. I earned enough through my loan, parental contributions and my bar money to live a good life. But I always managed to spend a little beyond my means. And it soon became a trend.

I left college with around £5K of debt. This meant I didn't take the step I wanted to: to study magazine journalism *(a wonderful course but a hefty fee)*. My parents weren't willing to lend me the cash, so I took a job instead.

This financial fork in the road is something I regretted for a long time. But my aversion to debt was always lurking, like a dark piglet snorting in the back of the room. And the idea of racking up more debt was impossible to comprehend. I felt I'd missed out on my true vocation of becoming a writer *(but obviously I got there in the end by a less-well-trodden path)*.

Throughout my 20s I lived hand-to-mouth. I moved to Australia, racking up more debt as I tried to keep up with my new wealthy friends. Early on I scored a job at Ogilvy, a fancy-pants advertising agency that paid well. But I still kept spending wildly beyond my income.

Clearly, I was taking the opposite stance to my parents. Credit cards were my thing. I had them all.

Note: I did ask my parents for loans on a few occasions and, while they weren't rolling in it, they possibly could have helped. But they firmly believed I had to learn the hard way as they had done, and so I did. Of course, at the time I was a tad bitter about this, but in hard times we do brave things. I ran out of money in Australia within weeks, and so the job at Ogilvy was a lucky break. Ultimately, though, it was the making of me and my future career. So, it's with a slight gnashing of teeth that I see my parents were kinda right.

I moved back to the UK in the early 2000s, leaving a trail of debt behind me. But over the next few years, simply because I had so much expendable income working as a digital marketing contractor, I managed to pay back all my debt and finally build some savings.

It was a good feeling. But it didn't last. I quickly whittled through my funds when I went travelling in my early 30s, and came back to Australia with my then partner *(and future husband)* with a full backpack and an empty bank balance.

It wasn't until I was about 33 that I felt I had a solid, consistent amount of money.

I remember heading to Double Bay *(a posh area of Sydney)* and spending a small fortune in a fancy lingerie shop on sucky-inny knickers and feeling like I was as rich as Croesus *(a Greek king who was, by all accounts, rather rich).*

But the sucky-inny pants were never going to work because I was pregnant.

My small-business money experience

Business and parenting are inextricably linked for me because I started my business when I was five months pregnant. My son has, therefore, always been a part of my business story, from the womb-kicking days of then to the grunty days of his now teendom.

Before my pregnancy, I was working on a fairly chunky contractor rate for four days a week and kind of dabbling in my side hustle of copywriting one day a week but not really achieving much. *(A side hustle is something that isn't your main business but you hope it will be one day.)*

When I discovered I was pregnant, I knew I had to sort my life out.

Pregnancy was a surprise for my partner and me. We'd been told by a specialist that we couldn't have kids, and my partner dismissed the idea of IVF, which he didn't feel we could afford. Instead, we'd planned a life of buying expensive white sofas and having exotic travel adventures, and I walked around for a few years looking at pregnant women and silently weeping. So, discovering we had a small human on the way threw us into a state of abject joy *(me)* and mild panic *(him).*

We had no savings. My husband had just started a French education business and had one client. We were renting a cramped, one-bedroom house in central Sydney.

The outlook was bleak.

So, of course, I decided to leave my cushy contracting job at five months and start a business. Genius, right? With literally zero business experience, no savings and no clients, and at a time of the worst financial stress in my life, I embarked on my small business adventure. What fun! What an absolute dick I was.

I started out doing everything I could to make money: graphic design (using PowerPoint to design logos – oh the horror!), website building and writing.

After the first year I niched into copywriting, and then further into SEO. I earned around $60K in my first year *(not bad)*, rising to $200K by the end of year four – an amount I'd never dreamed possible when I first started out.

It sounds dreamy, but it's not a pretty story. It was an incredibly difficult time.

In year two we moved to the Central Coast of New South Wales, and a year later scraped together enough to put a deposit down on a house *(with a helping hand from my partner's mum – thanks Hiwee)*. In year five I found out I was heavily in debt to the tax office, which threw us into yet more panic. A few months later we found my husband has also stuffed up his tax. Muppets, the pair of us.

We lived an extremely spartan life for what felt like eons. But it caused me to take stock, and the following year I made a big decision. All that financial strife and struggling caused me to think about not exchanging my time for money, and this was the thought that caused things to really take off.

Those early parenting years were a massive financial struggle. Moving out of Sydney meant we could afford to buy a property. Childcare was also cheaper *(and more accessible)* and the cost of living was much lower. But we totally lost our community and had to start again.

Yes, we missed everything Sydney had to offer, but it really helped us get on a path to a better financial future. And who doesn't make sacrifices as a parent?

My early years' business lessons

I'll talk more about my lessons and tips in later chapters, but here are some big-picture learnings from my early years in business.

Hard work

To a degree, I learned that earning money is a lot about hard work. But I also learned that working for 'the man' is a slow route to financial success. Working for myself, I matched my employed salary within two to three years and have exceeded it ever since. More importantly, *I* control how much I earn instead of someone else.

Risk

Starting my own business didn't feel particularly exciting or brave. It was simply a necessity. Time with my son was my priority, and I knew I wouldn't find any job that would let me work the hours I wanted and earn the money I needed. So, yes, I took a big risk. But I didn't have much of a choice.

Debt

In the early years of my business I was careful not to run up any debt. I didn't have a credit card and I didn't get a bank loan. I didn't buy anything until I could afford it, which meant for the entire first year of my business I worked with a slow MacBook and a pen and paper. No software, subscriptions, courses or memberships. *(Memberships didn't exist back then.)* I think now you'd call that 'bootstrapping', which makes it sound virile and edgy. It wasn't edgy. It was just a bit shit. But debt was still scary to me.

Frugality

Following on from the debt thing, I will add that I was careful with the money I had. For me there were no conferences or personal development days, and no retreats or masterminds. Such things felt like luxury. Damn, buying a new pack of highlighter pens felt luxurious. I was frugal to the point of ridiculousness because of my childhood and all the debt I accumulated in my 20s.

And this fear of spending definitely held me back in my early years.

Financial literacy

My financial literacy was zero. Maths had been my poorest subject at school; I didn't think of myself as a 'numbers' person. In fact, I foolishly wore this as a badge of pride, revelling in the fact I was an artsy, creative type. Finances were dull. Sure, I got myself a finance subscription *(Xero)* in the first year, and my first hire was an accountant, but I never looked at my numbers. I never thought about budgets or cash flow.

All the money went into one shared family bank account. I spent what was there and had panic attacks every time a tax demand came around.

This was nearly my absolute undoing. As I mentioned, I ended up owing the tax office around $50K, and it took a good couple of frugal years to recover.

Where I'm at now

In the following chapters I pass on my advice for managing money, achieving a steady income and hitting your six-figure goals, understanding profit and finding some passive income ideas. But first, I want to reiterate why understanding your numbers is so important.

As I said, my own personal money feels made this section of the book a little hard to write. But I think it's essential, so here goes.

Working on my money mindset and financial literacy allowed me to completely turn my finances around. I am now:

- **paying myself a set salary:** My business is now a company and I pay myself a regular salary.
- **relatively debt-free:** I have no credit cards or personal loans, and the mortgage on my home is paid off.
- **paying superannuation (the Australian version of a pension fund):** After years of not paying myself superannuation (*as a sole trader in Australia, you're not required to pay superannuation, so I just didn't for a long time*), I now pay the maximum amount possible each year.
- **an investor:** Since paying off my mortgage, I've been able to buy not one but two investment properties – one personally and one in a family trust. Both are rented and are 'neutral' in terms of debt as the rent covers the mortgage. I also have a *(baby)* share portfolio.
- **financially literate:** With the help of an excellent bookkeeper and accountant, I fully understand my financial reports, ask astute and annoying questions and no longer feel overwhelmed by numbers.
- **planned and organised:** I budget, have a clear plan for future cash flow and can react to ups and downs in my finances in a sensible, non-panicky way.
- **insured:** After years of neglecting insurance, I now have the full suite of income protection, professional indemnity, home, car, medical, illness and death insurance.

- **future-focused:** I'm working with a financial planner to secure my future and no longer live in fear I'll end up dying alone in a cold flat and being eaten by cats. *(I don't even like cats much, so they would be the neighbours' cats, which is even more insulting.)*
- **creating generational wealth:** I'm hopeful I can give my son a good start in his adult life: help him buy a car, help him at college, help him with a home deposit, and so on. While I don't want to make his life ridiculously luxurious *(the bumps in my road were kind of the making of me)*, I'd like to give him financial support to make positive choices.

On top of all this, it's a huge priority for me to educate my son about money as best I can *(acknowledging my own financial biases)*. I've instilled an understanding of money from an early age. He's earned pocket money and had to save for big things. He understands loans and credit cards, property and shares. He knows how much we earn, our family budget and where all that money comes from. He has his own bank account and, as I'll cover in a later chapter, has a job with a regular income.

My son is considering studying economics and finance at uni. Hopefully he will become hugely rich and I can give up my business and he can look after me *(joke)*.

My goal is to let him know that working for a financially secure life is important but that nothing is 100% secure, and that hard work is often necessary but it's not worth sacrificing everything to buy 'the thing'. I want him to realise life won't be handed to him on a platter, but that money doesn't have to be a constant juggle either.

Have I gotten it right? Only time will tell. But just by being open and honest I think I've made a good start.

This is the first time I've ever really dug deep into my feelings about money and acknowledged how far I've come, and I feel a little bit proud. I've gone from huge debt, constant anxiety and utter cluelessness about money to feeling financially secure and relatively confident.

It took me a lot longer than it should.

And I want it to take you less time.

TL;DR

Your financial history can dictate your current attitudes and behaviours around money. But you can also change the story. By examining parental attitudes, your own mindset and your previous 'mistakes', you can learn, move forward and build a brighter financial future.

Benefits

Thinking about your money mindset will help you:

- break free of ideas that will hold you back when it comes to creating the financial future you want
- understand your triggers, thoughts and feelings better
- change your behaviour around money and create new habits
- stop avoiding money and genuinely take control of your finances.

Over to you

I'd like you to take a little bit of time to reflect on your money feelings. At this point it's not about goals, but rather what's holding you back or getting you stuck in similar patterns that stop you moving forward. Try answering the following questions so you can dig deeper into your money mindset:

1. How did your parents approach money? What memories do you have about your parents and money?

   Example: 'My parents never took us on holiday. It was a luxury we couldn't afford.'

2. How do you think your parents' attitudes have influenced you?

   Example: 'I've gone the other way and decided to live for the now. This has meant racking up a little credit card debt.'

3. List five significant money events in your life and the impact they've had.

Example: '*Leaving college with student debt meant I didn't enrol in a course I wanted to do and it changed / slowed down my entire career path.*'

4. What are you most frustrated by when it comes to money?

Example: '*The feeling of overwhelm whenever I look at my figures.*'

5. How does that affect you?

Example: '*I work too many hours and never say no because I'm worried it will affect my income.*'

6. Do you self-sabotage when it comes to money, and what impact does that have?

Example: '*I don't like to spend money as it feels like I'm taking away from my dwindling pot, and this has held me back from getting the right tools and people in my business.*'

7. What new belief would you like to form about money?

Example: '*That I control my money rather than it controlling me.*'

8. What steps do you need to take to make this belief a reality?

Example: '*I need to improve my financial literacy, look at my figures more and have a budget.*'

Chapter 12

Getting real about your numbers

'It's good to have money and the things that money can buy,
but it's good, too, to check up once in a while and make sure
that you haven't lost the things that money can't buy.'
George Horace Lorimer *

Even when we've managed to get real about our time, be more productive and overcome our financial mindset issues, it's amazingly easy to make no money at all.

Most often it's *not* because of what we charge but because we refuse to create a budget and stick to it. We also relentlessly overestimate how much money we have and dramatically undercharge for our products and services.

And even those who *do* manage to achieve some modicum of financial control in their business still struggle to implement the same strategies in their own homes. So, in this chapter I'm going to tell you how to fix all that.

Recognising the feast-and-famine cycle

Many small businesses and freelancers live in a permanent state of feast and famine. It's the cycle of having too much and then not enough, and never feeling confident you'll have enough orders or cash in the bank to pay the bills in the long run.

This is also known as the rollercoaster of freelance/business/ ecommerce life.

To some degree, it's important to understand that feast and famine are part and parcel of being a small business owner, especially in the early years. We can't crave being free of 'the man' and immediately expect a regular wage. Running a business is about taking risks – this is the very definition of being an 'entrepreneur'.

But there are ways to mitigate the risks.

Calculating what you need to live on

It's a delightful reverie to plan how you'll spend your small business fortune, to imagine opening the floodgates and watching the money pour into your bank account. But the hard *(and slightly uncomfortable)* truth is that we need to focus on what we *need* before we can focus on what we *want*.

So, let me ask you a few questions:

- How much precisely do you need to live each month?
- How much do you need to cover life's essentials?
- What do you consider an 'essential'?

If a figure doesn't immediately pop into your noggin, it's likely you need to do the hard work of calculating your family outgoings.

I must admit that, while I now budget hard as a businessperson, I still struggle with setting a budget at home. I recently applied for a mortgage and my broker compiled a list of my spending for the previous three months. I was embarrassed and somewhat appalled. The amount I spent on coffee each month was frankly obscene. It gave me pause *(but not too much pause because, you know... coffee)*.

Creating a family budget

There are oodles of tools out there to help you calculate your living expenses. Just google 'living expenses calculator' to find one. I know it might feel overwhelming, but it's a necessary evil and a total non-negotiable if you want to turn this finance frown upside down.

My fave way to start is to look through the past three months of bank statements and highlight all the items you consider 'essentials', what you consider 'luxuries' and what is going towards your security and future. You can go more granular than this, but for me having three simple pots works well.

So first, highlight your essentials. For me these are:

- rent/home loan
- utilities
- food
- rates
- water
- school costs
- insurance.

Then, add all these up. The total figure is your essential baseline – how much you need to survive. I recommend adding 10% for wiggle room.

So, obviously, as a salaried human you'd:

1. confirm your salary
2. deduct the superannuation
3. deduct the tax.

This gives you your take-home salary.

Now deduct your essential baseline figure, and what you have left is for life's little pleasures. I like to budget for pleasure too. You could call them 'luxuries', but for me they're hardly Kim Kardashian–level items, so I'll call them 'nice-to-haves'.

> **TOON TIP** I find a monthly budget works best for essentials. We have set up monthly direct debits to pay most of our bills, and we made mortgage payments every fortnight to reduce interest payments ever so slightly.

Nice-to-haves

Okay here's my list of nice-to-haves, but remember that this list is yours, not mine, so add what you think works for your family:

- car
- Netflix

- after-school activities
- clothes
- beauty stuff
- cleaner
- holidays and outings.

Some of you may gasp in horror that I've included my child's after-school activities as a nice-to-have, but I feel that kids don't need weekly karate and flute lessons to be happy. I did zero activities as a child and still ended up a relatively normal human.

I also know some of you will also consider my first item, a car, an absolute necessity. It wasn't for me. *(I didn't learn to drive until I was 46, and our family didn't have a car until I was 47.)* But everyone's different.

Once you have your nice-to-have figure, you'll know how much you need to make your life both liveable and pleasurable.

And then it's onto security and the future.

Security and the future

While it's great to live in the moment, we must also plan for the future. And for me, the first steps here are to:

1. pay down any debt and get rid of credit cards
2. create a savings buffer
3. save and invest for the future.

In Australia, we self-employed people are encouraged to pay ourselves superannuation each year, but we're not actually required to, which is kind of daft. *(The amount we 'should' pay varies, so check with your accountant.)* I didn't save my super for many years, and I regret it now. I have a lot of catching up to do.

So, now you need to consider what you pay towards:

- superannuation
- debt repayment
- savings
- investments.

This is your 'security' budget. How much you put aside will completely depend on your income and other pressures, but even a small percentage will build up over time.

Now that you know these three figures, you know how much you need to earn. You'll want to start by covering essentials, then ideally ramping up to cover your security. After that comes luxuries *(although for me it was luxuries and then securities because I am a human).*

Creating a business budget

Obviously, business budgets can vary drastically depending on the business, but the process of creating one is the same: essentials, luxuries, security. Your essentials may look a lot different to mine when I started as a copywriter. I quite literally only needed a computer and an internet connection. You may need a lot more. You'll have to think really hard about what are essential costs and what are luxuries.

The essentials should be a pretty short list when you're starting out. And I would say the following are luxuries in a small business:

- office space
- courses
- retreats
- stationery
- memberships
- subscriptions
- fancy outfits.

I am still to this day reluctant to invest in any of these, partially due to my money hang-ups and partially because, when it comes to courses and memberships, I often can't see the value. I'm an insufferable know-it-all.

Security from a business perspective is about having a buffer – ideally three to six months of money to cover everything, and after that possibly some investments. It took me eight long years to get to the point when I could think about this.

It's important to get really clear on how much 'essential' money your business needs to make each month just to keep going. The problem is that many businesses never make much more than this, and the business owner never gets to pay themselves a salary. And paying myself a salary was a really big business step for me.

Financial milestones in your business

I believe the basic milestones for a small business are to:

- be clear on how much money you earn each month
- be clear on all your expenses *(essentials and luxuries)*
- pay yourself a regular salary
- pay yourself superannuation
- be able to project incomings and outgoings at least three months ahead.

Obviously, there are bigger goals as well, such as:

- employing a team of humans to help you
- investing in personal development
- building a financial buffer
- being able to financially plan a year or two ahead
- having spare business money to make investments.

It took me a few years to reach the basic milestones, and it may take you just as long. But there's no shame in that. Remember: patience is key when you're a business-owning parent.

Improving your financial literacy

As I mentioned earlier, financial literacy has been a problem for me. I wore my 'I'm not a numbers person' badge with foolish pride.

Yes, I've had financial software from the get-go. But for a long time I couldn't work out what any of the reports meant. Profit and loss? No idea. Net profit? Eh? It was all gobbledegook to me.

So, I never looked at my reports, didn't track expenses, didn't budget and didn't plan. And that got me into a lot of trouble:

- I went over the GST threshold – clueless *(according to the Australian Taxation Office website, the GST threshold is $75K, but check with your accountant)*, and then I had to pay back money I hadn't even charged
- I earned way more than I expected in one year and didn't save any of it for tax – panic

- I received a big payment from a client – spent it all
- I received a big bill – struggled to pay it.

And tax time became a hideous Russian roulette game of *Will I be hugely over?* or *Will I get a payout?* I wandered through the tax year blind and usually ended up in an absolute mess, scraping cash together just before the deadline or going on yet another 'payment schedule'.

Of course, my accountant back then could have done a better job of keeping me updated. But the onus was really on me.

TOON TIP Even when you outsource things in your small business, they're still *your* responsibility. Don't outsource and forget.

Over the past few years I've worked hard to learn how to:

- read my financial reports
- question anything I don't understand *(my bookkeeper is extremely patient)*
- check my finances regularly *(it's now the first thing I do each day)*
- follow up on outstanding payments quickly
- plan a budget based on previous years
- monitor my expenses and look for better deals.

How did I do this? I've invested in a great bookkeeper *(thanks Donna Sullivan)* and a great accountant *(thanks Bruce Whiting)*. I also watched a lot of YouTube videos and spent hours just fiddling around with my figures.

TOON TIP Just this morning *(at the time of writing)* I reviewed all my subscriptions and moved a few to annual payments, saving myself $800 in about two minutes.

Not one pot

My biggest recommendation for getting real on your numbers is to make sure your money doesn't all go into the same pot as your family money. And if you have a partner, make sure it doesn't go into your shared account.

If you don't separate the two, you'll never really be clear on what money belongs to you and what belongs to the business. And that's a huge problem.

I spent years working incredibly hard but not really seeing where my money was going. And when I hit six figures, I didn't feel any richer at all.

Using Parkinson's law again, our lifestyle expectations tend to fit, and then expand beyond, our income. I spent whatever I had without thinking about it.

These days, I recommend everyone create a separate account for their business money. In fact, it makes good business sense to set up five or six business accounts.

My potted Profit First summary

Profit First, the book by Mike Michalowicz, is a methodology much like the envelope system *(where you stuff money in different envelopes for different purposes)*. The idea has been around for yonks but gained popularity through Mike's book. It requires you to separate your money into different accounts and pay yourself a 'profit' first.

The idea is that thinking of your business in terms of 'profit first' enables you to manage cash better, relieve financial stress and have a more resilient business.

This book has been hugely influential in my business, and I credit it for my ability to pay off all my debts and get myself to the financial position I'm in today. So, thank you, Mike. *(Also a big thanks to Laura Elkaslassy, a* Profit First *pioneer who helped me get started.)*

Dale Beaumont from Business Blueprint, dad of two boys (15 and 12), agrees with me:

> 'One of the biggest things I recommend is to implement Profit First. You just never know what is around the corner, when there's the next, you know, GFC or pandemic or some technology. You might think, oh, won't happen to me, but you get totally wiped out. And all of that hard work just goes up in smoke. So, take 10% minimum off the table every single year and put it into other income-producing assets.'

For me, the key to having a financially healthy business hasn't just been about spending less than I make. It's been about spending money wisely and finding enjoyment in saving it, rather than wasting it on non-essentials.

Here's how to implement Profit First *(the quick version)*:

1. **Work out your percentages.** These will vary depending on the stage and structure of your business. Generally for up to around $250K you're probably going to go with the figures in table 12.1 *(although you can buy the book to get more detail)*:

Table 12.1: Profit First percentages for a sub-$250K business

Profit	5%
Your pay	50%
Tax	15%
Operating expenses	30%

Now I'll be honest: I think that 30% operating expenses is too high. I'd aim for 25%. I also started out with 1% profit while I got used to things. I would say, though, that you should stick to the figures above for the first six months and, after that, fiddle with them based on your business.

2. **Set up multiple bank accounts for:**
    - incoming account *(where all the money is paid into)*
    - profit
    - owner's salary and superannuation
    - tax *(and GST)*
    - expenses.

    TOON TIP If you have staff or subcontractors, you might want to split expenses into two pots: one for salaries and one for other expenses.

    If you have a company structure, you'll need to have a separate account for each company for tax purposes. Shop around for banks that don't charge a whole heap of fees to have multiple accounts.

HUGE disclaimer: Speak to your accountant before you do anything dramatic.

3. **Pick a payment duration and stick to it.** I started doing my Profit First transfers after each invoice was paid. Then I moved to daily, then weekly, and now I do it once a month. Yes, this means I'm paying myself a profit on a monthly basis. Of course, if there's nothing in there then I can't divvy anything up.

4. **Always pay the money into the separate accounts in the order I mentioned earlier.** It took me three months to implement the process properly and nearly six months to really get into the flow of it. At first, I found myself paying money into 'profit' and immediately having to transfer it to 'expenses' as I didn't have enough money to keep going. If this had continued to be a problem then I'd have clearly needed to cut costs.

> **TOON TIP** I highly recommend putting your profit into an account that's difficult to access so it's harder to borrow from.

Build reserves

Once you have the Profit First process working, you'll begin to see the money in your profit account increase. It's a glorious feeling. Over the years, taking a look at my growing profit account has helped me get through many a dark day.

It's also gives you an amazing superpower – the power of FU (*fuck you*)!

FU money is money that lets you say no to dodgy clients, not scramble to take every job and not live in a permanent state of financial panic. It's a buffer, and buffers bring a sense of calm.

Ideally, you want to keep building up your profit account until it covers at least three to six months' worth of business operating expenses. *(More on this in the next chapter.)* It acts as a pool of money for real emergencies when you need cash fast.

After that, I used mine to pay off credit cards and pay down my home loan. Then, I reformed my business as a company, and I now keep my profit in the company and use it for investments.

Manage your cash flow

An important part of getting real about your numbers is to stop living hand-to-mouth and pretending it's okay to live waiting with bated breath for your next invoice to be paid. While it's certainly part of the start-up phase of a business for most people, it shouldn't be an ongoing thing. Believe me, it's no way to live.

You need to start thinking about forecasting and budgeting. This can be as simple as mapping out what you earned in a previous year and planning to hit the same goals the following year plus, say, 5%.

You can keep the monthly income amounts regular or move them up and down to reflect the peaks and troughs in your business. And, of course, you should track your expenses alongside them.

You also need to think about cash flow – the amount of cash and cash equivalents (assets you can readily turn into cash) moving in and out of your business. Many business owners make the *mistake* of thinking this is the same as revenue minus expenses, but your business could have a turnover of millions but no cash available. *(We'll talk more about revenue and profit in Chapter 13.)*

Getting over yourself

Another big part of getting real with your numbers is getting over the daft stories you tell yourself. Yes, you can do the mindset work outlined in Chapter 11. But you also need to look at your day-to-day behaviour.

See if any of these phrases resonate:

'If I buy that tool, I'll be able to do this more efficiently.'

'When I win this next job, everything will be fine.'

'I'll have another sale to bring in some cash.'

'I really need to go to this conference to make it big.'

'I must rent an office space to look more professional.'

'If I do this course, I'll become a better...'

'I've hired a virtual assistant, but I'm not sure what they'll do yet.'

'It's normal not to pay yourself a salary.'

'I'm hoping for a big tax payout.'

All these statements speak to hope and whimsy when it comes to money, rather than to confidence, surety and planning.

Rather than pinning your hopes on an app, a mantra or a course, I want you to take control of your finances. At first it will feel like wrestling a recalcitrant, slippery eel, but after a while it will calm down and you'll see the smooth, calm waters of financial certainty.

TL;DR

As a small business owner and parent, you must face up to your money fears rather than hiding in the financial hole you've dug for yourself. This means understanding the stories you tell yourself and your financial habits, and planning for a better future.

Benefits

Thinking about the realities of money in your business will help you:

- conquer feast and famine
- stop thinking you have more money than you actually do
- stop overspending and making rash impulse purchases
- pay yourself a regular, reliable salary
- pay yourself superannuation
- become more patient by understanding you can have it all – just maybe not this week.

Over to you

Now it's time to do the work:

1. **Create a family budget:** List out your expenses and nice-to-haves, and map out what you'd like to put towards paying off debt and building savings.

2. **Create a business budget and map out expenses:** Again, list out what you spend each month, and perhaps make this an opportunity to set a limit on personal development costs. Also, review your subscriptions.

3. **Create a list of 'Aha!' moments:** What surprised you about where your money goes? Are there any easy budget cuts you can make immediately?

4. **Look at my list of 'getting over yourself' statements:** Which ones ring true? Or do you have one I missed? Write it on a Post-it Note and stick it somewhere noticeable. Note how many times you say it to yourself. What would your counterargument be?

   Example: 'If I buy this course, I'll finally be able to...'
   Counterargument: 'I should use what I already know to sell my products and services, and invest in that rather than doing another course. I need to believe in myself more and stop buying courses to make myself feel better.'

Chapter 13

The P word

'Profit is like oxygen, food, water, and blood for the body; they are not the point of life, but without them, there is no life.'

James C. Collins

You'll notice this book has 'six figures' in its title. That felt a little uncomfy for me.

I've never been one to bang the 'six figures' drum other entrepreneurial types like to bang on about. As you know from when I talked about my why *(in Chapter 3)*, I didn't start with a financial goal. And when I shifted to a finance focus, it didn't really live up to my expectations.

Also, when I mumbled about the title in my membership group, many said, 'Six figures? Pfft! I'm aiming for seven, or even eight'.

But I put a lot of thought into the title.

Why I put 'six figures' in the title of this book

I decided to run with it for two core reasons.

1. 'Six figures' means different things to different people

Many business coaches crap on about earning six figures but without any context or clarity because, obviously, six figures could be anything from $100,000 to $999,999.

More importantly, the distinction is rarely made between *revenue* and *profit*.

I know business owners who pull in six figures and don't pay themselves a cent. I know others who call themselves million-dollar business types but earned that figure over five years, and others who post about $100K launches but quietly spent $70K on Facebook ads.

It's not just smoke and mirrors. It's a lot of puff and piddle.

Six figures could mean your revenue, your take-home pay or your profit.

You may want to earn a lot more than six figures. But, obviously, to earn seven figures you need to earn six figures first, right?

2. I don't think a million dollars a year in revenue is achievable for most humans

There, I said it.

I know many business coaches *(and authors)* want you to believe earning $1 million a year is achievable. It's how they convince you to buy their expensive course or mentoring program *(which is how they made $1 million)*. But I believe most million-dollar business owners don't tell you the truth behind the figures.

They don't talk about:

· the privilege of having rich parents or a wealthy partner
· the compromises they made to achieve that goal
· the fact they're often burned out and miserable.

I personally know oodles of entrepreneur types, both male and female, who've hit the million-dollar mark *(if not more)* but are deeply unhappy and full of regrets, and who barely see their kids. They just hide it well in their pretty Instagram feeds.

And the point of this book is **balance**.

Not whipping yourself forward to achieve a goal so you can impress others. Not sacrificing your family life to earn more money to buy things you don't really need.

But of course, you picked up this book to find out how you could legitimately earn six figures in school hours, so let me break that down.

It starts with profit

In the previous chapter I talked about financial literacy. And, from my experience, one of the least understood aspects of business money is profit.

I know that, for many of you, talking about money in practical terms makes you squirm in your seat. Maybe learning about money makes your brain hurt. But please think of this as an important step up the financial literacy ladder.

Feeling comfortable with your numbers is a vital part of having a balanced business and family life. So, grab a crumpet and strap yourself in for a bit of solid money talk.

Ready? Let's go.

What is revenue?

Revenue is the money that comes into your business. It's what you charge for your products and services.

What is gross profit?

Gross profit is the money your business makes after you subtract all the costs from your revenue. These are the costs involved in manufacturing or selling your products and services, known in financial lingo as the 'cost of goods sold' (COGS):

Revenue – COGS = gross profit

COGS could include things like:

- materials
- labour costs directly involved in making the product or service
- credit card and transaction fees
- shipping
- equipment.

As you can see, all these costs can go up and down depending on your output; for example, if you sell more products, you pay more PayPal fees.

Generally, COGS doesn't include fixed costs – things you must pay for regardless of your level of output. My bookkeeper Donna told me this simple way to think about COGS: 'If you didn't make the sale, would you still be spending the money?' For example, I need to pay my electricity bill regardless of whether or not I sell the thing, but I only pay for shipping if I sell it.

Fixed costs can include:

- advertising
- insurance
- rent
- utilities
- subscriptions
- office supplies.

It also covers salaries for employees not directly involved in making the product or services you offer.

Knowing your gross profit helps you understand how well your business is managing production, staff costs and buying raw materials.

What is net profit?

Net profit – sometimes known as net income – is the amount of money your business earns after deducting *all* expenses. That includes all COGS, fixed costs, interest, salaries, taxes – the whole kit and kaboodle:

Revenue – (COGS + operating expenses) = net profit

Net profit helps you see the true financial health of your business and whether you're making more than you spend. You'll see two net profits on financial reports:

1. net profit before tax
2. net profit after tax.

TOON TIP Merchant fees (for example, PayPal and Stripe fees) are a funny one. I asked my members how they recorded theirs, and about half of them record it as COGS and the rest as operating expenses. I recommend checking with your accountant.

Absorption costing

Profit is fiddly because we also have to consider absorption costing, which is where a little blob of the fixed costs is assigned to each unit of production. *(Stick with me.)*

Let's say I make 30 jumpers a month and rent a studio for $500 a month to do all my knitting. Under absorption costing, I'd attribute a cost of $16.66 to each jumper to cover that rent.

Absorption costing is incredibly fiddly in my mind. So, I don't do it. For example, my email platform (*ActiveCampaign, a content relationship marketing and email tool*) would be a considered a fixed cost because, whether I sell one course or 100, I still need to pay for the platform. But how much I pay is based on the number of email subscribers I have, and the number of email subscribers I have influences how many courses I can sell. Confusing, right?

To make my life easier, I don't drill down to this level of absorption costing. I just lump all my software subscriptions under COGS assuming that, if I didn't sell such things, I wouldn't have them.

Profit and profitability

It's also important to know the difference between profit and profitability:

- **Profit is an absolute number.** It's a dollar amount (for example, a $5 profit on an item sold).
- **Profitability is a percentage.** It's the ratio between profit and revenue.

Profitability is also called 'profit margin', and I find this term easier to 'get', so we'll use that throughout this section.

Profit margin helps you compare your business to industry averages, competitors or your previous year's performances. It can also reveal positives or negatives in your business. An example is shown in table 13.1 with fictional piglet jumper manufacturing company Woolie Piggies.

Table 13.1: The profitability of piglet jumpers versus piglet pyjamas

	Piglet jumpers	Piglet pyjamas
Sale price	$100	$200
COGS	$50	$150
Gross profit	$50	$50
Gross profit margin	50%	25%

In this example, while each item brings home $50, jumpers are clearly more profitable. Why? Because the profit margin is higher. Knowing this may make the manager of Woolie Piggies think about dumping their pyjama line. *(But, of course, it's not always that simple. Piglet pyjamas might be a growing sector, or a luxury item, or something the business hasn't promoted enough yet.)*

Kate, this is giving me a nosebleed. Help!

I get it. Wrapping your head around these financial terms and what they mean took me yonks. But don't fret if it's a bit of a struggle. Let's use my fictional piglet apparel company to show how these figures actually work.

Last year Woolie Piggies made $600K from selling piglet outfits, and the COGS of producing those outfits was $200K.

All other costs – admin, sales, interest, taxes and salaries – came to $300K (see table 13.2).

Table 13.2: Piglet apparel company figures

Revenue	$600K
COGS	$200K
Gross profit	$400K ($600K revenue – $200K COGS)
Gross profit margin	66.7% ($400K gross profit ÷ $600K revenue)
Other income (grants and interest)	$0
Operating expenses	$300K
Net profit	$100K ($400K gross profit – $300K operating expenses)
Net profit margin	16.7% ($100K net profit – $600K revenue)

So, their gross profit margin was 66.7% and their net profit margin was 16.7%, which ain't bad at all.

Now let's look at an average month for me. (I've chosen November 2022; see table 13.3 overleaf.)

Table 13.3: My November 2022 figures

Revenue	$70,968.62
COGS	$2,843.96
Gross profit	$68,124.66
Gross profit margin	96%
Other income (grants and interest)	$227.54
Operating expenses	$54,499.75
Net profit	$13,852.45
Net profit margin	19.5%

So, my gross profit margin was 96% and my net profit margin was 19.5%, which means I'm doing better than Woolie Piggies (*most likely due to the fact that my business is largely virtual – no wool, no storage and no shipping to pay*).

Now, when you look at table 13.3 you might think $14K-ish net profit a month doesn't look like much, especially given all the work I do. But for September I recorded $51K net profit, October was $12K and December was $40K.

Profit is variable. Some months you win, some months you win a little less. But the idea is not to lose, and to try and keep your profit margin juicy.

TOON TIP It's best to view figures over each quarter, six months or year. That way, you won't panic after a bad month or celebrate too much after a good one.

What is a good profit margin for a small business?

Of course, what defines a 'good' amount of annual net profit will depend on the type of business you have. However, according to the Corporate Finance Institute the following profit margins are standard:

- **Low:** 5%
- **Average:** 10%
- **Good:** 20%[12]

Why I love bottoms

For me, the easiest figures to focus on are the bottom line and the profit margin. *(It's called the bottom line because it often contains two peachy zeros: 00. Nah, seriously, it's because it's usually the final or bottom figure on an income statement.)*

The bottom line tells me what money is mine at the end of the day.

Whether it's just me and the dog, or me and the dog and a raft of other humans, the figure I care about is how much money I can stuff into my sock drawer at the end of each month. And this makes it fiddlier, because I'm now an employee of my own company, and that means my salary is an expense, so it gets lumped into operating expenses. But to my mind it's also my sock-drawer money.

In the November 2022 example, when my business made about $14K profit, there were two payroll runs. Right now I'm paying myself around $10K a month before tax. And then there are dividends *(lumps of cash I take out of the business)* to consider. So, while $14K doesn't look that profitable, I took a fair blob of money home with me.

It took me a long time to accept that it's not just the money I take from the business that's mine. The money left in the business is also mine because it's my business and I'm the only shareholder. I don't need to take it all out and stuff it under the sofa cushions for it to be mine.

What does 'six figures' actually mean, then?

To some degree, what you define as 'six figures' is up to you.

For me it started as earning $100K revenue per year, which, using the Profit First figures I mentioned earlier, would have meant around $50K take-home pay (50% owners pay).

Then it became the dream of an after-tax salary of $100K. I needed to hit a revenue of way over $200K to achieve that.

When I moved to a company setup, selling digital products and courses (with relatively low operating expenses), I dreamed of $100K clear net profit. I managed to dial that figure up to around $200K net profit (plus my salary) after a year or so.

These days my annual revenue hovers just above or below the magic $1 million per year mark, and my profit hovers around $400K plus my salary.

But if I had my time again, I possibly wouldn't push it so high. On reflection, some of the compromises I made – especially the time not spent with my son – weren't worth it. I'll cover that more in later chapters.

Why not make more?

I could go further. I could push on and on from a seven-figure revenue to an eight-figure revenue. But I'm not willing to make the compromises it would take. In fact, next year I plan to dial down my income and, by doing so, free up my time.

Perhaps you are willing to make the compromises, at least for a little while. That's a decision you'll have to make.

If your starting goal is to earn $100K, like mine was, great. If your next goal is to hit $100K in your pocket after tax, great. And if you want to push on to more after that, that's your call.

This book isn't about a magic path to success; it's about choices. It's about understanding the exchange: what do you need to give up to get what you want? And is it worth it? It's about the level of profitability that makes you happy, gives you a comfy lifestyle and doesn't require you to sellotape an iPad into your kid's hands to achieve it.

TL;DR

Your business must be run at a profit or it won't last. But if you run your business just for profit, it will also fail, because it no longer has a reason to exist. *(This is a paraphrase of a Henry Ford quote.)*

Benefits

By understanding profit and profitability, you can set yourself more realistic goals for your business. Rather than just relentlessly pursuing more revenue, you can:

- decide on a business profitability goal
- review which products and services are most profitable
- review your expenses with a view to reducing them and improving profitability
- set financial goals for your business
- understand the exchange: what will you need to give up or do to reach your financial goals?

Over to you

Now it's time for you to do the work:

1. What is your revenue?
2. What is your COGS figure?
3. What is your gross profit?
4. What is your net profit?
5. Can you see which product or service makes the most profit, and which has the highest profit margin?
6. What is your first six-figure goal? *(Don't worry if you don't have one.)*

Chapter 14

Simple business money wins

'Do not save what is left after spending,
but spend what is left after saving.'
Warren Buffett

I spent a heap of time in Part II looking at ways to squeeze more out of the time we have. Which begs the question: can we do the same with our money?

Most people believe that, in business, we have to have that one big idea. The life changer. The amazing, innovative product. The killer launch. The smash hit. That one thing that finally tips the balance in our favour, opens the floodgates and lets the cash flow in.

I disagree. For me, it wasn't one big idea that helped me reach six figures *(and beyond)* but rather lots of small ideas – lots of little wins that added up over time. It was about fixing small failures and recognising opportunities for improvement. It's amazing how much money we can make while waiting for our big idea to strike. It's equally impressive how tiny, piddly-seeming ideas that seem insignificant at the time can grow into giant money trees.

In my business, I've learned to mop up the money crumbs rather than seek out some ultimate financial mega loaf. Or, as the old English proverb goes, 'Take care of the pennies and the pounds will take care of themselves'.

Yes, it may sound dull and not very entrepreneurial, but for me this approach has absolutely worked.

How to make more money in your business

Here are a few tactics I use in my daily business life to make more money *(or at least spend less of it)*.

1. Charge more

Charge more and you'll make more money. Yes, I know this sounds bloody obvious, but it's amazing how hard some business owners find it to increase their rates.

And often those rates are based on little more than a quick skim of their competitors' pricing. They set their prices without a thought as to whether those prices will support their cost of living or give them a decent profit margin.

We've already been through the nitty gritty of your numbers in Chapter 12 and your profit in Chapter 13, so I'll keep this short. I recommend upping your prices with inflation every year, but you should also consider a larger increase as your experience and abilities improve. Most clients and customers will wear a 10% increase without really noticing. It gets trickier at 20%, so I prefer a strategy of incremental increases rather than a giant leap.

2. Specialise

We're all happy to spend more on a specialist than a generalist. I'll wait three months and pay a premium to have a consultation with a renowned neurosurgeon. But I'm frustrated when I have to wait ten minutes to see my low-cost GP.

Specialising helps you:

- upskill on your area of expertise
- build a reputation in the market for what you do
- streamline your marketing so you can focus on your core customers
- clean up pricing and processes as you do the same work or make the same products again and again.

While it may feel scary to say, 'We only work with these people', keep in mind that you don't have to do that. Instead, you can reframe it as, 'We work with X, Y and Z but specialise in helping people do Y'. This lets you stay broad enough to take on customers as you need them but specialist enough to charge a premium for your best services or products.

3. Create recurring income

Nearly every business owner I speak to says their first goal is to replace the income they had in their old job. And I get this. While we love the freedom and autonomy of working for ourselves, we miss the regular salary.

A steady, regular income can help us feel safe and secure. It creates predictability, reassuring us that we've got our rent or mortgage payments and the essentials covered.

Here are a few forms of recurring income that have worked for both my members and me:

· **Retainers:** Retainers allow you to agree on a set price for a set amount of hours/product and bill at the start of each month. You might want to throw in a little sweetener, such as a 10% discount to thank the customer, and they should also get the benefit of being a VIP and being serviced before everyone else. These regular retainer amounts can help you plan and feel secure. They also give you the headspace to go after other opportunities because you know your day-to-day essential costs are covered – everything else is the fluffy icing on your business cake. It's hard to sell a retainer to a client from the get-go; you're more likely to win them over after the first project by suggesting you can keep helping at a VIP level for a set fee.

· **Maintenance plans:** Maintenance plans are similar to retainers and work for all kinds of service-based businesses, from developers to accountants. Rather than agreeing to work a set number of hours, you agree to complete a set number of tasks. This lets you charge a monthly fee for an agreed level of service or break down an annual fee into smaller chunks. For example, you may only use your accountant at tax time and get one monster bill at the end of the year, which is hard to budget for. Alternatively, you could ask if you can pay your accountant a little each month so you can budget it all out more effectively.

- **Memberships and subscriptions:** For service-based businesses, this can be a great way to support your clients in a more cost-effective way. Chances are you're giving similar *(if not the same)* advice to all your clients, so setting up some kind of membership or group for a monthly fee is a great way to turn that expensive one-to-one service into a more accessible one-to-many service. For ecommerce businesses, subscription boxes work really well to generate regular income. Subscriptions feel like an easier sell if you're offering something functional, like loo rolls, but they can also work for luxury items. People love receiving nice things in the mail, and the idea of getting an early-release item or carefully curated subscription box without having to think about it is super appealing to many.

- **Easy add-ons:** Selling advertising space on your website or building a simple directory for business owners *(and charging for listings)* can be a great way to add a little extra recurring revenue. It's also a great way to build loyalty and retention with your existing customers.

4. Create contras

Contras are exchanges of work – you do a set amount of work for someone and they do a set amount for you in return. While this may not seem like a revenue-generating idea, contras reduce the amount of marketing needed to win customers. They let you 'pay' for services without increasing your expenses budget.

Working with other like-minded business owners expands your customer circle and comes with built-in trust.

> **TOON TIP** Make sure to treat contras like real jobs. Be very clear about what you're offering and the price so you can manage expectations. I've had one or two contras go sour because one party felt hard done by and as if they had done more work.

5. Offer referrals

While back-scratching is nice, filling your bank account is better. So, ask yourself the question: how often do you find yourself recommending businesses?

It's great to make referrals out of the goodness of your heart and lovely if the other business reciprocates. But referrals are often a one-way street. I sent out hundreds of referrals but rarely got any back. And while the gifts of wine and biscuits were nice, it started to feel like a poor exchange.

My advice is to stop being squeamish about asking for a referral fee. It makes everything financially equal and more businesslike and stops things getting icky.

A standard referral rate among copywriters, for example, is 10%, which is a small price to pay for the copywriter who wins the job. They didn't need to do any marketing or build any trust; they just showed up and won the job based on someone's recommendation. The recommender also saved the client having to go back to the horror of Google and start searching all over again.

So, think about a village of useful suppliers you could build around your business – designers, accountants, printers, other businesses you love that complement your brand – and see if they're interested in a referral arrangement.

In my first year of business, when I had a brand-new baby, I only had a few hours to work but I got a lot of enquiries *(because I am an SEO goddess)*. Rather than turn these clients away, I decided to pass them on to other businesses I trusted. I asked for a 10% referral fee, which everyone was happy to pay. In that year, I earned nearly $18K in referral fees, which was around 30% of my income.

Referrals continued to be a part of my business model for years until I started my memberships. Now my members get all my referrals for free – an added incentive to join.

TOON TIP When working with other businesses in a contra, partnership or referral arrangement, put together a contract where you both agree on the parameters. It will help should things go awry. I have subcontracting, retainer and referral agreement templates on The Clever Copywriting School website.

6. Become an affiliate

Most of the software you use each day comes with an affiliate program and, while the payouts might not be mind-blowing, they all add up. Generally, you'll find a link to the affiliate program in the footer of the website.

Whenever you recommend a tool to someone else, you share your affiliate link. Using it doesn't cost them anything, but you get a small payment if they use your link to buy the product or service.

I make a small percentage of my income from affiliate links. But I only recommend software and companies I personally believe are great. There's no point eroding trust in my brand just to earn a few extra bucks.

TOON TIP If you're going to use affiliate links, it's always best to disclose them. Make it clear that the link is an affiliate link and you'll earn a small amount if they use it. Some people get a little funny about them, thinking you're only recommending the product or service to make a buck.

7. Reduce spending

Again, reducing spending sounds an obvious tactic, but it's a tactic lots of business types seem to avoid. You may spend hours poring through the Aldi catalogue looking for a great deal on ski suits but happily splurt money on things that don't really help your business.

I regularly look at my expenses to see what I can cut or reduce. Just yesterday *(at the time of writing)* I moved my podcast transcribing from Rev, at around $60 a transcript, to Otter.ai for around $100 a year. Sure, the quality isn't quite as high, but it's good enough for what I need.

Anu Sawhney from Bidiliia, mum of Eirya (9) and Daksh (2), said:

'I have a really clear divide between my needs and my wants, the essentials and the desirables. For example, I didn't have a PO box for the first year. I wait until I've crossed a monetary milestone, and then I can get what I want.'

And here's what Janine Leghissa from Desiderate and Taleeta, mum of Aaron (28), Charlotte (27) and Zeke (18), had to say:

'Before I invest in something new, I ask myself: Will it save me time in manual hours? Will it add professionalism to my brand? Will it add to the customer experience? Will it make more money than it cost, even if not immediately?'

8. Look for discounts

If you're currently paying for subscription services monthly, see if you can move to annual payments. They often offer hefty discounts *(up to 30%)*. Also *(and rather sadly)*, if you go ahead and cancel the company will often offer you incentives to come back.

9. Offer training and consultations

Yes, training and consultations still involve trading time for money. But we're talking substantially more money. I advise my members to charge three times their 'doing' rate to provide training.

Obviously, I had to build up trust and authority with my clients first. But after that, they were willing to pay a premium to be shown how to do something rather than have me do it for them – the argument being it would work out cheaper for them in the long term.

I started out with one-hour sessions, then expanded them to run over a few days. These days it's popular to offer VIP days, or 'Done with you' sessions, where you literally just have Zoom open with your client as you work through their problems.

Right now you might be fretting that training others to do the thing might mean they no longer want you to do the thing for them. I get it. But I've found that, even when I *do* train a client, they often don't have the time to do the do themselves long term and come nuzzling back to me.

From one-on-one training I moved into workshops and training events for groups, which was lucrative but stressful.

TOON TIP Be aware of how exhausting training is. Yes, you can charge three or more times your standard 'doing' rate. But you'll likely need a few hours to recover from each training session. I need an entire day off after doing in-house training and need to factor that into my costs.

Understanding passive income

As Warren Buffett said, 'If you don't find a way to make money while you sleep, you will work until you die'. Passive income is defined as income that requires minimal effort to obtain, such as income from a rental property, shares or any other activity in which a person isn't actively involved.

To be honest, I'm not a huge fan of the term 'passive income', as most of my methods are not entirely passive. But they are certainly easier than exchanging my time for money.

Also, I've only recently had the means to dabble in property and shares, but I reached my six figures without doing either. So, I'm not going to talk about investments but rather how I focused on selling my mind rather than selling my time.

To make this shift, I employed two core strategies.

1. Productising and packaging my services

Instead of quoting for every job and writing endless proposals, I retrofitted my services into a set range of prices. I did this by:

· looking for commonalities in the work
· tracking the time I took to complete that work
· finding low-cost value-adds to include
· working out pricing ranges for my projects (for example, knowing a five-page website would cost between X and Y).

I could then publish set productised pricing on my website, which in turn managed potential client expectations and reduced the number of 'tyre kickers' *(those who walk around your metaphorical car, kicking the tyres, asking lots of questions but never buying)*. It also allowed me to sell 'off my site' with minimal to-ing and fro-ing, which saved me time and therefore money.

2. Moving from a one-to-one model to a one-to-many model

I looked for anything in my business I could move from servicing one person at a time to servicing many. Obviously, if I was selling to many

I didn't charge as much as I did for one-on one. This reduced the entry point for my services substantially and, therefore, made my audience broader. *(Not everyone could afford to pay $3K for me to write their website, but they could very likely afford to pay $30 for my website copywriting template.)* It's more of a 'price 'em low, stack 'em high' model.

This one-to-many model translated into templates, courses, memberships and events.

*

For me, moving to so-called 'passive income' increased my earnings substantially. But it wasn't without its challenges and sacrifices. To pursue my dream of being woken from slumber by the 'PayPal ping' I had to:

- face a 50% income reduction income for a year because I didn't have time to do as much client work
- work long hours *(and sacrifice a lot of time with my son)* to get it all set up
- reach near-burnout (see Chapter 20).

This was partly due to my lack of patience. *(I wanted to get everything done as quickly as possible.)* But it's also just part of the process.

The biggest problem with passive income is the lack of understanding about how long it takes to create the income sources. So, here are a couple of examples of how much 'active' time it takes to creative passive income:

- Creating a template for my online shop can take up to eight hours of writing, proofing, editing and designing.
- Making one module's worth of content for my SEO course takes around 30 hours of researching, writing, proofing, designing, recording, editing and coding.

This is a heavy time investment, and when I apply an hourly rate to that time it would not seem profitable to begin with. A template, for example, may cost upwards of $1K to produce, meaning I need to sell 33-ish to cover my costs. This might take months. But it does happen and, once I hit that figure, everything after that is profit *(minus the cost of website hosting and marketing)*.

So, now that you understand the two core principles, let's dig into some of the 'easier' income ideas in more detail.

1. Creating templates

I'm sure your business has processes and templates that you use every day and, while they may seem obvious and easy to you, to a newcomer they might appear utterly magical.

I started creating templates when I worked in advertising at Ogilvy just to make my life easier. When I left to start my own business, I created new templates and adapted them for my needs. Not only were clients impressed, colleagues and competitors were also wowed when I showed them my templates.

I started a small copywriter community on Google way back in 2013 and invited several other copywriters to join. The first thing I showed them was my copy deck, which few of them had seen or used. *(A copy deck is a copywriting template that includes guidelines, revision grids, comments and the content for each page of whatever you're creating. They're used for websites, brochures, annual reports and more.)*

At first, I gave it away for free. Then I started selling it on my website. It's just a low-cost template, but over the years I've sold nearly 5000 copies, which provides me with a nice little trickle of cash.

I've since gone on to create nearly 100 templates in my digital marketing business and, while it takes a bit of effort to create them and market them, they're the purest form of passive income I've found so far.

(Many of my templates have been ripped off, repurposed and sold by both friends and competitors – that copy deck for example – but I try not to look or to think about it. And I firmly hope that karma lives up to its 'bitch' reputation.)

2. Courses

My first course was born out of my one-to-one SEO training sessions, which then evolved into one-day, in-person training events. I ran my first session in Sydney for about 20 people. It was nerve-racking, I can tell you. But it was also a great way to test not only my teaching skills but also the material, and the eight-hour session lent itself very easily to an eight-module course.

I created my first course, The Recipe for SEO Success, in 2016 and sold it to 20 existing clients and other copywriters. But, importantly, I sold it before I'd built it. Again, nerve-racking. I was often uploading training videos literally seconds before they were due to be delivered to my students. Why? Because I wasn't going to invest months building a course only to find that no-one wanted to buy it.

Since then, I've gone on to sell that course to more than 1200 humans. I've also built a range of other courses, a podcast, a resource library and more. That one course alone has earned me well over $3 million over six years.

The SEO course is a wonderful passive-income story, but the stress of creating it nearly ended me at the start, and maintaining it is one of my least favourite things to do. Still, if I had my time again, I'm not sure I'd have done it any differently. The 'seat of my pants' approach made sure I got it done and out there. I could have taken more time, sought more outside feedback and been more patient. But if I had, then I may never have launched, as that extra time would have given rise to more self-doubt and navel-gazing.

3. Memberships

At the same time that I created The Recipe for SEO Success course, I built my first copywriting membership, The Clever Copywriting School. This was borne out of a free group on Google that I decided to 'monetise'. Again, I started with a low price and gathered a few humans to join. It took a few years to gain traction and momentum, but it now has around 400 members.

After that I built a second membership – the Digital Marketing Collective – for digital marketing coaching, which currently has around 300 members and growing.

Memberships are often seen as the golden egg of passive income, but they still require a lot of work. New content, coaching, support and the technical apparatus all cost time and money. But they're far less effort than helping people one-on-one – and, for me, far more enjoyable.

Understanding business diversity

I also make income from:

- books *(such as the one you're reading)*
- podcast sponsorship
- conferences
- speaking gigs
- one-on-one coaching
- small group coaching
- retreats
- influencer arrangements.

The profit margin on each varies, but I never do anything that has a profit margin of less than 30%. That said, many I do for pure enjoyment rather than for buckets of cash.

By the way, this income diversity has been crucial to my success, especially during the dark times of global pandemics and economic crises. While this diversity sometimes makes it hard from a branding perspective, my ability to be good at more than one thing has several benefits.

1. It gives my customers more to buy

Customers may start with a simple template but then progress to courses and memberships. They may see me at an event and buy a book, then slip into the TOONIVERSE *(the rather pompous way I choose to refer to my little business empire / cul de sac)* and buy more things. I'm not a one-trick pony. People want to buy from businesses they trust; once I've built that trust with my high-quality products, it's much easier for me to sell more to the same customer.

2. It saves me in dark times

If I'd been purely a speaker, I'd have struggled during COVID. If I only wrote books, it would be a slow trek to financial success. *(I earn about $1 for each copy sold of the book you're now reading.)* My diverse range of products and services means I can adapt to market trends and dial elements of my business up and down as the world changes.

3. It keeps me interested

While I'd like to sound like a master business guru with a grand plan, a key reason I started developing passive income ideas was that I was bored. I'd spent six or so years being a successful copywriter and hit decent income targets, but the day-in and day-out of it was wearing, and I wanted something new to focus on.

So, you know I love shiny objects, and most of them have worked out great. (Okay, so that daft idea for a line of SEO tea towels didn't really eventuate, but now I have branded tea towels for my member gifts.)

Success is often a long game, and often it's not the brightest minds that make it but those who can cling on long enough. By having a diverse range of projects to work on and the ability to shift my focus from one to another on a daily or weekly basis, I keep things interesting for myself.

I'm now also lucky enough to have a team. So, while it may look like I have a lot to manage, it's not me doing all the do *(see Chapter 10)*.

Smarter, not harder

Business gurus everywhere talk about working smarter, not harder. And I get the idea. But I also want to acknowledge that often business is just hard work, and you're not 'dumb' if you're putting in the long hours.

Sometimes that's just the way it is: periods of hard yakka and periods of ease. Often it's only through the hard work that you realise there's a smarter way.

I've never gotten it right first time. I'm a huge believer in 'done is better than perfect' and iterative development. The key is not giving up after the first time and not dwelling *(too much)* on your mistakes.

Simple family money wins

Now, I could have included a whole chapter about simple money wins, but this book is primarily a business book, so I didn't. However, I do want to share a few top-level thoughts.

We all know family is an expensive business. While the figures vary, it costs between $159,120 and $548,400 to raise a child to 18 here in Australia[13]. Which sounds ridiculous until I remember that I spend nearly $7 a day just buying my son's yoghurts. *(He's really into health and fitness, and now has a penchant for YoPRO yoghurts.)*

This book is about money management, setting targets and managing your time to hit your desired income figure. But if you can reduce your family expenses, then maybe you can reduce your desired income too. Which would be nice, eh?

The spending shifts

When I spoke with John Cachia – founder of AFA Group Wealth and my financial advisor – for the *Six Figures in School Hours* podcast, we discussed the major shift that's happening in spending. Anyone who is 50-ish or younger has lived through a period when money has become cheaper and cheaper. During COVID, money felt essentially free. Our generation is living in a time when, if you want something, you get it immediately. Credit on tap. Everyone living beyond their means. Everyone in debt. *(If you're a Game of Thrones fan, it's kind of like we've lived through the summer and now our financial winter is coming.)* You earn more, you spend more, and saving has become a bit of an anathema for most.

As Morgan Housel wrote in *The Psychology of Money*, 'Saving money is the gap between your ego and your income'. For most of us, our ego is in the driving seat.

John Cachia from AFA Group Wealth, dad of two boys (6 and 3), told me:

> 'We're currently working with a client where the household earns $300K and they're going backwards $20K in the hole every year. So, we're talking to them about cutting back on spending and making trade-offs. It's not going to be easy.'

The cold, hard, uncomfortable truth is that we need to work out exactly how much we need to make ends meet, and we need to develop a more frugal mindset and make trade-offs.

John outlined:

> 'There are three things you can do to improve your cashflow. Number one: you can earn more – hard for some, easy for others. Number two: you can reduce your expenditure. Okay, once

again, easy for some, hard for others. The third one is revising your goals. For example, do we need to go on that holiday every year? Do we need to upgrade that car? Do we have to have that new car? Can we reduce?'

The mindset shifts

While cutting costs should be a straightforward and logical process, it's often not. No-one likes to feel a sense of deprivation. Just as kids don't like having their toys taken away from them, we adults don't like having our Netflix and coffee taken away from us.

As I mentioned in Chapter 12, I recently went through the process of creating a family budget when applying for a mortgage and was horrified at the amount I spend on shopping, coffee and subscriptions, but choosing which subscription to get rid of felt like a wretched choice. I had some stampy-feet moments as I planned to cut my daily coffee-shop purchases and make coffee at home *(with my amazingly expensive coffee machine, I might add)*.

I've generally found that, the more discontented I am, the more stuff I need to bolster my sense of self-esteem. The more exhausted I get, the more I rely on subscriptions and services to keep things running smoothly. The more guilt I feel, the more I lavish gifts on my son. When I'm happy, well rested and feeling balanced, I spend much less.

Is it the same for you?

So, while there are practical ways you can cut costs, the true challenge is asking yourself, 'Why do I feel the need to buy this in the first place?' and, 'If it's anything beyond a basic need – food, shelter, crisps – what is this item giving me?'

I'm not saying you need to push yourself through an existential survey every time you want to buy some new knickers, but it helps to stop and think before you whip out your credit card. Personally, I'm an ecommerce store owner's worst nightmare. I'll add something to the cart, then give myself a week to think about it. Yes, I'm that abandoned cart human you loathe. But for me it's the perfect way to delay the pleasure *(I enjoy the anticipation more than the actual item)* and evaluate my level of want *(was it just a momentary urge or a burning, long-lived desire?)*.

TL;DR

Making money in business isn't just about the simple exchange of time for money or goods for cash. It's about being inventive, looking for other opportunities, cutting costs and selling your mind.

Benefits

By looking for opportunities to save and make more money, to diversify and start selling your mind rather than your time, you can:

- increase your business's overall income (and profitability)
- reduce the amount of time you spend in your business
- ride out the ups and downs of the market and your industry
- keep things interesting and keep yourself motivated for the long term.

Over to you

Now it's time for you to get creative and think of some ways you could make or save money in your business:

1. Look at your business expenses and find three things you could cut.
2. Think about one specialist service or product you could offer.
3. Think about one other business you could partner or contra with, or refer work to.
4. Think of one passive income idea for your business.
5. Think about some at-home money savings you could make that won't leave you feeling too deprived.

Remember, if you'd like to work through these exercises in detail you can head to sixfiguresinschoolhours.com and grab the accompanying workbook.

PART IV

FAMILY

WHEN IT ALL FEELS TOO CLOSE TO HOME

FAMILIES ARE GREAT, RIGHT? I certainly wouldn't be without mine. We're like a little gang with our quirks, traditions and secret language.

But, while I love my family, I don't want to spend ALL my time with them. We're allowed to say that, right? And when we take the plunge into starting our own business, we're suddenly faced with the reality that we're going to be around our family *so* much more.

Thinking about how to work with family around was a huge challenge for me. If I was looking after my son, it was snatched minutes rushing through a task while he was briefly distracted. If I left the house to work, I was simultaneously too excited by the freedom to get anything done and desperate to get home because I missed him. And if I worked at home while someone else looked after my son, I was wracked with guilt, listening out for the slightest squeak of unhappiness.

I realised that being a working-from-home parent just wasn't going to work unless I could create some clear division between family and work life, and also get my family more involved in my business.

Now, I get that these two things seem somewhat in opposition to each other, but bear with me.

As I've mentioned before, I think the key to making this whole business parent thing work is being either 'on' or 'off'. Being either focused on your family or not. Focused on your business or not.

But the reality isn't so easy. I'd love to have solid periods of days and days to work with no interruptions, but that isn't going to happen. I dream of spending my time with my son just doing fun stuff, but there's always shopping and washing to do. I'd love to have a team of people making me snacks and cleaning my kitchen, but the budget won't stretch.

So, in this section, I want to talk through ways you can create both mental and physical boundaries for work. I want to give you strategies to reduce the household to-do list from the inside out. I also want to give you some tactics to get your kids more involved in your business so they stop seeing it as the enemy and start getting excited about what you do.

In this section we're going to cover:

· creating a great workspace
· the sweet joy of insourcing
· involving your kids in your business.

Ready? It's time to focus on the family.

Chapter 15

Finding your space

'In the midst of movement and chaos,
keep stillness inside of you.'

Deepak Chopra

We've talked about the why, the when and the how of your business, but now let's dig into the where.

I'm guessing many of you work from home. Most small businesses start from a home base because, in those early days, forking out cash for a private office or co-working space isn't realistic. And after those years of lockdown *(remember that?)*, many folk I know are taking a while to emerge from their caves and head into the office again.

While I place 'office space' very firmly on my luxuries list in Chapter 12, I'm rather willing to backstep on that. Having a separate office space can be an essential for many.

I'm proof of this. I can't tell you how much having a good work environment has helped my business and my family. Well, actually, I can and I will in this chapter. I'm going to run through what it takes to create a comfy working environment: the absolute essentials, the luxuries and whether having an 'open door' policy with your kids is the best strategy.

Working-at-home stress

In a study by CoSo Cloud, 77% of humans reported greater productivity when working from home and 52% said they were less likely to take time off. On top of that (and because who doesn't love a good statistic?), 74% said their family relationships improved, 82% said they were happier and more motivated, and 55% reported decreased stress levels.[14] And, of course, this all makes sense. No tedious commute. No Kevin from finance heating up tuna in the communal microwave. No hideous, forced after-work Friday drinks. Ugh.

But the survey didn't ask what it's like to work at home as a parent. I think that's an entirely different kettle of clams – and I think the statistics for parents working from home would look a little different:

- 84% of humans report discovering a mystery stain on their t-shirt two minutes before their Zoom begins
- 46% regularly have important documents used for kids' art projects
- 118% get interrupted at least 953 times per day by requests for snacks.

Working from home as a parent can actually be more stressful than working in an office because:

- there's zero separation between work and family life
- business feels less serious when it has to be cleared off the kitchen table before dinner
- it's impossible to concentrate and focus. It's all very well to talk about productivity and mapping out your day, but it's a tad harder to manage when you have a needy two-year-old glued to you 24 hours a day.

My space-finding adventures

I started my business in my lounge room. Admittedly, we had a desk *(which a neighbour was chucking out)*. But that was it. In our one-bedroom, matchbox-sized house in Sydney, my business began. And at first I was pregnant, so I had a few months of being child-free and having time to spare and space to stretch out. It was blissful after years in a vile open-plan office environment. But it didn't last.

Here are the stages of my space-finding journey:

1. After my son was born, I worked with him snuggled into my boobs in a body wrap, managing an hour or so whenever he napped *(which was never)*.

2. Next, he was rolling around on a playmat next to my desk with wiggly things dangling over him, and I was lucky to get 15 minutes of work done at a time.

3. After stern words and a bit of relationship counselling, my son's dad and I came to an agreement that he would care for our son for at least two days a week solo. This meant I could escape to a local co-working space. It was an indulgence financially and I felt a lot of pressure to get heaps done in the few hours I had there *(although I will also admit to using that time to just nap on the comfy sofa in the office)*.

4. When my son was about 18 months old, he went into day care two days a week. This made a huge difference. From here until school started, I worked well on those days and sketchily on the days he was home. Even if his dad was looking after him, my son would always want me, and I found it impossible to say no. I would occasionally try to work from the library or a cafe just to get some peace and quiet, but I never really found it productive. *(I am no J.K. Rowling.)*

5. My son starting school was the real game changer. It wasn't just that he was at school five days a week but that the mental load shifted hugely. I felt the responsibility level drop a little. Potty training – done. Sleepless nights – done. My son was able to grab his own snack, get himself dressed and use the remote control. It was also at this time that my son's dad and I converted a bedroom into an office, which we shared for a while. Fun times! *(More on that later.)*

6. In 2017, I invested in having a little shed built in the back garden *(which I dubbed my 'Tooncave' – you can google 'Kate Toon Tooncave' to see some pictures)*. It was a momentous moment, not just because of the cost – about $14K all up with painting, electrics and kit-out – but also because it felt like my business had

finally become a 'real thing': it had a permanent HQ. I still feel immense pleasure every time I commute across my backyard to my Tooncave. It's my own special place. I love it.

I've been working from my Tooncave ever since. Occasionally, I'll work from a co-working space for a change in the vibe, but I don't ever get lonely or crave the company of others.

And yes, I know I'm blessed.

All that being said, I feel that getting an ideal workspace is a progression – it doesn't happen all at once for most of us. We have to be adaptable creatures, especially in the early days, and exercise our patience bone.

Working from home essentials

So, what do I think are the most important factors when working from home, you ask? Well let me tell you.

1. Strong internet

How does the saying go? Before you marry a person, you should first make them use a computer with slow internet to see who they really are. I agree with this 100%. I am a MONSTER without good internet.

I started off with internet so bad I had to put videos on a USB and post them to my VA so she could upload them to YouTube as her internet was faster. Since then we've gotten a faster connection and I paid a fortune to have a cable run from the house to my office so I could have fresher, moister internet juice pumped into my Tooncave rather than rely on sketchy wi-fi.

Ironically, as I write this chapter, I'm enraged by our internet speed. It's school holidays and my son is using his new computer *(which he dutifully saved up for; see Chapter 17)*. His endless streaming of games and YouTube videos caused our internet to be rationed the other day: I got a text from the internet company saying our speed would be reduced. And here was me thinking we were on unlimited internet. We are now.

Our internet modem also happens to be in his bedroom and he has been known to accidentally kick the plug out of the socket just as I'm mid Zoom call.

I cannot stress this enough: If you want to maintain your sanity, get the best possible internet you can find.

2. A permanent space

Try to create an area to work in that you don't have to pack away at the end of each day.

Working from the kitchen table has an impact on the mindset – like your work is something to be squeezed in between cereal bowls and dirty lasagne dishes. Working from your bed or the sofa will not only break every work health and safety standard and give you backache, it will also make you feel a little less professional *(and might be a bit embarrassing for Zoom calls)*.

Even if you just get tiny desk in a corner of a room where you can set up your computer and your bits and bobs *(a friend of mine worked in a built-in wardrobe for many years)*, it will help you to focus and feel more productive.

3. Your own space

When my son's dad and I shared an office space, we had two little desks back to back in a small room. I bought a room divider in an effort to achieve some level of privacy but, if I'm honest, it was horrendous. Every single thing he did drove me to distraction.

He took endless phone calls in a loud French accent. *(He's French, but really, that's no excuse.)* He even typed excessively loudly. And he had this annoying habit of breathing.

After a few years of this fun, my options were either to smother him *(or myself)* with a pillow or get my own space. I tried to work out of libraries and drank far too much coffee working in cafes but, eventually, I had my Tooncave built.

Having a space to call your own is important. My office is a physical extension of my mind: colourful, creative, mostly neat and occasionally chaotic. I can work in my knickers, sing while typing, dance during my Pomodoro breaks *(which I talked about in Chapter 9)* and generally let it all hang out. And I often do.

Remember back in the introduction we talked about the little yellow-jumpered girl crashing her dad's interview? I think since then we've all softened on 'kidterupptions'. I make it clear to my members and students that I don't care if kids are present, and we'll often do coaching calls with 50% of the participants holding a small human of some description. A closeable door is great, but letting your kids open it is also important.

4. A door

For me, one non-negotiable when choosing a workspace was a closeable door. *(Can doors be uncloseable?)* It's important to avoid external distractions and to separate work life from home life.

At the end of a workday I can close the door and leave work behind. Alternatively, I can delight in being able to escape the rest of the house, closing my door and slipping into a delightful warm pool of work.

John Cachia from AFA Group Wealth, dad of two boys (6 and 3), told me:

> 'My door doesn't have a lock and people say it's crazy. But, you know, we have meetings, and my little boy will walk in, and he just wants a cuddle. And I'm fine with that.'

5. Noise-cancelling headphones

I already suffer from a little low-level aural anxiety and so wear my Bose noise-cancelling headphones almost permanently when out and about. It also stops people talking to me, which is fabulous as I have big eyes and this makes people feel I'm kind and approachable. While I am, I am not all the time. Especially not in supermarkets.

While working I take my ear protection a step further, wearing both earplugs and a rather fetching pair of bright orange tradie earphones.

Of course, when I'm in charge of my child, I can't wear these as I have to keep an ear out for disaster. But if I have some time to work while my son's dad is in charge or my son is at school, I don't want to be able to hear anything – not even my own breathing.

6. Good lighting

You probably know the dangers of blue light *(constant exposure to blue light can damage retinal cells and cause vision problems such as age-related macular degeneration)*, so, ideally, you don't want your only light source to be your screen. Natural light is best, so if you can set up your workspace near a window it will reduce strain on the old peepers and make your workplace more inviting. I also like to light a little candle, not to evoke some Dickens-esque work environment but rather because it feels cosy and keeps the smell of my senior dog's bottom at bay.

7. An ergonomic chair

Sitting in a random wooden-backed kitchen chair all day isn't going to feel great *(cue numb bum and backache)*. As soon as I'd scraped together a few pennies, I purchased a nice squishy chair with good back support. I also have an array of ergonomic doodahs for my wrists while I type.

I did try the stand-up desk thing, but it wasn't for me. I find it hard enough to concentrate when I'm sitting down. Standing up felt odd and unproductive.

I do, however, try to get up every 30 minutes or so and dance around my office to Taylor Swift; this helps ease my stress levels. And it annoys my neighbours to no end.

8. Outfits

While this doesn't sound like a work-from-home office essential, I think the topic needs to be covered. One way I save a lot of time in my day is by having a work wardrobe.

Now, I don't mean a natty little selection of mix-and-match pieces, pencil skirts and blouses carefully colour-coordinated with my shoes and clutch bag. Rather, I mean a range of leisurewear leggings and t-shirts – with the occasional nice top if I'm doing a Zoom. It's a bit like how Steve Jobs had a wardrobe packed with identical t-shirts and jeans *(and I think Mark Zuckerberg does this too)*. Basically, it's one less decision to make each day.

However, I know some folk find that dressing for work in proper business clothes puts them into a work mentality, so that might work for you too. I recently purchased a blouse to try this out but am yet to brave it.

9. Lunch and snacks

Okay, so it's not exactly an environment thing, but bringing your lunch and snacks to your work spot is a great way to stop procrastifaffing.

When our office was next to the kitchen, there were endless cups of tea and constant mindless gazing into the fridge seeking answers to all the questions in the universe. And also some cheese.

Now, when I make my son's lunch in the morning, I pack a second lunch for myself and head to my shed with plentiful food, snacks and liquids. This means I only really have to leave my shed for wees – and over the years I've developed a bladder of steel. I have considered putting a portaloo in my office, like the ones you take camping, but am terrified that one day I'll leave my camera on while Zooming and will broadcast my weeing to the world. So, as yet, I've held back. *(On reflection, this could be another passive income source. OnlyFans, anyone?)*

Woo-woo working from home requirements

Now, working from home is not just about having the perfect desk and pen pot but rather about having, as our mate Deepak (quoted at the beginning of this chapter) said, 'mental space'. I'll cover this more in Part V, but let's call out a few key points here.

1. Physical boundaries

I've covered the benefits of having a permanent space, a closeable door and, ideally, somewhere a little separated from the rest of the house. A few other tools I've used to help signpost that I'm working include:

- **A door tag:** I place an 'I'm working' tag on the door handle to signpost when I'm in deep work mode and when it's okay to come in and chat – a little like a hotel room-service sign.
- **An on-air light:** I have a light in my office window that I switch on when I'm recording a podcast or doing a Zoom.

Of course, it's not the end of the world if I'm interrupted, but these small changes cut down on accidental interruptions hugely.

Kara Lambert, mum of Imogen (17) and Brennan (15), said:

'I generally work with an open door. I tell the kids if I have a meeting coming up and they don't disturb. (The bonus of them now being teens is that they rarely disturb me anyway.) My hubby needs the visual clue of a closed door to indicate I'm working and not to disturb.'

2. Mental boundaries

I work hard to keep my business in the office. It's so easy to mix work life and personal life, especially if you also work with your family – especially if the laptop is open on the kitchen table.

'I'll just send a quick email before I make dinner', I say, and then an hour later I've only chopped one carrot and am knee-deep in work again. Dinner is late and my teen is frothing with hangry vibes.

These days, I delete all my work-related and social media apps off my phone at the weekend and lock my laptop in the office. *(Admittedly, sometimes I then look at Facebook via a phone web browser and have to sneak into my office to look at stuff, but at least I'm trying.)*

I also try to leave business 'thoughts' in my office. Ideally, I try to bundle up all negotiations, future business plans, work incidents and financial concerns in order to leave them behind as I start my family time. This isn't always easy, but I find writing down all my to-dos and concerns before I leave the office for the day kind of cathartic.

It's just as important to keep family issues reserved for the home. If you're in the midst of a family dispute, try to resolve this before going to work so it's not nagging at your brain all day. I also try to avoid lots of personal phone calls with my partner or my son's dad during the day. I'm not great at compartmentalising work and family, but it's a work in progress.

3. Patience

Of course, I've never met anyone who says, 'I love being interrupted; it's my favourite thing'. But working out how to respond to interruptions is so important.

As with difficult conversations, it's important to handle these situations calmly and clearly so that your child doesn't feel like they're in the way. You also don't want them to feel that your job is the enemy, but rather that it is something that helps your family thrive.

Of course there will be times when you blow your top after the 89th interruption; that's just being human. Remember, part of your goal in having your own business was to be able to spend more time with your kids, and that comes with compromises. When I'm starting to lose patience, I remember the hideous commute and the awkward conversations in the office kitchen waiting for the microwave to ping – and I feel a little better.

TL;DR

Creating your own area to work in isn't just about heading to Ikea to pick out the perfect pouffe. It's about giving yourself space, mentally and physically, to take your work seriously, focus and change gears.

Benefits

By defining and improving your work environment you can:

- reduce personal stress by separating work and family life
- make your business seem 'more serious' and make yourself feel more professional
- improve your productivity
- improve your focus
- switch off at the end of each day.

Over to you

Now it's time for you to consider how you can improve your working environment:

1. Consider what you find stressful about working from home.
2. List possible places to work where you could separate work from family life.
3. Review your working environment. Could you make it more work-focused?
4. What are some ideas around access to your workspace that you could agree upon with your family to reduce family tensions?

Chapter 16

Insourcing

'No one who achieves success does so without acknowledging the help of others. The wise and confident acknowledge this help with gratitude.'
Alfred North Whitehead

It was the most beautiful rah-rah skirt I'd ever seen – denim with little bits of broderie anglaise on each tier. *(To this day I don't understand why rah-rah skirts haven't made a comeback.)*

But I was ten, and it cost a huge £8. So, it was impossibly out of my reach, right?

Wrong. I had at least £12 saved up in my slightly balding koala money bank, so that beautiful rah-rah skirt of my dreams was mine, all mine.

I remember the sweet joy of counting out the coins on the store counter and taking this amazing item of clothing home. I felt glorious.

But how, you ask, did a young girl of ten manage to amass such a fortune?

Insourcing. As I mentioned in Chapter 11, my parents were early adopters, and I'm eternally grateful to them for this.

What is insourcing?

Back in Chapter 10 we discussed outsourcing. And, of course, out-sourcing is all very well and good if you've got the cash and the patience. But I know that, even after my detailed breakdown of how to make it work, some of you will still be resistant.

It's hard to spend money when you're barely scraping a living. And often the idea of outsourcing homey stuff feels even harder, because your home is your private space.

As I mentioned previously, I'm from working-class stock, and the idea of having 'staff' in any capacity feels like 'a rich-person thing'. It's all very 'posh' and 'extravagant'. Having a cleaner or gardener feels indulgent – 'Just do it yourself'. Hiring a babysitter feels like bad parenting – 'Don't leave your kids with strangers'.

And there's an awful lot of judgement on the interwebs if you even mention you have any kind of help. You may field accusations of privilege, showing off your wealth or being an uncaring parent.

But the truth is that we're not all lucky enough to have grandparents, relatives or friends to support us. And even if we do, they've often got better things to do. We need help.

But we also need to get over ourselves, because let's face it: we're usually our own harshest critics when it comes to asking for help. If you can't keep your own house clean, you're some kind of slovenly wench. If you don't walk your own dog, you're lazy. If you can't manage your kids, you're a bad mum or dad. And honestly, who wants a stranger washing their knickers?

The combination of external judgement, internal icks and sheer lack of money means we end up doing it all ourselves – and burning ourselves to an absolute crisp in the process. But we don't have to.

Let me introduce you to the glorious notion of insourcing.

Insourcing is the process of dividing up jobs into small chunks and assigning each one to a family member. It's all about recruiting your family *(and mainly your kids)* to help you run the home and keep things chugging along. Jobs for your partner. Jobs for your kids. *(And even jobs for your pets, if they're smart enough and have opposable thumbs.)*

The result? Less work and stress for you, and more time and energy for your business. It may seem obvious that your family should want to contribute to running the household but, of course, it isn't. We may think we've progressed since the 1950s housewife days, but often the stories my members tell me reveal quite a different story. So, insourcing is a concept that needs to be discussed, explained and made 'normal'.

The martyr complex

Now, before I go any further into this, I have to admit there's one big problem with insourcing: you won't get to be a martyr anymore. And I know you love it, 'cause I love it too.

'Don't worry. Just let ME do it,' you snipe as you reload the dishwasher so it's done 'properly'.

'Do I have to do everything around here?' you mutter as you finish a task before anyone even has a chance to do it.

Being a martyr, eating that burned chop and slamming dishes about in the sink – ooh, it feels *so* good! You're so unappreciated. You're more tired than EVERYONE.

I get it. You're so used to doing everything yourself and then whinging about it that it's become normal and feels like the only way. But now you need to stop flagellating yourself and start taking steps towards making insourcing work.

Insourcing to your partner

(Psst: Of course, this section rudely assumes you have a partner, which you may not. So, if this ain't you, then I salute you. Being a single parent is impossibly hard. Also, skip this bit.)

Insourcing to your partner is the best place to start because it should be easier.

Why? Well, hopefully, your partner is an adult and so will do a better job of things than your kids or pets. And, hopefully, they've developed a tad of emotional intelligence and can see that you're drowning under the weight of juggling family life and your business. They should care for you enough to understand that, if they don't start helping, you're going to crack.

But shoulda, coulda, woulda, right?

So, before I dig into the how, let me address a couple of elephants in the room.

Elephant 1: My partner doesn't see my job as a real job

If your partner doesn't see your job as a real job, then this is going to be tricky.

This is often the case when you work from home. There's an expectation that because you're home all day, you can still:

- put the washing on
- do the shopping
- whip up a seven-course degustation dinner.

Your partner doesn't get that those hours between pick-up and drop-off are precious, sacred time. Or that, as soon as the kids are back home, your brain is too busy preparing snacks and fielding questions about Minecraft to be focused on whipping up a soufflé.

There's also the idea that going out to work is *so* much harder. Don't get me wrong – for some jobs it is. But for many it isn't.

For me, going to work was spending an hour on the train listening to podcasts, wearing office-y outfits and having a nice lunch in some posh food court. I wasn't slaving away. I got ten hours a day away from home to be just me. Being at my 'real job' was way easier than being a work-from-home mum.

Have things gotten better? For some, maybe. I think the forced homestays of COVID allowed a lot of 'out of the home' working parents to see how the other half lived. The constant interruptions. The feeling of being trapped. The impossibility of achieving anything in the ten brief minutes your child is absorbed in some inane TV show.

And often, the realness of your job is measured by how much you contribute to the family coffers. Which makes it hard if you're just starting out and barely covering your costs.

> **TOON TIP** As we discussed in the money chapters, don't just plop your business money into the family account to be frittered away on treats. If you do, your hard-earned money will always have lesser value than the 'real' money that pays the mortgage. Separate accounts, people; you know it's the answer.

Elephant 2: I have an old-school partner

Of course, you could be married to some Don Draper throwback – the kind of person who expects to come home and find you in a negligee *(if you're a working dad with a 'power wife' then replace 'negligee' with 'clean undies')*, with dinner in the oven and the kids freshly scrubbed and tucked up in bed.

Or the slightly evolved partner who 'helps out' but acts as if they're doing you a favour. Announcing they've made dinner as if it's some big achievement. Taking the bins out and expecting a pat on the bottom. Referring to looking after their own kids as 'babysitting' rather than just parenting (and making you want to scream, 'They're your own bloody kids').

Suggesting insourcing to them might go down like a bag of dead frogs.

Of course, Rome wasn't built in an afternoon, and offloading all the laundry to your partner might not happen immediately. But, if you're determined, it will happen.

My son's dad was a little old school at the start. He's a modern metrosexual man but had traditional parents: mum was the homemaker and dad was the breadwinner. So, I know there was a degree of him thinking that women do the cooking and cleaning and men make the moolah.

Of course, it helped that it didn't take me long to make ten times what he earned. That gave me so much more say in how things were organised. But it wasn't always that way, especially in the early days.

So, here are some strategies that worked for me:

1. **Draw up a timetable for your day:** Break down all the things you need to do – both work-related and family-related – into tasks and assign times to them all. Then, sit down with your partner and take them through it so they understand what you do all day *(aside from watching Netflix).*

2. **Address the money issue:** Explain to your partner that, while you may not be making big bucks *(yet)*, your business has potential, but it will never become a serious business if they don't help you take it seriously.

TOON TIP Many people who have started a business have been able to 'retire' their partner with their income. So, you may want to dangle that tempting carrot.

3. **Ask for help:** Explain that you're feeling overwhelmed by everything you need to do, and that it's making you miserable. Then, ask where they think they can help. Ideally, your partner should want a happier version of you, even if that means they have to stack the dishwasher to get it.

4. **Start small:** Don't expect a reluctant partner to suddenly offer to cook dinner every night. Instead, start by asking them to do smaller tasks. They could warm up the oven, get the thing out to defrost, chop the veggies, nip to the shop for a missing ingredient. I know it sounds like I'm treating your partner like a big baby, but, well, if the baby cap fits…

5. **Play to their strengths:** If you're taking a softly-softly approach, ask your partner what chores they actually enjoy. You might like them to walk the dog, but if they hate it then it may be a battle you can't win. My son's dad was a reluctant cook and an ineffective cleaner but discovered a deep love of laundry. He honestly gets real pleasure from it, while I hate it. So, laundry became his thang.

6. **Accept imperfection:** The key to insourcing is to accept imperfection from your partner (*and even more so from your kids, but we'll get to that*). They won't do the job quite like you do it, but that's not the point. As you look at the slightly improperly stacked dishwasher, keep in mind that it's one less thing you need to do. Try not to be critical and instead offer positive affirmation.

7. **Don't jump in:** If you've handed a job over to your partner, let them actually do it. Every time you jump in, you're implying that they don't have to do it at all because you're 'there'. This could mean things not happening to the schedule you want them to. You'll also need to stop looking at the pile of dirty dishes and muttering under your breath. Believe me, it will get better with time.

Now, I get that, if you live with some prehistoric lump who has set ideas about who does what, then you might have chortled through this section. I guess it all depends on how persistent you can be in your insistence that you need help, even if it causes a few difficult conversations along the way.

Jennifer Crawford from Our New Home Coach, mum of two (16 and 12), told me this:

'Did I find insourcing to my partner challenging? Yes and no.

'He does most of the grocery shopping and a lot of the cooking. He also drives and does the garden. These tasks play to his strengths, so it's not challenging to get him to do them at all.

'I do all the washing. He says I'm obsessed with washing, but when he's out of undies it's my fault. Gah!

'In terms of cleaning, we both do it sporadically. Our house isn't a show home.

'For the past three years he's been home, so he's been able to help with things. But he's starting a new full-time job soon, so it will be interesting to see how it all pans out.

'He often asks, "What can I do for you today?" which sounds great but sometimes isn't, as it means I have to think of all the domestic things that need to be done. Often, I feel that, since I need to think about it, I might as well do it!'

(Kate note: OMG yes. I hate it when my partner asks me to write a shopping list. "You write the damn list!")

'When I complain about mental load, he just doesn't get it. His position is, "Tell me what to do and I'll do it".

'The kids help with setting the table and clearing up after dinner. Both of their rooms are a nightmare, but I can't get stuck into them for it when mine's not much better. We live in a small house. It's a constant battle with stuff. To be honest, the kids could probably help more. I need to get this happening!'

Insourcing to your kids

Insourcing to your kids might sound like a wild idea, especially if they're still at the blob-on-the-carpet stage. But it can happen, and it's miraculous when it does.

I started young with my son. I have a fabulous video of him mopping the lounge room floor, which essentially involved emptying an entire bucket of water onto the floorboards and sloshing it around with gleeful giggles.

But those were the early days. Now my son is 13 and his chores include:

- filling and emptying the dishwasher
- sweeping the kitchen
- emptying the bins
- feeding and walking the dog, and keeping his water bowls filled up
- popping to the shops to get things
- helping to unpack the shopping
- mowing the lawns
- washing the car
- cleaning the bathroom (I know, gasp!).

He does some of these tasks 'free of charge' as part of being a member of the Moussa-Toon clan. Others he gets paid for. *(We'll talk more about that later.)*

Now, that list might not sound momentous, but the morning chores alone – bins, dishwasher, dog, floor – save me around 30 minutes a day. That's 3.5 hours a week. And 182 hours a year. That's 182 hours I can invest in my business or in more fun stuff for our family.

But, again, before we dive into the how, let's discuss the 'why nots'.

Why not 1: Let kids be kids

Of course, we should give our kids plenty of time for play, self-discovery and mashing hummus into the carpet. But let's be clear here: I'm not advocating stuffing your seven-year-old up the chimney with a broom. I'm saying that getting kids involved in a few age-appropriate household chores is good for them – and for you.

I feel that folks who push the 'let the kids play' trolley forget that kids can get a lot of play and enjoyment from doing chores. If you make the chores feel like fun, then they *will* be fun. It's really that easy.

Furthermore, kids learn a lot from household chores, such as:

- the need to care for themselves and their home
- their role and importance in the family
- relationship skills with you and other siblings
- communication, cooperation and teamwork
- organisational skills and processes.

Finishing a task also gives kids a fantastic sense of achievement, which will make them feel more competent and responsible.

Why not 2: It's easier to do it myself

Absolutely, you're 2000% right that it's easier to do it yourself. Of course you'll do a better job of folding laundry than an absent-minded eight-year-old. Of course there'll be moments when your child throws the mop on the floor and tells you to do it yourself.

But that's not the point, is it? No-one is good at stuff straight off the mark.

Getting your kids involved in chores when they're young can test your patience and leave the kitchen floor dirtier than it was before you started. But, over time, they'll get better and better. Remember the outsourcing chapter *(Chapter 10)*? There I reminded you that the first three months of getting people involved in your business is an investment. Well, the same goes for getting your kids to do odd jobs around the house.

As some wise old badger once said, 'A patient parent is a happy parent'.

You're also setting your kid up with a good work ethic in the future. Imagine your child at 57: he's a high court judge, and he gets in a hissy fit, throws his gavel on the floor and tells the bailiff to do it himself 'cause it's too hard. It's not just about now – you're building a good future human.

Here are some tips to get you started:

1. **Chat it through:** Discuss the jobs as a family over dinner or during some other fun and relaxing time. Make it feel like a family project rather than a boring task or punishment.

    TOON TIP Never use chores as punishment, as you'll undo all your good work making them a positive thing.

2. **Choose age-appropriate chores:** Obviously, we don't want our two-year-olds carving the Sunday roast and four-year-olds cleaning leaves out of the gutters. We need to pick jobs that aren't too hard or dangerous. *(There's a helpful list later in this chapter.)*

3. **Start young:** Even little jobs like clearing the table or putting toys away can help teach young children that their contribution is important.

4. **Make the process clear:** Start by working on the task together so they feel confident and have you there to back them up. Provide clear instructions for older children; this could mean writing some notes, recording a little video or directing them to a handy YouTube video. *(My teen loves a good TikTok cleaning hack.)* Consider creating a timetable or list of jobs and sticking it to the fridge.

5. **Expect and accept imperfection:** Despite your instructions, they're obviously going to do a terrible job at the beginning. Expect spills, breakages and fumbles. Don't start them off with dusting Great Aunt Maud's prized china, and don't set them up to fail with impossibly complex tasks.

6. **Discuss the jobs in a fun way:** Ask questions about how they did each job, such as: 'What did you enjoy?' 'Was it hard?' and 'What might you do differently next time?'

7. **Be positive and reward:** Congratulate them on doing a good job rather than being critical. Consider creating a reward chart with small rewards, such as watching a movie, making their favourite food or small amounts of money to save for something they really want *(money is obviously a great incentive for older kids)*. Make a clear correlation between them helping and them getting to do fun things with you. And yes, this is still true of rolly-eyed teenagers.

Christina Parkin from Get Simply Sorted, mum of Daniel (32) and Stephanie (30), told me this:

> 'We had shiny white tiles, and it was my teenage son's job to vacuum and mop. So, I had to accept many instances of murky-looking tiles. But they were cleaner.

'Later he got a job at KFC and was eventually promoted to Head Mopping Trainer for his mopping skills. His boss was fantastic at creating "roles" out of responsibilities to make his teenage staff feel important in doing that job.

'He's now 32 and almost painful in his attention to detail in keeping his house clean. Honestly, his floors are cleaner than mine, although being an IT geek he's now invested in a Roomba.'

Paying for chores

Some people feel odd about giving kids pocket money. Others feel odd about rewarding kids for helping the family with money. Some hand out money willy-nilly and don't care about it.

What you do in your family is your call and no-one else's business.

As I mentioned earlier, my son has set chores he does just for being part of our family and others *(large jobs)* that earn him money. I think it's a good balance. It's certainly helped him understand the value of money and the time needed to make that money.

You might be thinking, *Well, how much do I pay?*

The answer will be different for everyone. Some parents do the tooth fairy thing and leave a dollar coin, while others leave a $100 note. *(If that's you, please adopt me. I'll willingly give you all my teeth.)*

I've found that age-band payments work well:

- **0–4 years old:** Enjoy this blissful period when they don't understand money
- **4–7 years old:** $2 per task
- **8–12 years old:** $5 per task
- **13–16 years old:** $10 per task

The prices above could be per week or, if your business is pulling in squillions, per day! (I was going to suggest paying by age – $1 for a one-year-old, $2 for a two-year-old, and so on. But that's obviously daft. One-year olds are so unhelpful around the house.)

Decide on a price and stick to it. Make a note of it somewhere and get your child to sign off on it so they don't constantly try to negotiate. *(My son is going to be a mean bargainer when he grows up.)*

TOON TIP Paying your teen $10 a task may sound like a lot, but it's probably cheaper than hiring a gardener or visiting the car wash.

TOON TIP Paying your child to work for you might be a better choice than having to drive them to and from a job – especially if you live in a remote area.

Age-appropriate insourcing jobs for small humans

Here are some jobs I gave my son at different ages. Obviously, their appropriateness will depend on the maturity and abilities of your child. You know them best.

Toddlers *(aged 2 to 3)* can:

- put away toys
- put dirty clothes in the laundry
- plump cushions *(the karate-chop bit is the best! Karate-chopping pillows so they have a little V in them is something interior designers do on those styling TV shows).*

Preschoolers *(aged 4 to 5)* can:

- help with the shopping
- put away the shopping when you get home
- help with dinner (under supervision)
- bake cakes (under supervision)
- water the garden
- put clean clothes in piles for each family member.

School-aged children *(aged 6 to 12)* can:

- feed the pets *(if you remind them 8978 times)*
- take out the bins
- sweep and vacuum
- help choose meals and make shopping lists
- wipe down kitchen surfaces
- load the dishwasher or wash the dishes
- mop the floors.

Teenagers *(aged 13 to 18)* can do all the jobs they did when they were younger, except now you can make them responsible for doing them all on their own, no supervision needed *(hopefully)*. At this age, teenagers can do more complex jobs with several steps *(but beware of the eye-roll factor – learning not to bite at grunts and 'whatevers' removes the temptation for them to get out of doing the job by starting an argument)*, such as:

· doing the washing
· washing the car
· preparing meals
· stacking and emptying the dishwasher
· mowing the lawn
· preparing their own lunch.

I think many parents find it easier getting their kids to help when they're older. They're more aware that you're working *(especially if you don't hide it from them)* and have a better understanding of how they can make your life easier, which in turn makes you a happier, more easygoing parent.

Angela Pickett from Angela Pickett Copywriter, mum of Angus (14) and Xavier (12), told me:

'From a young age, my boys had to pitch in with things like hanging up the washing and making their beds.

'With my partner and me it is usually a case of who has time. But sometimes at the weekends or after school, we'll write a list for the boys that might include vacuuming or cleaning the bathroom.

'Some tasks might look like a 'gender divide', such as me doing washing or making beds. But they're things Simon struggles with or things I enjoy.

'It was always a fairly even split between my partner and me, but now that the boys are older it's even between the four of us. They might not always do it perfectly, but I take a "done is better than perfect" approach.

'PS: While it sounds like we've got it all sorted, there's still the occasional banshee-yelling from me.'

The end result

I mentioned at the beginning of this chapter that I started young with my son. My parents are in the UK, I had few friends to help and we had zero money to spare. So, my son simply had to help.

He's done small chores from an early age and so doesn't question me when he's asked to do stuff. He's also learned a lot of life skills. He can cook a mean lasagne, wash his own clothes, paint a wall and handle a mop. His future partner, should he have one, will have a lot to thank me for.

I pay him for some chores, and he uses the money to invest in stocks and shares *(via a Raiz account, a mobile-first investment platform that enables easy investing)*, save for university *(I'm not joking)* and invest in computer bits and bobs.

The fact he helps out in the morning means I get to walk the dog, eat breakfast, make his lunch and start the day fresh, comfy in the knowledge that my kitchen isn't a war zone.

My son's dad does all the laundry and even hangs stuff on the line (which is a big deal for us English folk who are so used to using the tumble dryer), and I get a fresh pile of laundry on my bed every day. He's always willing to pop to the shops, and he shares cooking duty. *(It's mostly toasties and pasta, but still.)*

It took a lot longer for him to take over the mental load of things like bills, but we got there. I still make appointments, remember birthdays and plan holidays and occasions. The dog is 100% my responsibility, but I don't mind.

It hasn't always been fifty-fifty, but I'd say it is now.

TL;DR

Getting your kids involved in your business can be a glorious bonding experience, teaching them great life lessons and genuinely helping you out. But if it feels like a struggle then don't force it.

Benefits

Thinking about insourcing will help you:

- have one less job to do each month, week or day
- see your children take on new responsibilities and learn
- watch your partner actively support your business *(possibly)*
- transform your family into a team that works together towards goals
- create less stress in your home environment and more mental capacity to focus on work, life and family goals.

Over to you

1. Make a list of jobs your kids could complete.
2. Discuss with your family and write down the agreed job list.
3. Create a reward chart or similar to track when things are completed.

Chapter 17

Putting the kids to work

*'To be in your children's memories tomorrow,
you have to be in their lives today.'*

Barbara Johnson

Okay, so we've covered how we can get our kids to help more around the house. But how about we get them involved in the business? And is it even a good idea?

I thought I'd start this chapter by sharing my experiences of involving my son in the day-to-day running of my business.

The early years

From a young age my son saw that I was 'doing work' at home. I worked at the kitchen table, in our home office and, eventually, in my backyard shed. I always had an 'open door' policy so he could wander in and see me tapping away at the computer, even though it was challenging at times.

My son accompanied me to the post office to send parcels. He helped me unbox my books and branded goodies. He posed dutifully for shots with my I LOVE SEO cookies and featured in videos for my children's book *Wobbly Jim and a Parrot Named Sue*. From as soon as he could write, he was keen to help me with envelopes, carefully writing out addresses and sticking on stamps *(ever so cute for my members to receive a parcel with his huge handwriting scrawled across the envelope)*.

At around age eight, because I honestly had no choice, I took him to a conference *(thank you Elle from Artful Business)*. He sat and played on his iPad while I spoke, and a kind friend *(thanks Jo)* took him to the zoo for a few hours so I could focus on my talk. After that, we explored Adelaide – a great combination of work and fun.

As a pre-teen he was less embarrassed by everything I did and told me he was proud of me *(but, unsurprisingly, unimpressed by my low YouTube follower count)*.

But, in all honesty, it wasn't until my son was around 11 or 12 that he started to take a real interest in my business – not because he suddenly found it fascinating, but rather because he wanted to save up for much-desired things. This coincided with COVID, a drop in income for my son's dad and a decision by both of us that we would no longer be buying him anything, other than at Christmas and birthdays.

As discussed in Chapter 16, my son already does set chores around the house just because he's a member of our family and gets small blobs of pocket money for things like mowing the lawns. But he decided he wanted a supercomputer with all the bells and whistles, and his desire for money overrode his naturally lethargic teenage demeanour.

How we began

At age 12, my son already had a keen interest in videos *(he's from the TikTok generation)*, so I started off teaching him how to use my video editing software *(Camtasia)* and asking him to edit some testimonial videos for me.

He did an excellent job, improving on my efforts and learning new tips and tricks I hadn't known existed *(thanks to YouTube)*; and he was fast, so fast. I'm not sure if this was down to less overthinking or if modern children are just built better.

I shared a few of his videos with my membership and a few members offered to give him some work. He then went on to make several videos for other people, which he enjoyed. He even scored a regular social media job for an Aboriginal Education company, Koori Curriculum *(thanks Shannon and Jess)*.

But he didn't like the budget-quoting bit, the back and forth and the amends. *(Welcome to freelance life, buddy!)* He also didn't want to go to the effort of building a website and all that jazz, which is totally understandable.

So, after he'd shown this wasn't a passing fad, I decided to take him 'in-house' as a proper worker in my business. At first, he just did bits and bobs, and I gave him extra pocket money. But then I decided to make him a full-blown employee.

Why? Well, because he was racking up more hours, and it was becoming a legitimate business expense that I could claim. Also, I saw it as a way to give him a better understanding of money.

We took the following steps to get him set up:

1. We went to the bank and got him an online bank account (he can't use his card for online purchases until he's 14 but was able to set up an everyday and savings account).

2. I set him up with a tax file number *(for the non-Australians, this is how we register with the Australian Taxation Office to pay tax).*

3. I helped him implement a simple Profit First-style money split: 50% into long-term savings *(for car and university)*, 25% into short-term savings *(he puts some of this into a Raiz account, which I set up for him)* and 25% spending money.

4. We agreed on a set number of hours he has to commit to; he wanted to do eight, but I thought it was unrealistic, so we settled on five. So far, that's worked out just right.

As a salaried casual employee, he gets paid twice a month upfront, so he must learn to put away the money and budget for things he wants. He also has to keep track of his hours in a time sheet so he doesn't go wildly over or under – if he does, we balance the time in the following month.

With the videos, the social media and work from me – as well as some money from his grandparents – he was able to save up enough for his computer in about a year. He built it with my partner over a long weekend and the result is kind of amazing. He also managed to save more to buy a new desk and chair and even fancy bedding. His bedroom is now a state-of-the-art gamer's paradise and much the envy of his friends – and, better still, he has the LED glow of knowing that he paid for every little bit of it.

The positives

I have found so many good things in employing my son in the business:

1. **Financial literacy:** My son has better financial literacy at 13 than I had in my late 30s. He has the ability to split out his money and know exactly what is his, an understanding of long and short-term savings, and a grasp of the differences between investing in shares and in a traditional savings account.

2. **Confidence:** My son is confident talking to other members of my team: he filled out his tax file number declaration form online via Zoom with my bookkeeper, my Digital Manager Kat takes him through his social media jobs and he interacts with everyone via our Slack channel. He's also happy to go to the post office and chat to staff, which is a biggie for a teen boy.

3. **Communication:** Although still occasionally a monosyllabic teen, my son has learned the art of writing a short, polite email, of explaining his processes and of articulating anything he's struggling with in a clear way.

4. **Ease:** On my side of things, I know I'm providing my son with great life lessons, but I don't have to drive him to and from a job *(saving me a lot of time)*; this also gives me huge peace of mind given I'm a bit of a helicopter parent.

5. **Quality time:** Remember how I dismissed the notion of quality time back in Chapter 5? We talked about how all time could be considered quality, not just trips to the zoo. Well, here's another example. You might not think sitting together addressing envelopes or working out why our social media tool isn't connecting properly is quality time, but it most definitely is.

We're working together on a common goal, working out issues, arguing sometimes and having a giggle.

6. **Reduced workload:** My son working five hours a week is now five hours I don't have to work myself. Obviously, at first it wasn't a huge time saving – I could have done it quicker myself and I was investing time in helping him through things. But now he's up to speed and much faster than I am. My post *(I send a lot of parcels)* was always last on my list, and physically having to go to the post office felt like a huge drain in my day. So, as well as it being a great bonding experience, it genuinely helps me day to day.

The challenges

Of course, not everything is smooth sailing, and there have been challenges along the way:

1. **It's a bit of a faff:** Him doing the odd job and me giving him pocket money was, of course, easier than setting him up as a casual employee. We had to organise tax, WorkCover, time sheets and payroll. It took some time for us to get all our paperwork ducks in a row and I needed the help of my bookkeeper to do it all properly, which was a cost to my business.

2. **We don't always agree:** Obviously, at 13 my son knows everything about everything and often questions why I'm telling him to do things a certain way. This can be challenging when you just want to get things done, and even more challenging when you realise he's right and has far better ideas than you.

3. **I sometimes have to nag:** While my son is mature – possibly because he's an only child – he is still a teenager and, while he talks a big talk about wanting to work five hours a week, in reality, when the work needs doing, he'd much prefer to be out with his friends or gaming. I do sometimes have to remind him to get it done, which causes friction when he'd rather lie on his bed, but generally we work it out.

4. **It's too easy:** Having been brought up with a 'you won't have it handed to you on a plate' mentality, I do sometimes feel I've made it a tad too easy for my son. He hasn't had to apply for a job, work with odd people or deal with a difficult boss. *(Okay, scratch that last one – I'm a super difficult boss.)* And perhaps he'll have a rude awakening when he goes out into the 'real world'. Or possibly not; even working in my small team he's learning how to be diplomatic, communicate and meet other people's expectations. I guess we'll see in a few years' time.

5. **It's not social:** Other parents have questioned my plans because of the lack of social interaction and the fact that the work is majority screen-based. My belief is that my son gets plenty of social interaction at school, and plenty of exercise both there and in our gym visits. As far as the screen is concerned, I don't see working in a shop or cafe as any more wholesome than working in front of a computer.

My recommendations

Here are a few things that helped us navigate the working together adventure.

1. Let them come to you

There were a few times when I suggested my son might want to help do things and he wasn't keen. I didn't push but rather waited until he decided it was his idea. Forcing your kid to be involved won't be fun or valuable for either of you.

Tony Cosentino from The WordPress Guy, dad of Josh (33), Kat (30), Fynn (13) and Sam (10), agrees:

'My son, who is 13, is very driven by what he needs in the moment. So, if he needs to get a new thing, then he comes and asks me for work to do. And then he'll use all that money until it's gone. He's not motivated to plan ahead and save for the long term. Even if I say to him, "Why don't you just do the work for when this thing comes up next time?" it doesn't compute, and I can't really knock that because that's how my brain works.'

2. Build up slowly

We started early with small tasks and built up to bigger things, and we continue to push it further:

- **Age 5 to 7:** sticking on stamps, packing envelopes, writing addresses
- **Age 8 to 10:** making Canva graphics
- **Age 11 to 12:** video editing using Camtasia.

TOON TIP Of course, I had to monitor the output and ensure it looked great. If I had amends, I handled them gently; my son preferred me to just make a little list of things I wanted changed. Sometimes he disagreed and I took that on board. Obviously, you can't feel bad about giving your kid feedback; it's all part of it.

Now, at 13, with a strong grasp of technology, here are a few things my son does:

- Schedules social media posts using Agorapulse
- Makes and resizes graphics for social media
- Edits and adds subtitles to videos
- Manages all post, including tracking on a spreadsheet, packing and going to the post office
- Pulls together social media copy decks.

Now that he's 13, he can have a Facebook account and so is also setting up events for my membership. *(He only uses Facebook for this as, obviously, in his opinion, 'Facebook is for old people'.)*

I'll soon be training him in how to use our email marketing software and how to use WordPress to do minor text updates on the website.

3. Create standard operating procedures

I spend time writing out really detailed standard operating procedures for every task. So, every job he has to do is listed with numbered steps to completion. I also make short Loom videos to train him on tasks. It's not realistic to expect him to remember everything, and it saves him having to ask me question after question. I also pass responsibility for briefing him to Kat, my Digital Manager; they get on great, and that degree of separation really helps my son and me.

4. Use good tools

My son has an email address set up; we use Slack to communicate, Asana to manage tasks, Google Docs for writing and Canva for graphics, as well as other tools. *(I've included a full list of tools I use in the Extra Bits section at the back of the book.)*

Technology comes easily to my son, and he has apps on his phone for all of these desktop tools and can flip between them with the ease of a damp otter sliding off a log.

5. Manage expectations

My biggest tip is to manage your own expectations. My son's level of keenness has changed over the months, but also changes day to day. Some days he just can't be bothered, and while I'll push him *(and explain why that wouldn't fly for a real job)*, I also give him a little grace: I ensure the tasks I give him aren't too time sensitive, and I always have a back-up plan. He's only human. I regularly don't feel like doing my job, so I can't expect him to be motivated all the damn time.

Some practicalities

I want to cover some common HR and tax questions before we wrap up. *(Now, of course, this section is Australia-specific, so you'll need to do your own research if you're based elsewhere.)*

Employment rules are the same across Australia, but rules about long service leave, workers compensation and health and safety vary between states and territories.

I'm not an accountant or HR person so, rather than just gleefully fling my opinions about, I sought the professional thoughts of veteran HR manager Karen Hillen from My HR Partner and Diana Todd, founder of Balance Tax Accountants and an amazing Australian accountant.

Let's cover off some common questions.

Does your child need a tax file number?

A tax file number or TFN is a requirement for Australian residents. According to the ATO website[15], you can apply for a TFN at any age, but if you are:

- **12 years old or under:** your parent or guardian must sign on your behalf
- **13 to 15 years old:** you or your parent or guardian can sign
- **16 years or older:** you must sign your application yourself.

Do you need to do a tax return?

The current tax-free threshold in Australia is $18,200, which means your child won't have to pay any tax if they earn under that amount each year and will be able to get back all the tax that was taken from their pay.

Diana Todd added:

'Educate your child on the tax deductions they're eligible to claim against their employment income from the start. While they're earning under the tax-free threshold, these deductions may not increase their refund amount, but the awareness and habit of record keeping from the beginning will support them in minimising future tax when their taxable income increases.'

Do you need to pay superannuation?

Generally, if you're under 18 years old, superannuation is only paid if you work more than 30 hours in a week, so it is likely that this won't impact you or your child.

Diana Todd said:

'While employers may not be required by law to pay super-annuation guarantee for some employees under 18 years old, many employers are opting to contribute to employees' superannuation above the minimum requirement as a staff retention strategy.'

Do you need WorkCover?

If you're taking on an employee, you'll likely have to consider workers compensation insurance, which is a form of insurance payment to cover employees if they are injured at work or become sick due to their work[16]. I've included a link to more information in the references section at the back of the book *(or you can Google 'Fair Work workers compensation')*. Karen Hillen from My HR Partner, mum of Dan (35) and Mark (33), confirmed:

> 'Workers compensation insurance is compulsory when you have employees; it's not something that you can decide not to have. Make sure you check what insurance options you have in your particular state.'

Do you need a contract?

Karen Hillen told me this:

> 'When you're employing family, it's really a judgement call. You probably don't really need an employment contract for your son or daughter because there's less likelihood that there's going to end up being a drama. But if you're employing someone, a contract is a good idea as things do go wrong. For example, if you're employing your brother, sister, cousin – a contract is a very good idea. So, I think it's good to have something written down even if it's not a formal traditional contract.'

With my son, we both agreed a simple one-pager of bullet points covering hours, what he was doing and what was expected of him was appropriate. That's what we did, but really for us it's more about day-to-day communication.

Should you take your kids on as permanent part-time or casual?

My son is employed as a casual human. Karen explained why this is a good idea:

> 'Permanent employees have a guarantee of ongoing hours, and they get annual leave, sick leave, public holidays, etc. They can be permanent part-time but still be entitled to those benefits.
>
> 'A casual employee has no guarantee of any sort of regularity of hours or ongoing employment. So, it's a bit freer and easier. It's a great way to start off with kids, especially if you're not sure how many hours you need them to work.'

What should you pay?

Obviously, what you choose to pay is largely up to you if it's an informal arrangement. But if it becomes an employee relationship and you're doing formal payroll, you must follow award rates.

Karen Hillen added this:

> 'Australia has different "awards", or levels of pay. (An award is a legal document that outlines minimum rates of pay and entitlements.) So, currently, the minimum wage is $21.38 an hour for permanent employees. Casuals get a 25% loading on top of that. Many awards have junior rates of pay based on age, but some don't – for example, the award that covers an employee on a building site doesn't have junior rates, so if you're employing a junior you need to pay them adult rates.'

Now, you might think, *Who's to know?* But the Fair Work Commission can check up on you at any time, and there are penalties for not paying award rates, so it's best to play by the rules. People can also report you if they think you are doing the wrong thing. My son and I agreed on a rate we felt was fair; he tried to negotiate but I'm a tough cookie. It's more than he'd earn in a shop or cafe, so he's happy.

Is it worth the faff?

After all this, you might be thinking that it's hardly worth all the fuss to get your child involved in your business, or you might decide it's easier if you keep it simple and not go down the formal route. I'd say, each to their own. It totally depends on the type of business you have, your relationship with your child and the child themselves.

My son was super keen to take these steps and become part of my business; it was 'child-led' employment, so it worked for us. But he could easily change his mind tomorrow and decide to get a real job. If he does, I'll be absolutely fine with that. *(Funny that even I still sometimes consider a job in the big wide world more real than one working at home when, in fact, working for my business might be considered much more serious and 'real' than working at Maccas.)* As with all the ideas in this book, I recommend you read through them, 'try them on' and see if they fit your business or family life. Employing your child might seem a ridiculous idea right now but, as your child and your business grow, things might change.

TL;DR

Employing your child is a great learning experience for both of you, but only if you're both up for the challenge.

Benefits

By considering employing your child you can:

- give them a great sense of purpose and involvement in your business
- help them get a better grasp of financial literacy, including tax, superannuation and managing their money
- provide them with useful skills for future life
- boost their confidence and interpersonal skills
- reduce the load on yourself by farming out minor tasks *(if you manage expectations)*
- give them an insight into your working life, work ethic and relationships with colleagues and customers.

Over to you

Now it's time to see whether this would really work for your business and your child or children:

1. What sort of jobs do you think you could pass to your child?
2. Think about how many hours they could work each week and what sort of rate you want to pay.
3. Talk to your accountant about the requirements in terms of tax, superannuation, WorkCover and the type of employment status that would work best.
4. Talk to your child about their level of interest, and possibly start off with a trial of a few hours a week.

Remember, if you'd like to work through these exercises in detail you can head to sixfiguresinschoolhours.com and grab the accompanying workbook.

PART V

COMMUNICATION AND SELF-CARE

PUT YOUR OWN OXYGEN MASK ON FIRST

IF YOU'RE ANYTHING LIKE ME, you've put yourself firmly at the bottom of a long list of things and humans in your life. The kids come first, of course. Then, it's a toss-up between your dog, your partner and your business. After that, it's the house, the extended family, friends… you name it. Where are you on the list? And why is it that I can always remember to feed the dog but rarely remember to take my vitamins or drink any kind of fluid?

Sound familiar?

I spent the first eight years of my business life sacrificing myself on some imagined business altar. Working every minute I could. Trying to have an immaculate kitchen. Holding in wee so long it reabsorbed into my body. I spent many, many days screaming expletives at my computer, weeping into my dog's soft fur, snapping at my poor child and collapsing in a heap at the end of the day. I gained weight and became a habitual wine drinker *(celebrating with booze on any day that had a 'Y' in it)*.

Why? Because I wanted to have it all, no matter what it cost me. No matter how exhausted or ill I got. And then I realised I could have it all, just not at the same time, and that I had to put myself first at least some of the time.

Because the truth is that without you, your family and your business is nothing.

I realised I'd been holding myself to an impossible standard: trying to impress people who didn't even like me and working towards a financial goal I didn't care about. And quite literally no-one cared. No-one was in awe of my late-night manic work sessions. No-one was applauding my sparkling cooker hob. No-one gave even the tiniest of shits. It was just me, myself and I.

And here's the thing: the work I was doing wasn't even my best because I took no time at all to recharge, rethink or *(shudders)* relax.

We're sold an idea of hustle culture: 4 a.m. wake-ups, ice baths and efficiency. But maintaining this level of super humanness just isn't possible for most regular business-owning parents, and thinking it is will set you on a fast track to illness, mental health issues and burnout.

So while it may pain you as it did me, I want you to face that truth. To help you do that, I want to wrap up this book by focusing on how to handle the other side of business – beyond the emails and spreadsheets, beyond the money and the to-do lists. I want to show you that prioritising 'you' isn't selfish or wasteful. It's absolutely essential in creating the parenting and business lifestyle you want.

In this section we'll think about:

· how to have difficult conversations
· filling your empty cup
· banishing burnout.

It's time to get our woo on and do the deep work.

Chapter 18

Difficult conversations

'The way we talk to our children becomes their inner voice.'
Peggy O'Mara

When combining the roles of awesome business human and serene parent, the biggest challenge I came up against was communication. How to persuade my son that mummy locking herself in the office was a good thing. How to explain why I was 'always on my phone' but that he shouldn't always be on his iPad. Why I was one of the mums who never helped out at the school sports carnival. Why I couldn't just drop everything and play Minecraft.

And if making my son understand was tricky, it was even harder with my family and friends. Oh, those judgy parents at the school gate. One mum in particular really got on my tits. I can still remember her gently resting a hand on my arm and telling me in soothing tones, 'Hi hun, I took some photos of your son at the Splashathon because I saw you weren't there again this year. Shall I AirDrop them to you?' Gah! AirDrop *this*, sweet pea! *(Raises middle finger.)*

Then there are the friends who want to pop over for a cup of tea because you're at home doing 'nothing'. And the partner who can't believe the house isn't a sparkling palace when they return from work.

And, of course, the dreaded clients – how do we admit that we actually have children and can't make that breakfast meeting in the city at 8 a.m.?

If we want to run successful businesses and still be good parents, we need to get better at communication, even if having those difficult conversations gives us the icks. We need to be clear about our priorities and explain our needs, because it can make the difference between flourishing and flopping.

In this chapter, I want to give you some strategies to help you have better, less difficult conversations with the people who matter to you most – including yourself.

It all starts with you

Let's get one thing straight: If you go into this 'running your own business' thing with the attitude that it's 'stealing time from your family' then it's going to be a struggle.

How you frame your business and its place in your life is critical.

Many of us feel that time spent doing anything other than nurturing our small humans somehow makes us poor parents. *(This is a throwback to historical notions of motherhood, our own childhood and societal pressures, as discussed back in Chapter 5.)*

The stories we tell ourselves matter. If you decide that working conflicts with your role as a parent, then it will. If you believe it's impossible to juggle a successful business with being a good parent, then it will be.

It all starts with us having a difficult conversation with ourselves.

I find it helps to create a little list of business and parenting mantras. Here are a few of mine:

- I'm allowed to fulfill my own intellectual and psychological needs.
- Good parenting doesn't mean not working.
- Working is a way of supporting my family.
- It's okay for me to enjoy my business – even more than spending time with my child sometimes.

I mean, it's not like we need to be with our children 24 hours a day, right? We can't spend the whole day gazing at them and feeding them carrot sticks.

For most of us, time is the biggest sticking point. The longer we work, the more guilty we feel. And, even with all the productivity tips and time management skills, working will necessitate us being away from our kids for some portion of the day.

How much is 'allowable'? How much is too much? This, I believe, is a deeply personal thing.

Many parents don't have a choice when it comes to organising their time. They're up at dawn to do the parenting things, then commute, work a long day and commute home for dinners, baths and bedtime routines.

And here's what I realised about having your own business: It's the fact we can choose our hours that makes us feel more guilty. We're not being pressured into working long hours by some big, bad boss but by ourselves. And that's why it feels suckier.

The rose workers

I began thinking about working hours way before I had my son.

I'd left a rather horrendous job at an advertising agency and decided to take a break before plunging into a new role. I saw a casual job going at a well-known florist warehouse, packing roses for Valentine's Day. It involved shift work, and the money wasn't exactly amazing, but for some slightly crazy reason I thought it would be a good experience.

Looking back, I have no idea what I was thinking. Perhaps I was somewhat traumatised by my previous advertising role and needed to shake things up.

I applied, and I got the job. What followed was three of the hardest days of my working life.

We worked standing at long tables cutting the ends off roses straight from the freezer (*they were shipped in from South America*). First, we pulled off the limp petals. Then, we stripped the stalks of thorns, stabbed them into little plastic packs of plant food and passed them down to be wrapped in cellophane and shoved in a cardboard box. So romantic.

We were given flimsy plastic gloves to protect our hands, which quickly filled with blood from the thorns pricking our fingers until we just stripped them off and accepted the mess and pain. We weren't given loo breaks, and I became adept at holding in wee for hours at a time *(still an amazingly useful life skill)*. Lunch was a 30-minute break sitting on boxes in the warehouse carpark.

It was gruelling on the legs and lower back. It was monotonous and dull.

But here's the thing: my fellow workers – nearly all first-generation immigrants from the outer west of Sydney – were incredibly grateful for the job. Many of them got up at 5 a.m. to prepare breakfast and lunch for their kids before dropping them off at whatever childcare they could arrange and getting on the train. They wouldn't get home again until late into the night. And then they had to shop, cook, clean and get their kids into bed.

And they repeated the routine six days a week, month after month. As casual workers, they had no sick leave or holiday pay. Miss a day and make no money; it was as simple as that.

As we chatted around the table, I asked them about their kids and their families. They told me their husbands worked long hours too or had two jobs to make ends meet. Some were lucky enough to have relatives or community friends to look after their children. Most were not. For all of them, the difference between their childcare fees and their wages was painfully slim.

But every single one of them felt working this hard was worth it because it would give their kids a better future. Did they feel guilty about not spending as much time as they'd like with their children? Absolutely. Did they think the end justified the means? Yes, 100%.

I'm ashamed to say I quit after three days – not to return to my child *(he was a mere figment of my imagination back then)* but because I couldn't hack it. Embarrassing to admit, but true.

Years later, when I was sitting in my comfy backyard office worrying I hadn't chopped enough carrot sticks for my child or completed a wooden jigsaw with him that day, I remembered those rose workers. It helped me keep things in perspective.

So, what's the point of my little flowery allegory?

Well, it's to say that you have to start with the difficult task of forgiving yourself. I know. Hideous, right?

You need to realise it's okay to work, and that it doesn't make you a terrible parent. It's actually rather beautiful and amazing to build something that's completely your own, and to show your child what's possible. To explain to your child *(and yourself)* that you're not someone else's creature and working just to pay the bills. Instead, you have your own business and are creating a future on your own terms. That makes you a role model, whether you like it or not.

If you don't forgive yourself, it's going to be hard. And your child will feel it. Kids are smart little buggers. They smell guilt. More importantly, the joy of having your own business will be eaten away by the feeling that your business is in a constant wrestling match with your parental duties.

Repeat after me: 'It's okay for me to work.'

Or make up your own mantras to mutter next time you're feeling crap about 'just finishing that one last thing'.

Love languages

You've probably heard of *The 5 Love Languages*. It's a book by Dr Gary Chapman published in the 1990s that essentially attempts to help couples love each other better. Because, while love is a many-splendoured thing, it can also be a very confusing thing.

There are love-language quizzes you can do online that I think are genuinely helpful. They gave me a real insight into how people love and what they need to feel love.

The five love languages are:

- words of affirmation
- acts of service
- receiving gifts
- quality time
- physical touch.

(As an aside, I did these quizzes with my current partner and we had similar scores in the same places, which of course means we're perfect for each other. Right, Tony?)

I think it's easy enough to see how we can apply these love languages to our children. In fact, five years later Gary wrote a book called *The 5 Love Languages of Children*, and a version for teenagers three years after that. The books talk about getting practical *(and real)* about your child's love languages and, by working though and understanding this, building a stronger relationship.

With my son, I'm all about physical touching. What can I say? I'm a hugger. It was great when he was little but doesn't work so well now he's a teen – I get a few hugs a day but most of my physical affection is borne rather than enjoyed *(although I firmly believe that teenagers need and want parental affection).*

I'd say acts of service are a given as a parent. We have no choice. I know how much my son appreciates it when I make him a snack after school, but I'd do it even if he didn't. And I've always been a big one for words of affirmation – I relentlessly tell my son he's kind, funny and awesome and that I love him *(and he regularly begs me to stop).* But I know that, over the years, when I've felt guilty, I've often compensated for my lack of 'quality time' by overdoing the gifts thing. *(LEGO was my go-to; my son could now buy a Lamborghini based on the resale value of the LEGO in our loft.)*

Taking the time to think about how you love, and how that differs from how your kids want to be loved, is vital for good communication and a solid relationship. You might think your kid desperately wants you to watch telly with them, but all they might need is a reassuring hug and a snack. After that, they'll happily go back to solo play. Time isn't everything. Gifts won't soothe the guilt long-term. Remember: presence, not presents.

Flipping the script

I work with a lot of small business owners, and one of the toughest challenges they encounter is knowing what to say in difficult situations. I give out endless advice on how to draft the right email response and even make a decent living selling templates to handle every business eventuality.

So, I know the value of having someone tell you exactly what to say in tricky situations.

Rather than giving wafty, froo-froo advice here, I decided to write these little scripts to provide you some thought starters. Obviously you can adapt them to your tone and vibe.

Scripts for you

Let's start by dealing with the most difficult person in the room – you:

- **When you feel guilty:** 'Hey me. It's normal to feel guilty when I can't be here for my kids as much as I'd like to be. Being a working parent is a balancing act, and I'm doing my best. I'm setting a good example for my kids by teaching them strong work ethics, and I'm providing for my family.'
- **When you miss the swimming carnival:** 'No, it's not great that I can't make the school carnival. But think of all the time I've spent with my kids. We cooked dinner together yesterday and had a fun bath time at the weekend. I can't make every special occasion, but I can be fully present for my kids when I'm with them.'
- **When comparing yourself to other parents:** 'Yes, it appears that Maureen is a better parent, and she actually makes cakes for cake day rather than buying them from the supermarket and messing up the icing to make them look homemade. But who knows what support Maureen has? Maybe Maureen is sick of being a full-time mum and would love a business. We can't all be Maureen – rather, we need to appreciate being ourselves.'

Scripts for kids

As we discussed way back in Chapter 5, even at a young age kids can understand what we tell them, even if they can't always articulate the perfect response.

Explaining to your kids that you need to work can feel challenging. So, I've written a few scripts here to help you:

1. **'Why are you always on your phone?'** 'You know when you're at day care/school and you talk and play with your friends? Well, when I work, I need to talk to people and help them do things. Sometimes I call them on the phone or send them messages

to help them with their problems and make sure everything is running smoothly. Just like you have toys and books to play with, I have my phone to do my work. And when I'm done with work, I'll have more time to play with you.'

2. **'It doesn't look like work, though.'** *(Usually from a savvy tween or teen.)* 'Yes, I know I'm on Instagram or Facebook. But social media is an important part of my job. I use it to build relationships with my customers, answer questions and sell my products and services. So, while it might look like I'm just having fun, I really am working.' *(P.S. If you're just doomscrolling, it's fine to admit it and put your phone down.)*

3. **'Why can't you play with me?'** 'I need to work now so we have money to buy things we need, like food, our house and toys. When I work, I'm helping to take care of our family. I enjoy my work just like you enjoy [insert kid's favourite activity]. When I finish work, I'll be free to have some fun with you. Work is important, but so is spending time with the people I love. And that's you!'

4. **'Why haven't you finished yet?'** 'I'm sorry, but I'm working right now. Remember, we agreed that I'd stop at 1 p.m. and we'd have lunch together. How about you go [insert activity] and then we can do something nice when I'm done. I can't wait to spend time with you.'

5. **'Why don't you have a real job?** 'I do have real job. But, instead of going to an office or a shop or a factory to work like some people do, I work from home. I work from home on a computer and a phone, which means I don't have to leave the house to go to work. I like this because it means I get to spend more time with you. Even though I don't leave home and work somewhere else, I still do important work that helps take care of our family.'

6. **'Why can't I come into your office?'** 'I understand it can be hard to know when I need to work and when it's okay to come and talk to me. When my door is closed, it means I'm in the middle of something important and need to focus. I love you very much, and I'm always here to listen and spend time with you. But right now, I need to finish this work so I can be around for you later.'

Of course, this won't cut it with smaller kids, and you'll need to have an agreed list of 'you can come in' emergencies. But these don't include:

- looking for a crucial bit of LEGO
- needing a different snack to the one provided
- sibling doing something sibling-ish.

My son and I had an emergency word: 'hedgehog'. Saying 'hedgehog' meant the door could be opened no matter what I was doing.

Having a few stock responses will help your kids understand that while work is important, so are they, and you're doing your best to be a good parent *and* run your business.

Now my son is a teen, I talk to him much like any other adult. He understands the pressures I'm under and that generally I'm doing my best. He's the first to call me out on my bull poop, too. It's hard for me to criticise him for looking at YouTube videos when I've just spent an hour watching Dr Pimple Popper videos on TikTok. *(Don't look, they're horrific; I'm so ashamed.)* So, I just keep it honest with him, and that seems to work.

Sam Jockel, Founder and CEO of ParentTV, mum of Eden (15), Maisie (13) and Ellis (9), offered this advice:

> 'My advice when communicating with a teenager is to tell them the truth – that work is a part of life and, as much as it feels like it can get in the way, having your own business often asks more of me than having a job. But what it does give you is the ability to choose. I have had to work hard, which comes at a cost sometimes, but it has also given me flexibility with our holidays and pick-up and drop-offs and pretty much anything I actually choose to do.'

Scripts for partners

There are eleventy billion books about communicating better with your partner, and it would be impossible for me to cover it all here. As I said, I've written this book with only a vague nod to 'partners' since you may or may not have one. But if you do, having them accept your business is its own delicious can of worms.

So, I'm just going to give you one script to use here – the 'Why didn't you put the washing on?' script:

'Hey, sweet cheeks. No, I didn't put the washing on today. Between drop-off and pick-up I need to concentrate on my business, and I don't have time to take a break to do household chores. I want to get as much done as possible to make my business a success, and I really need your support with this.'

An alternative I like to use is this script:

'You've got arms. Do it yourself.'

Or, for extra conflict-causing juice:

'What did your last slave die of?'

Scripts for friends

Friends are wonderful things, or so I hear. To be honest, I often struggle to maintain friendships because after my son, the house, my relationship, my job and, most importantly, my dog, it feels like I have nothing left to give. And when you try to fit in a little self-care time as well, it's really difficult to make friendships a priority. *(If my friendships were houseplants, they'd die pretty quickly.)* This makes it tough when I genuinely need another adult human to talk to. *(The dog is great, but he's a bit short on useful advice.)*

What has helped me hugely has been finding friends in a similar situation – other working parents – and those who don't need a lot of attention. I call these 'succulent friends'. We give what we can give when we can give it, and that works fine.

There's a common understanding and an honesty. We know we'd like to see each other more but accept that right now it's just not possible. That mutual understanding is everything.

But if you have a buddy who is always pressing you to go for a coffee in the middle of your working day, here's a script that might help:

'Hey Sue, I really appreciate you thinking of me but I'm afraid I won't be able to make it for coffee this time. I'm really snowed under with work and need to focus on getting it done. I'm sorry I can't join you but hope we can catch up soon.'

My tips here are to be honest and direct, be polite and apologetic, and avoid committing to a future date as you'll probably have to cancel anyway. Explaining the reason you can't meet up helps them understand that it's not personal.

Scripts for school parents

It's easy to feel judged by parents who have more time with their kids than you do, who may have chosen not to work or who don't even have to. But we have no idea what lies behind their decision.

As I said earlier, you may well feel like an imposter, standing there at the bake sale with a supermarket cake you quickly iced and squished a bit to make it look homemade. But Maureen, with her perfect, nutritious oatmeal buns, might be envious that you have your own business.

We all choose different paths. Life is only a competition if you choose to compete.

But if the snidey remarks about not attending school events get to you, here's a script you can use. You can also use it if you simply want to explain to your kid's teacher why you're not available to help out:

> 'Hey Janine, I'm afraid I won't be able to attend the [name of event] as I have to work at that time. I understand the importance of school events and am committed to supporting our school community. I will do my best to be involved in other ways. Thanks for understanding.'

The tips about being direct, polite and apologetic – but not too apologetic – apply here. Not being able to make an event in the middle of the workday is perfectly normal. Almost 70% of two-parent families in Australia with dependents have two working parents[17], so being unavailable is the norm rather than the anomaly.

Just because you work from home doesn't mean it's not work. And if all else fails, wear noise-cancelling headphones to the school gate and pretend you're on a work call.

Scripts for clients and customers

Ridiculously, letting your clients know you've actually produced a human seems like a bad thing. I see so many small-business-owning parents trying to hide their 'parentness' – trying to work 'normal hours', taking calls while their child is literally climbing all over them, or sneaking into the bathroom and covering themselves with a towel to drown out the noise of their kids.

The truth is that society expects parents, especially women, to work like they don't have children and raise children as if they don't work. But we shouldn't. And guess what? Your clients probably have kids too, so they probably totally understand your challenges. In my view, it's best to be honest and set expectations from the get-go:

· Talk to your clients about your family on the first call.

· Explain that you work restricted hours.

· Include your working hours in your email footer.

· Set up a clear out-of-office email that explains when you do and don't work.

· Stick to your working hours as much as possible. Don't take calls at 8 p.m. if it doesn't work for you.

And when the kids get sick, or something comes up that affects your ability to work, own it.

It's important to set realistic, generous timelines of when you'll complete the work. I hear about *so* many business owners saying, 'My child is sick, so I can't deliver today. But I can send through tomorrow'. No, you won't. The child will be sick again, then you'll get sick too, and you'll have to keep pushing back the deadline. Give yourself a decent breather instead.

Of course, you should be prepared for some clients to push back. However, in all my 14 years as a small-business-owning parent, I've never lost a client through being honest about the challenges of having a child. People will generally be kind if you communicate.

Kristy Wright, from Kristy Wright Copywriter, mum of Stevo (10) and dog (13), told me:

'They say honesty is the best policy, but this can be really tricky to let clients know that a family emergency has come up when their time and money is important too. What I've found is, if you let them know as soon as possible, generally people are understanding. They have families and know these things happen to everyone. Communicating honestly and as early as possible is key.'

And Angela Denly, mum to Georgie (14) and Iris (10), added:

'I've never tried to hide that I'm a working parent, and on the occasional time when "kid stuff" has thrown a spanner in the works, it's been okay. I aim to communicate quickly and clearly so we can find an outcome that works for everyone. Having a policy not to work with arseholes helps too!'

Here's a script you can use the next time you have a poorly child:

'Hi Bob,

'Just getting in touch to let you know that unfortunately I won't be able to deliver [the thing] on [the date] as agreed. My child, [name], is unwell and I need to look after them, and that's going to affect my ability to work.

'I'd like to be realistic and set a new deadline of [date – at least a week later] to make sure I can fully focus and deliver the best possible work. I hope that works for you.'

Having a child and a business is not something to be ashamed of. It's a glorious thing and, with a little open, confident communication, hopefully everyone will get it and leave you the hell alone.

TL;DR

Deciding how we'll frame our work to kids, partners, friends and random humans is important. We need to communicate the role our business plays clearly and unapologetically – even to ourselves.

Benefits

Working out our communication issues will mean:

- more understanding from your family and friends
- less stress and guilt about your relationships with your kids, partner and friends
- getting to grips with the 'school gate' scenario
- better tactics for handling those difficult conversations with your family and friends
- strategies for having tough conversations with yourself.

Over to you

Now it's time for you to write some scripts of your own, or at least get clear on what you want to say to whom:

1. Which script feels the most fitting for the chat you need to have with yourself? Take the time to write it out and keep it somewhere handy for those dark, parent-guilt days.
2. Which script would work well for your partner?
3. Which script would work well for your child?
4. Which script would be perfect for your customers or clients?

Chapter 19

The empty cup

'*The thing that is really hard, and really amazing, is giving up on being perfect and beginning the work of becoming yourself.*'

Anna Quindlen

As business-owning parents, we know we can't drink from an empty cup. We'll inevitably feel as if we're running dry – so exhausted that we want to give up and go back to work for the 'man'.

And let's get real here. Even with all the productivity hacks in the world, this feeling of exhaustion won't go away until we solve the root problem: not prioritising self-care.

What is self-care?

Self-care isn't about being selfish or self-indulgent. It's about looking after yourself so you can be healthy, mentally well-rested and content. This in turn helps you be a good parent, run your business and achieve everything *(or almost everything)* you want to achieve for the day.

The World Health Organization defines self-care as 'the ability of individuals, families and communities to promote health, prevent disease, maintain health and cope with illness and disability with or without the support of a health-care provider'.[18]

While self-care is often dismissed as being in the zone of aromatherapy massages and 'woo-woo' mantras, it's so much more than that. Self-care includes anything and everything related to being physically and mentally healthy. And self-care is deeply personal: what works for you might not work for someone else. *(Aromatherapy does nothing for me, but watching Netflix in the bath while eating crisps does everything.)*

Self-care can be anything that brings consistent contentment to your life. And it doesn't need to involve luxurious experiences or expensive treats.

Creating a third space

As a reluctant self-carer, I resisted making it a priority for many years. I think it's because I have a bad case of what I like to call 'Burned Chop Syndrome', where you take the less attractive thing on offer *(the burned chop)* so others can have the better ones.

Oh, how I love to be a martyr.

But, as we know from our discussion about parent guilt back in Chapter 5, many parents also feel guilty about taking any time or money away from their children. If they're not working, they're parenting, and vice versa. There's no room to introduce a third element.

In his book *The Third Space*, Dr Adam Fraser opens up the idea of creating a third space that fits between parenting and business. Instead of habitually carrying our mindset and emotional state from one activity to another, we can create a moment of 'space' or transition between activity A and activity B.

As a work-at-home parent, I used to pat myself on the bottom, delighted I no longer had to commute. But I now realise that commute had an important purpose. The commute – if it's not too stressful – allows us to move from the state of working to the state of parenting *(and vice versa)*. It gives us time to process the day before we launch ourselves into parenting. Whether we're listening to a podcast on the train or sitting in the driveway for a few minutes before we head inside, it's a moment *(or longer)* to pause that helps us mentally 'show up' for whatever comes next.

My commute now is a few quick steps across my back garden, which doesn't give me enough time to transition from bad-ass business mogul to patient, loving mum. So instead, one important part of my self-care is carving out small chunks of 'me' time. It started with simply locking the loo door for a few precious moments when my son was small and has now blossomed into, among other things, long walks listening to an Audible book before dinner. This gives me a little pause after my son gets home from school and before I start the evening routine of dinner and family time.

Why are we so poor at self-care?

After discussing this topic with dozens of my members, it seems most of us have similar reasons for putting ourselves last and not prioritising self-care. We want to be liked and appreciated. We want to do good things for other people. And we don't feel we have enough time for that list of people to include ourselves.

And, while you might not have identified as a 'Permissive Parent' *(see Chapter 4)*, you firmly believe your kids should come first. A long way before yourself. Always.

The idea of putting your own oxygen mask on first is unimaginable. You'd rather put everyone else's mask on and even give your mask to the person next to you, which, of course, leaves you breathless.

As a busy parent, I acknowledge that self-care can even feel like one more bloody thing on an already long to-do list. And, ridiculously, I often add it to the list of things I'm not good enough at, which makes me feel even worse and more in need of self-care. *(Oh, the never-ending spiral.)*

I find that if you're poor at self-care, it likely comes down to one of the following reasons.

1. Perfectionism

Maybe your parents were the type who held you to a high standard, and that's been baked into you. Or, perhaps they were more permissive and had few expectations of you, and you've grown up determined to be different.

Buddha forbid that anything you do should be less than perfect. Your house must be immaculately clean. Your children must be entertained within an inch of their lives. Your spreadsheets must be formatted. Your inbox must be empty.

So you're up at 5 a.m. icing those damned cupcakes, or working until midnight to meet a client deadline.

It must be done right, whatever it takes. And so it takes everything.

2. A 'suffer first' mentality

You have a mindset that, to be successful in anything, you must first make a sacrifice. You must suffer before you can have the prize. This turns everything in your life, parenting and business into a trial. And if anything good happens without the necessary suffering, you question whether you deserve it or you expect it to disappear in a puff of smoke.

3. Poor stress recognition

Yes, you're fine, fine, fine *(if 'FINE' stands for 'fucked up, insecure, neurotic and emotional')*. And then suddenly you're not. You manage to juggle everything for a period of time, and then it all comes crashing down.

So it's balance and harmony, then resentment quietly building up, and then... boom! The outburst. The pressure release.

In a never-ending cycle.

Yes, you can feel the rising sense of angst and overwhelm. But you push it down, determined to cope, to not ask for help and to 'manage'.

Until you can't.

*

I believe these feelings all stem from the same root cause: the feeling of not being 'enough'. The deep-rooted feeling that something isn't quite right, that something is missing. You have a somewhat bottomless pit of need that's likely impossible to fill.

Everyone must like you – because you don't like yourself enough. Everything must be perfect – because otherwise people will realise you have no idea what you're doing.

On some level, you feel you're not capable and you're not coping. And I can say this with confidence because I was this person *(and still am occasionally)*: one way I stopped the endless loop was to explore the Think, Feel, Act Cycle.

The Think, Feel, Act Cycle

I picked this up from Annie Grace's The Alcohol Experiment *(you can find out more about this at thisnakedmind.com)*, but it's not a new thing. In fact, it's rather Buddhist *(and I've done my share of meditation and silent retreats)*.

The Think, Feel, Act Cycle concept proposes that how we think creates our feelings, and how we feel drives our actions:

1. We have a thought.
2. That thought turns into a feeling.
3. That feeling causes us to act in some way.

So perhaps it's a positive thought:

1. I look nice today.
2. Therefore, I feel more confident.
3. Therefore, I act confidently and enjoy an experience more.

Or perhaps it's a negative thought:

1. I am not a good parent.
2. Therefore, I feel more worried and down.
3. Therefore, I am less able to enjoy time with my child.

It starts with a thought – something we've conjured up in our brain. A belief. But beliefs are slippery little suckers.

A belief is *an idea that we hold as being correct*. It is an acceptance that something exists or is true, whether or not there is proof or evidence: for example, a belief that the earth is flat, that Father Christmas exists or that we're not measuring up to some imagined parental standard.

We know beliefs aren't definitive or true. We know they're subjective. But, unless we pause, examine them and hold them up to the light, it's so easy to fall into the trap of believing all the daft little thoughts our brains conjure up. And recognising the Think, Feel, Act Cycle helps me with that.

Some of us lean towards the 'cup half empty' approach to life. I know I do.

So often in business I've thought I'm not enough, which makes me feel insecure and anxious about my abilities, which then makes me work harder for a client to make them like me. Which leads to late nights and exhaustion.

In my personal life I tried so hard to please friends and family, and to accommodate their needs at the expense of my own – so much so that it became a way of life. And I'd think my efforts weren't noticed, and I'd feel unappreciated, which would lead me to act in a disgruntled or emotional way. It's a draining way to live.

It might sound obvious to you that if you can control your thoughts, you can control how you feel and act. But it was a lightbulb moment for me. I'm getting better at recognising these negative thoughts and shutting them down. It stops me from wasting time in a spiral of self-doubt and helps me get on with tasks.

I'm getting better at pushing the positive thoughts and letting them flourish, which makes me feel more confident about what I'm working on. I'm also getting much better at cutting off the thought before it turns into a feeling, or acknowledging the feeling before it turns into an action.

Or, as William Ernest Henley wrote, 'I am the master of my fate, I am the captain of my soul'.

I'm the captain. I can control my thoughts, feelings and actions. I just need to be aware of them and manage them. Using these self-care strategies frees me from so much faffing about and helps me feel 'enough'.

Annie Grace counters the Think, Feel, Act Cycle with the ACT technique:

- **Awareness** of the thought – taking a moment to pause and observe what's going on
- **Clarity** around the thought – investigating the effect of the thought and how it makes you feel

- The **turnaround** – designing a new thought that's true enough for you to believe and helpful enough for your brain to seek it out when it's in need.

Using this method, our previous negative thoughts would look like this:

1. **Awareness:** 'I am not a good parent' – I am judging myself harshly.
2. **Clarity:** This is likely because I'm tired and because I failed to meet a commitment to my child.
3. **Turnaround:** I can't be a perfect parent all the time. Things happen. I will be more realistic about my commitments in future.

Of course, this kind of sane, rational thinking isn't possible every day. But the more you try to employ the ACT technique, the more it becomes natural and habitual.

Trying to be 'happier'

If you're anything like me, you spend a fair amount of time thinking about how to be happier. And, while a good night's sleep and drinking more water may help to a degree, understanding the science behind happiness is crucial to attaining it.

Why does a warm firm hug from a loved one make you feel one way, and a good sweaty workout make you feel another? It's all about the chemicals and understanding your daily DOSE.

'DOSE' is an acronym of dopamine, oxytocin, serotonin and endorphins. These are the four primary chemicals that fuel positive emotions. By understanding how these chemicals work, we can make better choices about activities and actions that help or hurt our general level of contentment and happiness.

Dopamine is the happy chemical that's often released when we achieve small tasks such as:

- someone liking our post on Instagram
- finally seeing the bottom of the laundry basket (*I know this sounds mythical but I've heard of it happening*)
- ticking off something on our to-do list.

Unfortunately, our desire for dopamine can also be problematic, as it's closely linked to addictive behaviour, poor technology habits, over-eating and excessive drinking.

Oxytocin is often referred to as the hugging drug and is released by the brain during physical contact. It also helps us build relationships, trust and loving feelings. We gather our oxytocin through things like:

- sharing a family meal
- having a long hug or *(gasp)* sex
- opening up emotionally
- stroking dogs.

Unlike dopamine, which is all about instant gratification, oxytocin gives us lasting feelings of safety and calmness.

Serotonin is another social chemical creating strong positive emotions. It plays a crucial role in our feeling of wellbeing, our sleep and our mood. *(It's also believed to have an impact on our digestion and even organ development.)* Interestingly, around 90% of your body's serotonin is produced by your gut and about 10% by your brain[19].

You can increase serotonin levels by:

- eating well
- getting more sunlight
- exercising
- reducing stress
- taking certain supplements *(personally, I swear by 5-HTP dietary supplements, which help raise serotonin levels in the brain).*

Endorphins are released in response to pain or stress. They help us push ourselves beyond our comfort levels and keep functioning even when we're in pain and feeling stressed. They help ease symptoms of depression, reduce stress and anxiety, and improve self-image. *(Okay, give me all the endorphins please.)*

You can stock up on endorphins by:

- listening to music
- exercising *(I know, I know, it's all about the exercise, right?)*
- receiving massages and other treatments

- eating *(but healthy food, because remember that gut stuff from the serotonin chunk)*
- laughing with friends
- watching your favourite TV show.

Each of these chemicals plays a huge part in our day-to-day experiences, physically, mentally and emotionally. So being conscious of your daily DOSE is important.

Instead of just thinking, 'Oh, I feel awful today', and dismissing it as a normal part of being a business-owning parent, dig a little deeper. What behaviours could be creating this feeling? What did you do today that led to these feelings of ick?

But more importantly, what could you do today to build a better tomorrow?

A little nod to hormones

I've never really thought about my periods or how they affect my work. The arrival of my period each month was still a hideous surprise *('What, this again?')* even after 30 years. I found myself feeling low and weepy at work a fair bit and didn't connect the dots. Doh!

Then my partner advised me to get an app that tracks my cycle *(imaginatively called 'Cycles')*. Suddenly I could see what was happening: I was riding the rollercoaster of my hormones every dang month.

The app even sends a text to me and him informing us both that 'stormy days are ahead'. How cool is that? Now I'm much more aware of how my hormones impact my day-to-day.

One of my team members also suffers terribly with period stuff, so we made 'P Days' a thing – additional sick days where we could just be honest that we had our period and felt crap *(rather than pretending it was something else)*.

And men, don't think you don't have cycles. I'm sure there are days when the testosterone is pumping and you feel angry for no damn reason, right?

For me, realising these moods are somewhat out of my control took a lot of pressure off me to be 'perfectly balanced' every day and just go with the (Aunt) flow. *(Aunt Flo was a euphemism used when I was younger to refer to the arrival of your period – the embarrassment of being caught off guard by 'a surprise visit from Aunt Flo'.)*

Right now, hormones are raging in the Toon household with a teenage son and a perimenopausal mum. It's fun, I can tell ya. But recognising that sometimes it's beyond our control makes it all a little easier to deal with.

Living in the moment

While we all know we can't change the past or control the future, we do spend an inordinate amount of time thinking about both.

As parents, we mostly live in the moment. We lurch from one thing to another, rarely getting the headspace to plan ahead or dwell on past mistakes. We're simply too tired and too busy.

But there's a big difference between being wrapped up in a million things to do and being present and aware of the moment. And often, those future and past thoughts *do* sneak in. In fact, as you read this book you may be thinking about your parenting efforts so far and questioning what you've done. You may be planning how you can do things better.

That's all fine and natural. But all you're really in control of is the now: this minute, or the next hour or so.

While it's great to review previous actions and think about improvements, it's important not to live in a state of perpetual guilt about previous mistakes. While it's great to make plans, it's not good to get too attached to them. Instead, let life unfold with the knowledge that you'll cope with whatever comes your way.

So how do you live in the moment? Of course, there are whole books dedicated to answering this question, but here are my three quick tips.

1. Be thankful

I know it sounds trite, but putting actual time aside to be grateful and think about the positives in your life genuinely helps you appreciate the now. I keep a little gratitude journal and try to write down one positive thing each day.

Another tactic I've picked up along the way is to follow the Rose, Rose, Thorn, Bud approach. *(I'm not sure who invented this; I've seen it attributed to lots of different people.)* It's something my partner and I share over text messages just before bedtime. It works like this:

- **Rose:** A highlight from your day; for example, 'My daughter did a wee in the loo for the first time,' or, 'My teenager talked to me about school in the car'.

- **Rose:** Another highlight *(because hopefully there were at least two)*; for example, 'I found time to read my book,' or, 'I finally got that thing ticked off my to-do list'.

- **Thorn:** Something that didn't go well *(we don't need to be endlessly positive, and sometimes getting it off your chest helps)*; for example, 'I forgot to book the kids' dental appointments again'.

- **Bud:** Something you're looking forward to; for example, 'Can't wait for a stay-at-home day on Saturday, just to potter about'.

I like this structure of recognising that life isn't perfect but there's a little light at the end of the tunnel. It's a lovely habit to get into, even if you just say it to yourself out loud before you go to sleep. But if you can write it down, it's also lovely to look back on. It helps you remember all the micro good times rather than the big, flashy things.

2. Pay attention to the small things

It's easy to look forward to the big things, the events and the achievements, but I've found that appreciating the small things brings me back to the here and now. I seriously live for the small pleasures:

- my first coffee in the morning
- a hot bath at night
- a hug from my teen
- stroking my dog in front of the TV.

These days it's the micro joys that make me really feel present and content rather than flashy award ceremonies or big occasions. *(I actually find big occasions a little stressful.)* So, my advice is to focus on the day-to-day joys rather than lusting for the big life extravaganzas.

3. Connect to the senses

When I'm feeling flappy or anxious, I've found that I need to bring myself back to the present moment. Generally, I'm stressing about a deadline or something I need to complete and totally forgetting where I am or what I'm doing now.

So, I stop what I'm doing and start naming what's around me *(in my head, so I don't sound like a loony Toon)*. It calms me down and brings me into the moment.

One example of when this occurs is during my daily walk. Even when I'm listening to an audiobook or podcast, I often find myself all up in my head worrying about the day ahead *(and missing whole chapters and having to rewind)*. So, I stop myself and start observing, listing out what I can see or how I feel *(I'm lucky enough to live by the ocean, so there are a lot of lovely things to see)*:

·   I see the blue ocean.
·   I feel rested and well.
·   I can smell the jasmine.
·   I can hear the crash of the waves.

I know this feels woo-woo, but it really works, even for this cynical British human.

*

This is a relatively short chapter on the huge topic of self-care, but I wanted to give you a few practical ways I've managed to look after myself while being a working parent.

What's the line – if you don't make time to be well, you'll have to make time to be poorly? This was the case for me. I neglected self-care for many years, and it led me down a dark path to almost absolute burnout *(which I cover in the next chapter)*.

TL;DR

We may not be able to drink from our empty cup, but we can work hard to fill it.

Benefits

By taking time to focus our own mental and physical wellbeing, we can:

- improve our physical wellbeing
- manage and reduce stress in both our family and business lives
- form better relationships with ourselves and like ourselves more
- be more present both in the family and at work
- reduce the chance of burnout.

Over to you

Now it's time to set yourself up for self-care success:

1. Work out one third-space activity a day you could use to separate parenting and your business; for example, perhaps you could take 10 minutes before you wrap up work to listen to some music while you clear things away.
2. Identify two *Think, Feel, Act* flows you often find yourself cycling through.
3. Write down one way you can get your daily DOSE (dopamine, oxytocin, serotonin and endorphins).
4. Write down your Rose, Rose, Thorn, Bud for today.

Chapter 20

Banishing burnout

*'Almost everything will work again if you unplug it for
a few minutes, including you.'*

Anne Lamott

I'm going to assume you read the previous chapter and took everything on board, and so you'll never, *ever* face burnout in your business ever again.

Pffft! Let's get real. Burnout is always lurking in the corner of the room, like a dark otter, ready to jump out and consume us at any moment. So, how do we keep the burnout otter at bay?

For me, true success in business isn't about being the smartest or the most talented human but rather the most persistent. If we are to maintain our persistence, we need to avoid burnout at all costs.

What is burnout?

Burnout is defined as a state of emotional, physical and mental exhaustion caused by prolonged stress. And, obviously, it has a huge impact on our personal wellbeing.

According to the World Health Organization, burnout in working life is characterised by three dimensions:

1. feelings of energy depletion or exhaustion

2. increased mental distance from your job *(or business)*, or feelings of negativity or cynicism related to it
3. reduced professional efficacy[20].

It's easy to see that these dimensions can also apply to our family life. In my experience, men find it even harder than women to admit burnout *(because they see it as a sign of weakness)*.

Stress and burnout are strongly linked. However, while stress often makes me feel hyper and frantic, burnout for me feels different. It's more about lethargy, lack of motivation and not caring.

As someone who's struggled with depression her entire life, I can tell the difference between burnout and depression. But you might find it a little harder, so if you're in any doubt, go chat to a doctor. Best to be cautious.

What causes burnout?

We talked in the previous chapter about brain chemicals and our general inability to live in the now and at least occasionally put ourselves first. But I think the other big factor when it comes to burnout is ego.

Ego is our sense of self, our self-esteem and our self-importance. And boy, is it a fragile little flower.

As humans, we're on a constant search for something better. It's this insatiability that makes us what we are. If someone hadn't sat in a cave and thought, *This cave is nice and all, but it could be warmer*, we wouldn't have fire. Or, *This sled is hard to pull, but those round rock things seem to roll quite easily; perhaps I could...*

You get the idea.

But while our ego and need for self-esteem can be a powerful force in helping us build a happy family and business life, it can also be our Achilles heel. Because our ego often has us believing our happiness lives in a different time period. It has us believing we were happier in the past, or that we could be happier in the future.

It also believes it can predict the future: 'Things will be great when I can...' or, 'If only I could achieve X, then I'd be happy', or, 'As soon as I tick off everything on my to-do list I can properly relax'.

Our ego also believes our happiness lies in the hands of others, and so we constantly seek approval and affirmation from our friends or peers. We compare ourselves unfavourably to others. We feel like imposters around 'successful' people. And we go out of our way to show everyone how happy and successful we are. All signs our ego is in the driver's seat.

Again I come back to that feeling of 'enoughness'. If we feel 'enough', we can happily survey our business kingdom *(or cul-de-sac)*, our family and our life, patting our belly with pride and contentment. But if we don't feel 'enough', there's a constant itch of dissatisfaction. We're always looking for some 'other' thing or the 'next' thing to tick off before we can reach our happy little nirvana *(the place, not the band)*.

The price of ego

While many of us admire great business leaders, we often admire only the obvious bits rather than the whole of them. We desperately crave their business acumen, their drive and their wealth. But their personal lives, their sacrifices and their flaws? Not so much.

Many of the richest humans in the world are also divorced:

- Elon Musk famously slept on the Tesla factory floor for a year, barely seeing his family.
- Steve Jobs had a deeply complex relationship with his kids.
- Bill Gates speaks of having worked seven days a week for more than 30 years, which is hardly conducive to a happy family life.

So, while they're often rolled out as great examples of business leaders, they're clearly not great examples of successful family men. While the ego may want the life of Musk, the head and heart need to realise that it comes with a heavy price tag.

The problem of appearance

Another factor of burnout is the importance of social show – the need to appear happy, wealthy, healthy and successful to impress others. Pride often overrides common sense.

Back in the day, it was only our neighbours, the ubiquitous Joneses, we had to keep up with. Now it's the entire world via a sea of glossy Instagram pictures. We can't just measure ourselves against our co-workers and friends; now we need to measure ourselves against mega-famous millionaires.

We want to have the nice car, the nice house, the nice... whatever. And then we get the nice car and wait for the admiring glances. But here's the problem: when people see you in your fancy car, they're usually admiring the car, not you. They don't want to be *you*; they're thinking about how great *they* would look in your car.

All that work you put in to make people think *more of you* is for nothing. Your admirers just want what you have. And, if we're honest with ourselves, disgruntled admiration or even jealousy from others doesn't materially improve our lives in any way whatsoever.

So why are we pushing so hard?

Recognising the signs of burnout

As business-owning parents, we're often so busy running about after everyone else that we find it hard to spot the signs that something isn't quite right. Furthermore, we often dismiss these signs as 'just part of being a parent'. We're meant to be permanently exhausted, right? Drinking a bottle of wine every other night is 'normal'. And all parents are grumpy and snappy.

Nope.

It's important to spot the signs of burnout early so you can *(hopefully)* head them off at the pass. Some key indicators of burnout *(or that you're on the brink of something big and messy)* include:

· **Exhaustion:** You're feeling physically and emotionally tired every day.
· **Lack of motivation:** You're struggling to get out of bed each day or follow your usual routine.
· **Difficulty concentrating:** You're struggling to focus on anything and finding it hard to concentrate on relatively simple tasks.

- **Irritability:** You're feeling fits of temper, suddenly bursting into tears or screaming expletives at your computer *(or other drivers while in your car).*

- **Loss of interest:** Things that used to make you happy or excited lose their appeal, or you feel creatively numb.

- **Insomnia:** You're struggling to fall asleep or stay asleep *(which, of course, leads to more exhaustion).*

- **Depression or anxiety:** You're feeling low even when there's nothing hugely wrong, or you constantly feel the fear that something terrible is going to happen.

- **Decrease in productivity:** You're struggling to get things done and finding it hard to maintain a sense of accomplishment.

- **Decrease in work satisfaction:** You've lost the usual satisfaction in your work, or you feel you have no real sense of purpose.

- **Illness:** You're more susceptible to illness, both physical and mental, such as colds, flu and tummy upsets.

- **Alcohol and eating more:** You find yourself drinking more regularly or using food to self-soothe.

While experiencing one or two of these might just be a sign of a bad day or a difficult week, any more than that could mean something's not quite right and you're heading for a bigger crash.

The stages of burnout

Now that I've listed them, the signs of burnout might seem obvious. But in my experience, it kinda sneaks up on you. For me, the phases run something like this:

1. **Buoyant phase:** I'm full of energy, optimism and enthusiasm.
2. **A whiff of stress phase:** The buoyancy dwindles and I start to feel a slight edge of stress. I find it a little harder to focus, I jump from task to task and I find myself waking up during the night.
3. **Full-on stress phase:** I feel stressed most of the time, get snappy with my family, burst into tears and find it hard to work through anything for longer than 20 minutes.

4. **Burnout phase:** This is when I've reached my limit and I'm obsessing over everything. The self-doubt is high and I start to get headaches, tummy upsets and a tight feeling in my chest.

5. **Ongoing burnout:** I know that if I keep feeling this way and don't make change, I could sink into genuine depression, and my family and business life would start to suffer.

It can be pretty scary to feel this way and it may leave you feeling helpless, but there are ways through it and strategies to mitigate the feelings.

My burnout story

I was teetering on the brink of burnout for years, my toes on the edge of the cliff, ignoring the signs and clinging on for dear life. I had been quietly unhappy in my marriage for several years and used work as my escape. I felt I had far more control of my business life than of my personal life either as a partner or a mum.

And so my business became my everything. It was my source of pleasure, connection, achievement and pride. It was my safe place when my personal life was in turmoil. My business seeped into every available crack of my life and was an ever-drumming beat in my brain.

But it wasn't truly safe at all, because most of the time I didn't have a clue what I was doing and was terrified of being 'caught out'.

So I lived in permanent sphincter-clenched terror. Trying to keep everyone happy. Trying to make everything just right. Worried about what everyone else was doing and what everyone thought of me.

And because this was stressful, I ate too much, drank too much and slept too little. (*The only tools in my emotional toolkit were wine, coffee and crisps.*) I was frazzled, snappy and difficult to live with. I also put on more than 30 kilos and started developing some health issues. My anxiety and depression spiralled.

It was not a good time, I can tell you.

And I'm not sure what changed. Because I didn't reach rock bottom, but I damn well glimpsed that boulder. There was no sunrise meditation brain flash or 'come to Jesus' moment, but rather a slow, steady realisation. And it was this: *no-one was coming to save me.*

And so I decided to save myself. I did so using a lot of the practical lessons I've talked about in the book so far:

- I rethought my approach to parenting and mum guilt.
- I recognised the true reasons I started my business – money, freedom and flexibility.
- I employed oodles of productivity tactics and outsourced tasks.
- I sorted out my financials.
- I created my own office space, got some help and involved my family.
- I worked out ways to communicate better.

But most importantly, I worked on me. And I gave myself the time for self-care.

After years of fad diets, boot camps and speedy solutions, I gave myself a distant deadline. There were no hairpin turns, just a gentle lazy arc into a better place:

- I started eating better and less.
- I began prioritising exercise.
- I thought more about my needs and wants.
- I judged myself more gently.
- I chipped away at my mindset issues.

It took about two years to shed the kilos and far longer to cut back on the booze. And yes, of course, I often still struggle to put myself first. My son *(and my dog)* will always occupy the top spot on the podium, and my business and I jostle for second position. *(My poor partner comes in a close third, but he's cool with that.)*

I've made massive improvements, and you can too.

Burnout banishers

Most of us recognise that if we burn the candle at both ends, it will burn out twice as fast and make a gooey, waxy mess of everything. But we do eff-all to mitigate the effect stress has on our daily lives.

So I've made a list of some ways I fill up my empty cup, beat burnout and stay perky *(but not too perky, because relentlessly perky people get on my tits)*.

I take time for me

Although it often feels selfish, I try to do one thing for myself each day. That could mean:

- a piping-hot bubble bath
- an early bedtime to read my book
- a long walk with a good podcast
- something crafty, like art or sewing.

Some days I may only get 30 minutes of 'me' time. But it's precious, and it helps.

I ration my creative energy

I believe we only have so much creative energy each day and that we can use it up in any number of ways, even when we're not actually creating anything. We burn up our creative energy when we:

- consume content – online browsing, listening to podcasts, reading books
- talk to others in person or on the phone
- use social media, which not only burns our creative energy but also messes with our mindset.

By limiting my exposure to these things, I'm more able to store up my creative energy for when I need it. I do this by:

- taking the social media apps off my phone completely each Friday afternoon for the weekend
- not having my inbox connected to my phone
- not looking at my inbox or socials at the start of each day so I can lick that frog instead
- setting strict boundaries about when I talk to friends and other people.

Socially, I think I'm somewhat of an ambivert – a combination of both introvert and extrovert. Yes, I get energy from other people, but only on shorter exposures. Any longer and I quickly run out of steam and need to run away. Recognising this and accepting it has helped me a lot.

I book treats

I book in occasional treats and rewards: a foot massage, a facial, getting my toes done, a quiet coffee in a bookshop or a new Audible book. Not huge, not pricey, but perfect little pats on my own big bottom.

I parent myself

My parents live in the UK and, while I know I'm so lucky to still have them, I do miss them. *(Skype is great but not quite the same.)* I miss someone looking after me, worrying about what I have for dinner and making me feel safe and cared for.

So instead, I try to parent myself:

· I cook myself nutritious meals. *(Why does soup always feel so wholesome?)*
· I make sure I'm in bed at a good time.
· I take my vitamins.
· I give myself time to do things that give me pleasure.

Parenting myself makes me feel looked after and gives me more energy to look after others.

I share with others

Who doesn't love a good whinge? I know I do. And it's comforting to know others feel the same way.

Ironically, while social media is often the cause of my burnout feelings, I do find solace in sharing ups and downs online and always have. *(There's something cathartic about posting something on Facebook and getting some help and advice – even given the odd shitgibbon comment.)*

After several social media blackouts *(when I don't use it for weeks)*, I've found I do become a little lonely. So, for me it's often a fine balance between too much social media and too little.

I avoid draining relationships

While it's hard to let friends or people in my life go *(because I want everyone to like me)*, I've learned that some people just aren't great for your mental health. Some people suck the life out of you, draining all hope and happiness in the process. You know the sort: the casual snipes, the constant weeing on your bonfire of excitement.

Better to have fewer friends than fake friends, if you ask me.

I eat the elephant one bite at a time

When life is overwhelming, I try to take a step back and break the overwhelm down into small, bite-sized chunks. I take a month-long task and break it into weeks. I take an hour-long job and snip it into 25-minute sections. It makes everything feel more doable and digestible.

I separate business issues and personal issues

It's so easy to let the lines blur and have home issues affect work *(and vice versa)*. I try to keep them both in separate boxes, with the lids pressed firmly down, to avoid carrying the emotions from one part of my life to another. *(The 'third space' concept in the previous chapter helps with this.)*

It's taken me a long time to make this emotional compartmentalisation stick, but it's a brain saver for sure.

My mum, Freda Toon, mum of Chris (53), and me (48), said:

'I think it's hard to separate personal issues from business issues at times. If you've just had a flaming row with a member of your family, or poor service in a coffee shop, you can sometimes transfer that anger into your business day (and vice versa). It's important to give yourself time to settle.'

I sit in the uncomfortable feelings

Sometimes there's no escaping the bad feelings. You can't use productivity hacks. You can't distract yourself. And you don't want to block them out with booze *(or whatever your blocker of choice is)*.

In these times, it's often good to just sit in the uncomfortable feelings. Feel them, submerge yourself in them, and let them pass. And of course they *do* pass. If you really observe them, it often happens in a matter of minutes. It just feels longer when you're in the eye of the storm.

'This too shall pass' is a much-used mantra in my life.

I learned how to say 'no'

Setting boundaries is relatively easy. Enforcing them is a little harder, especially with yourself. I can't tell you the number of times I've been furious at Yesterday Me who committed to a certain event or project when it's poor Today Me who has to deliver it.

Remember:

- Saying 'no' to some things allows you to say 'yes' to others.
- In most cases, you don't really owe anyone anything.
- With customers, you owe them exactly what they paid for and nothing more.
- You don't have to respond to everything immediately.

Next time someone asks you to do something and you find it hard to say 'no', simply reply with, 'Can I take a day to think about that?'

Most people will say 'yes', giving you time to reflect. And if they push for a response, saying 'no' becomes somewhat easier.

I keep a journal

I've found that writing down your negative thoughts and worries is not only cathartic, it also helps you recognise patterns. It took me ages to connect the dots of my mood swings to my periods, for example, but when I started tracking them it became bleeding obvious.

Journalling also helps me see how many of my thoughts were impacted by lack of sleep, poor diet, booze or lack of exercise. This, in turn, allows me to make micro changes and improvements.

It also helps me spot important triggers – things that set me off and get me spiralling – which makes it easier for me to avoid those triggers.

And finally, seeing recurrent thoughts pop up again and again (*I tend to worry about the same five or six things all the time*) helps me dig into them and find the root cause of these anxieties.

I keep a business journal

While lots of folk keep a personal journal, few keep a business journal or track any of their business wins and fails.

I have a journal on my desk where I write down one good thing that has happened each day, no matter how small. It helps me to read through them on a Friday afternoon when often I've completely forgotten what I did *(or who I even was)* on Monday. At the end of the month or year, it's amazing to read back and see my progress.

Change can feel glacial in business. And when we can't see our improvements, journalling helps.

I meditate

I once did a 10-day silent retreat with my son's dad *(pre-child)*. It was the making – and very nearly the breaking – of me. We weren't allowed to talk *(obviously)*, or make eye contact, or have any physical contact. Being alone with my own brain for an extended period was uncomfortable, but it was worth the pain. It taught me the importance of silence and processing thoughts, and of taking control of the constant babble in my mind.

I'm not great at meditating. But when I set aside the time, I always feel better for it. I've tried a few different apps – Calm, Headspace, Balance, Bloom – all of which were good. But in general, I find simply observing my breathing works best.

I also enjoy mindless and repetitive tasks such as sweeping or cleaning. They allow my brain to slip sideways and focus on the activity at hand rather than the constant narrative in my brain.

I take regular breaks

I'm not someone who likes to take a month off each year. I'd rather take smaller weekend getaways or micro breaks during the week. While I know I could push on and achieve more, there's a certain point – we all feel it – when we know working more won't be productive and that we should take a step back.

As I mentioned in chapter 7, I set aside Fridays as free days – I can choose to work on Fridays, but I often choose not to. This gives me time to do some self-care and personal admin.

I eat well

Yes, I'm one of those revolting people who eats a mostly healthy, well-balanced diet.

Although I was brought up to use food as a treat and a reward, I try to use other things now. I'll have a nice massage or a hot bath. I watch my macros *(macronutrients, the three nutrients we need most of: protein, carbohydrates and fats)*. I try to eat wholefoods and not overindulge. Of course, I'm human and as susceptible to a hot buttered crumpet as the next person. But I try not to binge-eat or use food for comfort too much. I often plan a nice meal for the end of the day, taking time to enjoy the cooking process, and knowing it's on my list of to-dos gives me something to look forward to.

I exercise

I make time to exercise every day, usually aiming to hit 10,000 steps. It's often incidental exercise rather than time at the gym, but it all adds up. When my son was younger, even though I was heavily overweight and often struggled to run about, I did my best. Now my son is older we go to the gym together about four times a week. It's great bonding time for us *(in the car, at least – I'm not allowed to talk to him at the actual gym)*.

I prioritise sleep

I've always underestimated the power of sleep, but my partner is obsessed with it and reminds me of it all the time. I also read *Why We Sleep* by Matthew Walker[21], which was a real eye-opener *(or should that be closer?)*. Now I push to get at least 7.5 hours of sleep a night, have a night-time routine, try to limit screen time *(often failing)* and keep my bedtimes regular.

Understanding HALT

Another coping mechanism that's helped me avoid burnout and negative behaviour in general is HALT, which stands for 'hungry, angry, lonely, tired'. It's an acronym that's often used in sobriety programs, but I think it works well as a parenting and business tool.

Next time you feel a bubble of anger, sadness, irritability or whatever, take a minute to work out whether you're hungry, angry, lonely or tired *(or all four)*. Did you skip breakfast? Did you have a bad night's sleep? When was the last time you had a good hug?

Taking a minute to assess the cause of your emotions can stop you in your tracks because there's usually a rational explanation for how you're feeling.

I often work like an utter demon fuelled only by coffee and spite. Then I wonder why, by 3 p.m., I am a raging ball of irritation. A little food in my belly or a short nap often changes everything. Suddenly, I'm a happy little badger again and everything is right with the world.

My biggest change

Obviously there are lots of tips in this chapter that might work for you, but here's the thing that really changed my life: I gave up drinking.

I don't want to get all preachy and self-righteous here. I know that, when I was drinking, if anyone had suggested I give up my precious wine I'd have wanted to stab them in the leg with a fork. It's a deeply personal decision. So, I'm not going to go into my booze-free journey, but suffice to say it's been one of the most difficult things I've done. I wasn't a big drinker but it had become a habit. Those few glasses of wine on a Friday night became a few glasses of wine every night. Booze, without doubt, contributed to my anxiety, weight gain, irritability, poor sleep, bad diet... you name it.

Eliminating booze has also pretty much eliminated all my anxiety, my stress and my bad temper. It's allowed me to sleep more, eat better and exercise regularly. I can now regulate my moods, anticipate negative feelings and head them off at the pass.

I regret all the years I drank as a parent, desperately craving my wine after the struggles of dinner, bath time and getting my son to go to sleep. I regret thinking for so long that booze was a relaxing solution when really it was the problem. But we can't relive the past. So instead, I look to the future.

If you think giving up booze may be for you, I highly recommend googling 'The Alcohol Experiment'. There, that's all I'm going to say.

*

I credit my ability to keep on keeping on for a large part of my business success. With kids, you have no choice but to get up each morning and do the do; with a business, not so much. I've seen so many business owners fall along the way, and that's why I think it's so important to look after yourself, make good choices and not judge yourself too harshly.

TL;DR

If we're the captains of our ships, we have a responsibility to look after ourselves, notice the signs that something isn't right and course-correct.

Benefits

By considering the risk of burnout we can:

- recognise the signs early and seek help
- implement small strategies that can keep us on track each day
- avoid the rollercoaster of emotions that come with parenting and running a business
- be calmer and more present in our day-to-day lives
- feel that we're in control of our show and not a slave to our negative emotions.

Over to you

Now it's time for you to consider your burnout status and what tactics you can use to avoid reaching full flame:

1. Review the list of burnout signs. How many apply to you?
2. Review the anti-burnout strategies and pick four. Aim to implement one new strategy a week for the next month.
3. Buy a beautiful personal and business journal and commit to writing one line in it every day for at least ten days.
4. Write 'HALT' and 'This Too Shall Pass' on Post-it Notes and stick them somewhere prominent *(and send me a photo of them via social media)*.

Remember, if you'd like to work through these exercises in detail you can head to sixfiguresinschoolhours.com and grab the accompanying workbook.

$

Conclusion

So... what next?

Well, here we are at the end of the book. Whether you read it in one sitting *(dream on, Kate)* or over many months, I hope it's given you some food *(and snacks)* for thought.

For me it was an epic journey. The writing of this book was also the lived experience of the challenges and ideas put forth in this book.

I imagined writing it in a cosy cottage in the Blue Mountains, my days filled with long, contemplative walks, cups of tea and satisfying writing sessions. I pictured myself wearing a turtleneck jumper and sitting in a big armchair before a roaring fire *(even in the 30-degree heat)*.

But, of course, life doesn't work out that way. I wrote this book over the Christmas school holidays in stolen moments at my desk, in bed, in cafes, on trains and even in the bath.

A member of staff resigned the day before school broke up for the Christmas hols. So, on top of the book, I had to take over the 30 hours a week she was doing for me and manage my memberships – oh, and launch my flagship SEO course. And then we also decided to have all the floors ripped up in our house. And I caught COVID.

Life, eh? What a poo storm!

So, I had to use all my own tips and advice *(wise goddess that I am)*. I had to acknowledge that some things would suffer. I didn't make it to the gym as much, I gained a few kilos, my son was delighted to spend a ridiculous amount of time on his computer and my home looked like a medieval slop house for most of the summer.

But we survived. My son finally got so bored he formed a friend group and started going to the beach with them, as well as getting back into playing the piano and doing a lot of work for my business. Instead of going to the gym, I took long walks to process my book thoughts. My team stepped up and became more autonomous in managing their own work. And the launch of my flagship course went just fine – not as amazing as previous ones, but fine.

And it all brings me back to the idea of balance. For me, having a business and being a parent will forever feel like balancing on a tightrope. Sometimes I'm wobbling wildly, flapping my arms in terror trying to right myself again. Sometimes I'm taking big, confident strides from one podium to the other. Most often, I'm just taking tiny, tentative steps and doing my best.

Because, yes, you can be a successful business owner and a good parent. But maybe not all on the same day.

Some days your kids win: you're present, focused and that fun parent you see in the movies. On other days your business wins: you're a sleek otter of efficiency, gliding through your tasks, mastering your money and kicking goal after goal.

Understanding the exchange

For me, it all comes back to understanding the exchange and the consequence: namely, what are you prepared to give up and is it worth what you get in return?

Author, TED Talker and *The New York Times* columnist David Brooks talks about trying to balance the two selves. He talks about those who crave success and have résumé skills (being efficient, smart and financially savvy), and those who seek connection and love and have eulogy skills (being loving, dependable and consistent).

Of course, most of us would likely rate eulogy skills higher than résumé skills. But which do you think more about? Which do you work harder on, your family or your business?

To have a solid business and a solid family life, we have to work on both.

The goal is not to be perfect. We've already established there's no such thing as a perfect parent, and measures of business 'perfection' are fleeting and often dissatisfying. Perhaps all we can aim for is to remove as many bad days as possible, to achieve a level of general contentment both in the office and at home *(which may be the exact same place for some of us)*.

Yes, we need money – maybe six figures, maybe more or less. Yes, we want to have autonomy and a degree of security. But we have to be careful that our lifestyle expectations grow slower than our income. We don't want to spend more than we earn. We don't want to sacrifice our family happiness on the altar of our business success.

Yes, we want success – however we define it – and we want to be happy. But we have to be careful that our pursuit of happiness doesn't make us unhappy.

The importance of patience

I think patience is another key factor. How quickly do you want to achieve your goals? And is the journey as important as the destination?

For me, persistence has been the most important character trait in my business success: a willingness to get up each and every day and try again, to overcome failure and fraughtness and do my best no matter how exhausted I feel. And I'm in it for the long game. I never want to return to working for 'the man'. My business was my escape, and I don't have a back-up plan. So, it has to work, and I appreciate that will take time. I've set myself destination after destination, arrived and felt a bit meh, so now I think less about the end of the road and more about enjoying the road itself.

The importance of astonishment

I used to think I was humble. I'm not into expensive goods or fancy brands. I never really quite believed it when my business was doing well. I'm not overly good at tooting my own horn.

But being humble isn't often seen as an admirable attribute. As a parent, maybe. But in business, not so much.

What I've realised is that it's not humbleness that matters, it's astonishment. And I now realise that I've managed to maintain that level of astonishment as a parent and as a business owner. I'm astonished I was able to make a human after so many years of trying and failing. I'm astonished I've built a business that lets me work at home in my undies and provides enough to give me a good life. Keeping that astonishment helps me stay motivated on the toughest days.

Aren't you fairly astonished at how good your life is when you take a good, hard look at it? Everything you have now is what you long ago dreamed of. And there's more to come.

YOLO and FIRE

Being a successful business-owning parent is also about the shifting importance of YOLO (you only live once) and FIRE (financial independence, retire early).

The fact we only live once dictates that we should seize the day. Push harder. Squeeze the most out of life. Be present. Live in the moment.

Financial independence and the desire to retire – early or at all – calls for more caution, reducing spending and putting in the hard yards over the long term.

But really, we don't want to be too focused on either YOLO *or* FIRE. *(Or, we perhaps we want to combine the two. YORE?)*

There can be a fear that if we don't make the proverbial hay while the sun's at its peak, if we don't hustle, we'll miss the 'moment' with our business. On the flip side, we're constantly told that if we don't enjoy our kids, they'll be grown and gone, and we fear that when we look back our hearts will be heavy with regret.

Both fears are only as true as we want them to be. Yes, our kids will only be kids for a short time, but if we play our cards right, they'll be in our lives forever. Yes, businesses can grow quickly, but hopefully they'll also grow slowly and steadily and support us for the long term.

The world will wait

I live by own personal mantra: the world will wait.

There are so many things I want to achieve, but I don't have to achieve them today. I have days and weeks and months to get them all ticked off. And I don't want to sacrifice the time I have with my son to get them achieved any faster.

It struck me only recently that 'family' is a short-term thing.

Having spent so long trying to find a good partner and have a child, I think I felt it would last forever. But my son is almost 14. He's likely to be at home full-time for another four years, and then our little family will separate. Sure, he might come back. He might still be living in my garage when he's 47. But we'll never have *this* time again. It's precious.

My priorities have also shifted. I now care far less about what other people think of me and my social standing than I ever did before. And you're probably the same, if you're honest with yourself. Do you admire someone because they have a great car or because they have a great relationship with their child? Do you admire someone's follower count more than their family life?

And what matters most? Your glorious spreadsheets or your glorious post-baking kitchen mess? Your business bank balance or fun bath time with your kiddos?

You can enjoy both. But you have to ask yourself what it comes down to: what is your pride and joy?

Yes, being a parent and having a business is hard. We put far too much pressure on ourselves to be all things to all people. And we may look with wistful eyes at our old child-free selves or other child-free humans living their best business lives. We may imagine what our businesses could be if we didn't have to worry about our kids.

But we need to have a realistic perspective. It's important to remember our whys and that, every day, we get to hug these amazing little beings we created.

So that's why I say the world will wait. Don't be in a rush to achieve everything in your business at the cost of your family.

Everyone told me when my son was small that 'the time would fly by' and I should 'enjoy every minute'. And of course it did. And of course I tried. But I couldn't sit staring at my son appreciating him every minute of the day. I needed something for me, I needed to feel fulfilled and, to be frank, I needed bloody money.

Now he's a teenager, there's a part of me that regrets all the time my business took away. And I think all parents feel this way to some degree. Teenager years are hard. My son is forging his own life, which is glorious, but I miss him. He needs me when he needs me and I have to be okay when he doesn't. *(And yes, I know he still loves me truly, madly and deeply.)*

These days, I have so much more time to work on my business. Hours of it. More than I've ever had before. And I'd swap it all to take my giggly six-year-old to the park one more time, or have him snuggle into me watching *Finding Nemo*, or be able to organise pieces with him for his latest LEGO set.

But I'm also proud that I've been able to support my family for the last 14 years. I'm proud of what I've built. I feel I've set a good example for my son and taught him some important life lessons.

At the time of writing I'm about to take my son on a trip to Europe. I'm speaking at events in The Netherlands, Paris, London and York, and we're swinging by my parents in Scotland. I couldn't have afforded this trip without my business. I feel immensely proud that I can do this for him, although I'm sure we'll have our challenges along the way.

Running your own business is the ultimate struggle/juggle for parents *(especially single parents)*. It feels impossible to do well in both worlds at the same time. We never know if we're making the right decisions and only time will tell.

But, when you're feeling overwhelmed by the mess, exhausted by your kids or wishing you could focus more on your business, I think it's important to remember that yes, the time will fly by, and yes, you should enjoy every minute – **but it's okay to love your family AND your business**.

Thanks for reading and I wish you all the best with your business parenting adventures.

Kate

Extra bits

Tools

ActiveCampaign (activecampaign.com) is a customer experience automation platform that helps businesses connect and engage with customers. It creates optimised customer experiences by automating many behind-the-scenes marketing, sales and support processes.

Asana (asana.com) helps you manage projects, focus on what's important and organise work in one place for seamless collaboration.

Calm (calm.com), **Headspace** (headspace.com/headspace-meditation-app), **Balance** (balanceapp.com) and **Bloom** (enjoybloom.com) are all apps that provide meditation services.

Canva (canva.com) is a free-to-use online graphic design tool. Use it to create social media posts, presentations, posters, videos, logos and more.

Freedom (freedom.to) is the app and website blocker for Mac, Windows, Android, iOS and Chrome, used by over 2.5 million people to reclaim focus and productivity.

Google Docs (docs.google.com) enables you to create and collaborate on online documents. Edit together with secure sharing in real time and from any device.

Instagram (instagram.com) is a simple, fun and creative way to capture, edit and share photos, videos and messages with friends and family.

LastPass (lastpass.com) is a password manager that secures your passwords and personal information in an encrypted vault.

Loom (loom.com) records quick videos of your screen and camera. Explain anything clearly and easily – and skip the meeting. An essential tool for hybrid workplaces.

Raiz (raizinvest.com.au) is an app that automatically invests your spare change.

Rounded (rounded.com.au) is accounting and invoicing software made just for freelancers and sole traders.

Slack (slack.com) is a better way to communicate with your team. It's faster, better organised and more secure than email.

Toggl Track (toggl.com) is a time-tracking app that allows you to track your daily activities across different platforms, providing you with detailed insights and an opportunity to optimise your workflow by identifying areas where you can improve.

Xero (xero.com) is online accounting software for your business that connects you to your bank, accountant, bookkeeper, and other business apps.

Books

G Chapman, *The 5 Love Languages: How to Express Heartfelt Commitment to Your Mate*, Northfield, 1992.

id., *The 5 Love Languages of Children*, Moody, 1997.

id., *The 5 Love Languages of Teenagers*, Moody, 2000.

A Fraser, *The Third Space: Using Life's Little Transitions to find Balance and Happiness*, Penguin Random House, 2012.

M Michalowicz, *Profit First: Transform Your Business from a Cash-Eating Monster to a Money-Making Machine*, Portfolio, 2014.

S Pape, *The Barefoot Investor: The Only Money Guide You'll Ever Need*, John Wiley & Sons Australia, 2016.

W Sears & M Sears, *The Attachment Parenting Book: A Commonsense Guide to Understanding and Nurturing Your Baby*, Little, Brown, 1993.

K Toon, *Confessions of a Misfit Entrepreneur: How to Succeed in Business Despite Yourself*, 2017.

B Tracy, *Eat that Frog! 21 Great Ways to Stop Procrastinating and Get More Done in Less Time*, 3rd edition, Berrett-Koehler, 2017.

M Walker, *Why We Sleep: Unlocking the Power of Sleep and Dreams*, Scribner, 2017.

About the author

Kate Toon is an award-winning entrepreneur and parent to one human and one fur baby. From her humble backyard shed on the Central Coast of NSW she masterminds an ambitious business universe, helping thousands of other humans to build their own version of success through digital marketing and business know-how.

Kate is a renowned speaker, mentor, educator and podcaster. She was named Australia's Most Influential Small Business Woman (2022), one of Australia's Top 50 Small Business Leaders (2022), and Businesswoman of the Year and Training & Education Provider of the Year at the national MyBusiness Awards (2020). She's also the founder of CopyCon and The Digital Marketing Collective Conference, and is a resident expert on *Kochie's Business Builders*.

In her spare time Kate is often found taking gym selfies and roller-skating, much to the embarrassment of her teenage son.

Acknowledgements

I'd like to shout out the following humans:

- **My mum and dad,** who were the first readers of this book and obviously helped me become the parent and business human I am today. I love you, thanks, and 'rocks ahead'.
- **My partner Tony,** for his daily encouragement and love, and 1.5-hour back rubs.
- **My son's dad, Hichem,** who has been a great partner in raising our wonderful small human and a wonderful dad. Thank you for doing the washing so well.
- **Caroline Malloy,** the patient book coach who helped me put my book pitch together and dealt with much gnashing of teeth and wailing by me.
- **Bronwen Whyatt, Erin Huckle, Lauren Minns and Wendy Brown**, my faithful book readers, who provided so much insight, witty feedback and motivation to keep going.
- **Will Allen, Bill Harper and Christina Parkin,** for their help editing bits of the book and proofing the crap out of it.
- The fabulous members of the **Digital Marketing Collective,** for all their awesome quotes and endless encouragement.
- **Kate Christie,** for being an awesome, helpful human and giving me the inside track.
- **Mel Schilling, Kelly Irving, Andrew Griffiths, Fiona Killackey, Lucy Bloom and Annie McDermott,** for their fab booky advice.
- **Jade Warne and Emma Lovell,** for my fabulous back cover snap.
- **Tess McCabe,** for the rad cover design and for taking my many rounds of amendments.

- **Lesley and the team at Major Street Publishing,** who took a chance on me and my book idea.

- **My dog Pomplemousse** *(okay, so, not officially human),* for being my constant furry companion and muse as I wrote. Legend.

- **My son**, who is, of course, my absolute everything. Anything I write here will make you cringe, but you really are the best of people – kind, smart, thoughtful and loving. I'm so very proud of you, and guess what? I love you.

References

1   https://www.afr.com/companies/financial-services/
    funding-options-widen-for-smes-20221123-p5c0le

2   http://www.aplen.pages.ontraport.net/WorkingFamiliesReport2019

3   Baumrind D. Differentiating between Confrontive and Coercive
    Kinds of Parental Power-Assertive Disciplinary Practices. *Human
    Development.* Published online 2012:35-51. doi:10.1159/000337962

4   Baumrind D. Child care practices anteceding three patterns of
    preschool behavior. *Genetic Psychology Monographs.* 1967;75(1):43-88.
    https://www.ncbi.nlm.nih.gov/pubmed/6032134

5   Maccoby EE, Martin JA. Socialization in the Context of the Family:
    Parent-Child Interaction. In: *Handbook of Child Psychology.*
    Socialization, Personality, and Social Development. 1983

6   Steinberg L, Lamborn SD, Dornbusch SM, Darling N. Impact of
    Parenting Practices on Adolescent Achievement: Authoritative
    Parenting, School Involvement, and Encouragement to Succeed.
    Child Development. Published online October 1992:1266.
    doi:10.2307/1131532

    Spera C. A Review of the Relationship Among Parenting Practices,
    Parenting Styles, and Adolescent School Achievement. *Educational
    Psychology Review.* Published online June 2005:125-146. doi:10.1007/
    s10648-005-3950-1

    Nyarko K. The influence of authoritative parenting style on adolescents'
    academic achievement. *AJSMS.* Published online September 2011:278-
    282. doi:10.5251/ajsms.2011.2.3.278.282

7   Strage A, Brandt TS. Authoritative parenting and college students'
    academic adjustment and success. *Journal of Educational Psychology.*
    Published online 1999:146-156. doi:10.1037/0022-0663.91.1.146

8   Rankin Williams L, Degnan KA, Perez-Edgar KE, et al. Impact
    of Behavioral Inhibition and Parenting Style on Internalizing and

Externalizing Problems from Early Childhood through Adolescence. J Abnormal Child Psychology. Published online June 12, 2009:1063-1075. doi:10.1007/s10802-009-9331-3

9   https://www.medicaldaily.com/nature-vs-nurture-debate-50-year-twin-study-proves-it-takes-two-determine-human-334686

10 https://archive.org/details/cassellshousehol02londuoft

11 Brian Tracy, Eat That Frog! 21 Great Ways to Stop Procrastinating and Get More Done in Less Time.

12 https://corporatefinanceinstitute.com/resources/accounting/profit-margin/#:~:text=You%20may%20be%20asking%20yourself,a%205%25%20margin%20is%20low..

13 https://www.finder.com.au/life-insurance-and-the-cost-of-raising-children#:~:text=The%20Australian%20government%20estimates%20that,it%20probably%20costs%20far%20more.&text=Updated%20Oct%2013%2C%202022%20.

14 https://www.cosocloud.com/press-releases/coso-survey-shows-working-remotely-benefits-employers-and-employees

15 https://www.ato.gov.au/Forms/TFN---application-for-individual-living-outside-Australia/?page=2

16 https://www.fairwork.gov.au/employment-conditions/workers-compensation

17 https://www.abs.gov.au/statistics/labour/employment-and-unemployment/labour-force-status-families/latest-release

18 https://www.vu.edu.au/mitchell-institute/prevention-risk/state-of-self-care-in-australia#:~:text=Self%2Dcare%20is%20defined%20by,a%20health%2Dcare%20provider'

19 https://my.clevelandclinic.org/health/articles/22572-serotonin

20 https://www.who.int/news/item/28-05-2019-burn-out-an-occupational-phenomenon-international-classification-of-diseases

21 https://www.amazon.com/Why-We-Sleep-Unlocking-Dreams/dp/1501144316

Be better with business books

MAJOR STREET

We hope you enjoy reading this book. We'd love you to post a review on social media or your favourite bookseller site. Please include the hashtag #majorstreetpublishing.

Major Street Publishing specialises in business, leadership, personal finance and motivational non-fiction books. If you'd like to receive regular updates about new Major Street books, email info@majorstreet.com.au and ask to be added to our mailing list.

Visit majorstreet.com.au to find out more about our books (print, audio and ebooks) and authors, read reviews and find links to our Your Next Read podcast.

We'd love you to follow us on social media.

in linkedin.com/company/major-street-publishing

f facebook.com/MajorStreetPublishing

⊙ instagram.com/majorstreetpublishing

🐦 @MajorStreetPub